*Hispanic Linguistic Studies
in Honour of F. W. Hodcroft*

HISPANIC LINGUISTIC STUDIES IN HONOUR OF F. W. HODCROFT

Edited by David Mackenzie
&
Ian Michael

THE DOLPHIN BOOK CO.
1993

This volume has been produced with the aid of a generous grant from the Fiedler Memorial Fund made by the Curators of the Taylor Institution in the University of Oxford

ISBN 0 85215 079 2

Printed in Wales by J. D. Lewis and Sons Ltd., Llandysul,
for the Dolphin Book Co. (Tredwr) Ltd., Llangrannog.

CONTENTS

Contents

PREFACE

With astonishing erudition, which nothing seemed to have escaped, he united an infectious enthusiasm and a power of lucid and fruitful exposition that made him one of the greatest of teachers, and a warmth and openness of heart that won the affection of all those who knew him... In his case, the scholar and the man cannot be separated. His life and his learning were one; his work was the expression of himself... [His] humour was not only one of his most striking characteristics of a man; it was of constant service to his scholarly researches. Keenly alive to any incongruity in thought or fact, and the least self-conscious of men, he scrutinized his own nascent theories with the same humorous shrewdness with which he looked at the ideas of others.

These words, written almost a century ago by G. L. Kittredge about his mentor Francis James Child of Harvard, the great Anglo-Germanic philologist, can, if put in the present tense, so remarkably stand as a description of Fred Hodcroft that the origins and training of the two philologists would merit closer comparison.

Frederick William Hodcroft was born on 22 February 1923 at Stretford, near Manchester, the fourth of five sons of a chartered accountant, and was educated at Stretford Grammar School where he took his Higher School Certificate in the first year of the Second World War. After leaving school he briefly, in November 1940, became a postboy at Tootal Broadhursts, but in 1941 was appointed audit clerk with a Manchester firm of Incorporated Accountants. In 1942 he joined the RAF and the following year was sent to Canada for Air Crew Training. For almost two years he served with 27 Squadron RAF in Burma as

Wireless Telegraphist/Navigator, taking part in twenty-one operations in Beaufighters against the Japanese Forces. Holding the rank of Warrant Officer (First Class), he was repatriated as medically unfit for duty in August 1945, and was demobilized in 1946.

He went up to the University of Manchester in October 1946 to read Spanish under J. W. Rees, taking his First in 1949. There he completed his MA by thesis on the language of the *Crónica de Morea* in one year, while holding the appointment of Assistant in Spanish in the Department; he was promoted Assistant Lecturer in 1952. In 1953 he was elected to a University Lectureship in Spanish at Oxford, where his duties included all the teaching of Spanish Philology, formerly undertaken by W. J. Entwistle.

Now it is impossible to understand Fred's scholarly formation without knowing something of that of Rees, who read classics at Aberystwyth before the First World War, served in Flanders, studied Romance philology in Germany, learned French from a baroness in a castle, and then came up to read Modern Languages at Oxford, where he was greatly influenced by Barber of Exeter—the classical philologist who was his moral tutor.

If Fred has many of the characteristics of F. J. Child, he has far more in common with Jo Rees: the vast reading cloaked in scholarly modesty, the scientific application of philological principles, the keen sense of humour at all times, the righteous indignation at any injustice committed on others, the constant dedication to his pupils, and even some of the Reesian hobbies such as hill-walking, carpentry and other practical tasks.

Above all, they both managed to become legendary in their own life-times for their eccentricity. I shall only give one example of Fred's, of which he alone will know the truth: it is said that a neighbour, a retired consultant, trudging one day through the snow along St Mary's Close,

Kidlington, was mildly surprised to see Fred working at his desk wearing a woollen tea-cosy on his head. Perhaps this was during the 'winter of discontent'.

My own most treasured memory is from the late sixties of Jo Rees and Fred Hodcroft poring over maps while navigating me through Betwys-y-Coed in a dense autumnal fog on our way to one of Rees' famous Harlech weekends, only to find that they had opened sheets of the Spanish IGC maps and were trying to locate Alcocer.

All three scholars had something else in common: they carried most of their vast knowledge in their heads and were too painstaking to get it all down in print. Jo Rees, apart from two published articles and his famously unpublished edition of *La vida de Santa María Egipciaca*, the text of which was set up in page-proof in 1938, left Fred his famous system of card-files and note-books, which constitute a corpus of Old Spanish phonology, morphology, syntax and semantics to which neither the efforts of the Real Academia or the Madison Medieval Seminary can yet aspire. The trouble is that only Rees knew how the complex system of cross-references involved in looking it up actually worked, and he failed to leave the instructions:

Messis quidem multis, operarii autem pauci.

Fred's co-edition of the *Textos lingüísticos del medioevo español* has received the accolade of being fully integrated into the Real Academia's card-files of the *Diccionario histórico de la lengua española*, together with various notes he has sent to the Academia; one of his other publications [*AFA* 14/15] contains a lengthy footnote which is very *sui generis*: an account—very useful for editors of medieval texts, and known to so few of them—of meaningless dots and tittles in Old Spanish manuscripts. Now, in his well-earned retirement, Fred has the opportunity to publish all

he knows in a thesaurus of Old Spanish, for few scholars—
in Spain or elsewhere—entirely possess his grasp of the old
language in all its variety and in its relation to the modern
form of Spanish of which he is likewise so much the master.

It is typical of a scholar of Fred's formation to have spent
much of his time correcting and checking the work of
others, as countless expressions of gratitude in prefaces will
attest. It is also a mark of his wife Joan's tremendous
concern for all Fred's colleagues, friends and pupils, that
they both should have consistently offered such warm
hospitality to so many of the more than seven hundred
pupils to whom Fred has given tutorials and supervisions
in Oxford since 1952, as well as to Hispanic colleagues past
and present from the world over.

The love and respect in which Fred is held were shown by
his extraordinarily popular Presidency of the Association of
Hispanists of Great Britain and Ireland from 1981 to 1983,
and are profoundly felt too in his own Oxford College, St
Cross, of which he is a Founding Fellow (now Emeritus),
and in those other Colleges where he has been Lecturer: St
Anne's, Exeter, Regent's Park, St Peter's and New College,
as well as in the Faculty of Medieval and Modern
Languages, and in the larger University beyond.

This volume of essays reflects the wide range of Fred's
linguistic area of research and teaching, though not his
literary interests, which are considerable. The distinguished
contributions herein by the leading Romance philologists,
Professors Yakov Malkiel and Rebecca Posner, that by the
Royal Spanish Academy's Director of the Historical
Dictionary, Don Manuel Seco, and those by Professors Ian
Macpherson and Ralph Penny, and Drs John England,
Christopher Pountain and Stephen Parkinson, provide no
better testimonial of the esteem in which Fred Hodcroft is
held in Spain, the United States (where he spent a fruitful
semester at the University of Texas at Austin from

September 1969 to January 1970) and the United Kingdom. The remaining contributions are all by his own pupils: *ex fructu arbor agnoscitur.*

Ian Michael
University of Oxford

Publications of F. W. Hodcroft

Books

[with D. J. Gifford] *Textos lingüísticos del medioevo español*, Oxford: Dolphin Book Co., 1959; 2nd ed., revised, 1966.

[ed. with D. G. Pattison, R. D. F. Pring-Mill, R. W. Truman] *Medieval and Renaissance studies on Spain and Portugal in honour of P. E. Russell*, Oxford: Society for the Study of Medieval Languages and Literature, 1981.

Articles

'Se desea informes', *BHS*, 38 (1961), 25-27.

'Notas sobre la *Crónica de Morea*: fonética', *AFA*, 14/15 (1963-4), 83-102.

'*La Celestina*: errores de interpretación en el estudio de su sintaxis', *Filología Moderna*, 14 (1964), 154-56.

'Theses in Hispanic studies approved for higher degrees by British and Irish Universities, 1972-74 (with some additional earlier titles)', *BHS*, 52 (1975), 325-44.

'Elpha: nombre enigmático del *Cantar de Mío Cid*,' *AFA*, 34/35 (1985-86), 39-63.

[*in press:*] '*¿A·mí un él?*: observations on *vos* and *él/ella* as forms of address in peninsular Spanish', *Journal of Hispanic Research*.

Reviews

Criado de Val, M., *Análisis verbal del estilo*, Madrid: RFE, 1953 (Anejo 57): *BHS*, 32 (1955), 61.

Criado de Val, M., *Indice verbal de 'La Celestina'*, Madrid: RFE, 1955 (Anejo 64): *BHS*, 34 (1957),108-10.

Roca Pons, J., *Estudios sobre perífrasis verbales del español*, Madrid: CSIC, 1958: *BHS*, 37 (1960),116-18.

Mendeloff, H., *The evolution of the conditional sentence contrary to fact in Old Spanish*, Washington, DC: Catholic University of America, 1960: *BHS*, 38 (1961), 242-43.

Tilander, G. [ed.], *Vidal mayor: traducción aragonesa de la obra* In excelsis Dei thesaurus *de Vidal de Canellas*, Lund: Hakan Ohlssons Boktryckeri, 1956 (Leges Hispanicae Medii Aevi, 4-6) 3 vols: *MAe*, 30 (1961), 136-38.

Alvar, M., *Textos hispánicos dialectales: antología histórica* Madrid: CSIC, 1960, 2 vols: *BHS*, 39 (1962), 239-43.

Zamora Vicente, A., *Dialectología española*, Madrid: Gredos, 1960: *BHS*, 41 (1964), 250-52.

Fotitch, T., *An anthology of Old Spanish*, Washington DC: Catholic University of America, 1962:*BHS*, 43 (1966), 57-59.

Pottier, B., *Systématique des éléments de relations: étude de morphosyntaxe structurale romane*, Paris: Klincksieck, 1962: *BHS*, 43 (1966), 214-16.

Montgomery, T., *El evangelio según San Mateo según el manuscrito escurialense I. I. 6: texto, gramática, vocabulario*, Madrid: *BRAE*, 1962 (Anejo 7): *BHS*, 43 (1966), 221-22.

Moliner, M., *Diccionario del uso del español*, Madrid: Gredos, 1966, vol 1: *MLR*, 43 (1968), 492-94.

Pey, S., & J Ruiz Calonja, *Diccionario de sinónimos, ideas afines y contrarios*, London: Harrap, 1966: *MLR*, 43 (1968), 492-94.

Russell-Gebbett, P. [ed.], *Mediaeval Catalan linguistic texts*, Oxford: Dolphin Book Co., 1965.

Lorenzo, E., *El español de hoy: lengua en ebullición*, Madrid: Gredos, 1966: *BHS*, 46 (1969), 48-49.

López Blanquet, M., *El estilo indirecto libre en español*, Montevideo, 1968: *BHS*, 46 (1969), 241-42.

Chasca, E. de, *El arte juglaresco en el 'Cantar de mio Cid'*, Madrid: Gredos, 1967: *MAe*, 39 (1970), 336-38.

Penny, R. J., *El habla pasiega: ensayo de dialectología montañesa*, London: Tamesis, 1969: *BHS*, 49 (1972), 290-92.

Alcina Franch, J., & J. M. Blecua, *Grámatica española*, Barcelona: Ariel, 1975: *MLR*, 53 (1978), 207-10.

Deyermond, A. D. [ed.], *Medieval Hispanic studies presented to Rita Hamilton*, London: Tamesis, 1976: *BHS*, 56 (1979), 55-56.

Sampson, R. [ed.], *Early Romance texts: an anthology*, Cambridge: CUP, 1980: *MAe*, 52 (1983), 166-67.

Los clíticos en el español actual, Amsterdam: Universiteit Amsterdam, 1980 (Diálogos hispánicos de Amsterdam, 1): *Notes & Queries*, 30 (1983), 1-2.

Wright, R., *Late Latin and early Romance in Spain and Carolingian France*, Liverpool: ARCA, 1982: *MAe*, 54 (1985), 132-33.

Blecua, A., *Manual de crítica textual*, Madrid: Castalia, 1983: *BHS*, 63 (1986), 149.

Gilkison Mackenzie, J., *A lexicon of the 14th-century Aragonese manuscripts of Juan Fernández de Heredia*, Madison: HSMS, 1984 (Dialect Series, 8): *BHS*, 64 (1987), 252.

Steel, B., *A textbook of colloquial Spanish*, Madrid: SGEL, 1985: *Quinquereme*, 11 (1988), 109-10.

Pharies, D. A., *Structure and analogy in the playful lexicon of Spanish*, Tübingen: ZRP, 1986 (Beihefte zur ZRP, band 210): *JHP*, 13 (1988), 67-68.

Obituaries

'Cyril Albert Jones (1924-74)', *BHS*, 51 (1974), 272-76.

'J W Rees', *The Times*, 18 September 1976.

'Alan Robson (1915-1987)', *The Postmaster*, 56 (1990), 39.

'Kits van Heyningen', *Oxford Magazine*, 56 (1990), 3 & 5.

'Douglas Juan Gifford (1924-1991)', *BHS*, 69 (1992), 175-77.

Subject position in Old Spanish prose, 1250-1450

N E I T H E R the linguistic historian wishing to describe the evolution of Spanish nor the literary critic wishing to make value judgements on the style of individual writers has a great deal of data on the evolution of word order in Spanish to assist them in their analyses. In this article I wish to set out some basic data on the position of the subject in Old Spanish prose texts of the thirteenth, fourteenth, and fifteenth centuries, a period in which Castilian was becoming established as a major cultural and standard language.

The following tables give the overall figures for seven texts from this period; they are based on declarative sentences only, and I have excluded from consideration subject pronouns, as there is a marked difference between the position of subject pronouns and that of subjects which have a noun as the head-word.[1]

table 1: subject position in independent clauses

text	order S - V		order V - S	
Calila	594	(32%)	1259	(68%)
Engaños	181	(41%)	262	(59%)
Castigos	948	(60%)	634	(40%)
Lucanor	652	(60%)	432	(40%)
Gatos	298	(52%)	278	(48%)
A B C	733	(66%)	369	(34%)
Espéculo	1085	(52%)	989	(48%)

[1] The texts analysed are: *El libro de Calila e Digna* [1967]; *El libro de los engaños* [1959]; *Castigos e documentos* [1952]; *El conde Lucanor* [1971]; *El libro de los gatos* [1958]; *Libro de los exemplos* [1961]; *El espéculo de los legos* [1951].

table 2: subject position in dependent clauses

text	order S - V		order V - S	
Calila	680	(57%)	520	(43%)
Engaños	83	(48%)	90	(52%)
Castigos	770	(58%)	562	(42%)
Lucanor	988	(67%)	495	(33%)
Gatos	148	(62%)	89	(38%)
A B C	448	(68%)	209	(32%)
Espéculo	579	(45%)	705	(55%)

table 3: combined totals (independent and dependent clauses)

text	order S - V		order V - S	
Calila	1274	(42%)	1779	(58%)
Engaños	264	(43%)	352	(57%)
Castigos	1718	(59%)	1196	(41%)
Lucanor	1640	(64%)	927	(36%)
Gatos	446	(55%)	367	(45%)
A B C	1181	(67%)	578	(33%)
Espéculo	1664	(50%)	1694	(50%)

It is immediately apparent from these figures that there was great flexibility in the position of the subject throughout the Old Spanish period, with combined totals for subject anteposition ranging from 42% [*Calila*] to 67% [*ABC*].[2] This range might initially suggest a diachronic progression from the thirteenth-century *Calila* to the fifteenth-century *ABC*, but this assumption is difficult to support in view of the figures for the other texts, particularly as the fifteenth-century *Espéculo* has

[2] The range of figures differs considerably from those given by Crabb [1955] and Pardo Huber [1973], both of whom used very much more limited samples.

the relatively low figure of 50% for subject anteposition. It is, in fact, clear that the texts vary more according to source than date of composition, especially in the case of the two works translated from Arabic, *Calila* and *Engaños*, the only two texts in which the V–S order predominates. The other texts do not show such close similarities, but some importance may be attached to the fact that the two works with the lowest frequency of subject anteposition after the Arabic texts are *Espéculo* and *Gatos*, both translated from Latin works written outside Spain, whilst the three works which show the greatest preference for the order S–V are *Castigos*, *Lucanor*, and *ABC*, the three works in which one would expect the least influence from other languages. I have dealt elsewhere with the main factors influencing subject position in Old Spanish prose as they can be deduced from an analysis of *El conde Lucanor*;[3] in the present study I wish to focus on the extent to which Old Spanish prose texts varied, and in particular on the possible influence of Arabic and Latin on the syntax and style of works translated from those languages.

1 *Libro de Calila e Dimna; Libro de los engaños*

Both texts show a clear preference for subject postposition, and they are the only texts which show such a clear tendency. The predominance of postposed subjects in works translated from Arabic and Hebrew has been observed by both Crabb [1955] and Pardo Huber [1973], and Hottinger [1958] includes in his study of *Calila* a detailed analysis of the ways in which various Arabic constructions are rendered by different patterns of word order in the Castilian translation. There is no known Arabic

[3] See England [forthcoming].

version of *Engaños* sufficiently close to the Castilian to allow a similarly detailed syntactic study, but the similarities between *Engaños* and *Calila* suggest that many of Hottinger's findings could be applied to *Engaños*. A detailed comparison of word order in the Arabic and Castilian texts would have to be made by a specialist in Arabic, and in any case the differences in structure between the two languages increase the difficulties in making any such comparison. However, an analysis of the Arabic and Castilian texts of chapter II of *Calila* as it appears in Galmés de Fuentes [1956:21-61], shows that the translators usually retained the order S–V or V–S of the original, but occasionally replaced the predominant Arabic V–S order by S–V in Castilian. The following expressions all have postposed subjects in the Arabic text:

...di a mi alma a escoger en estas quatro cosas que **los omnes** demandan en este siglo... [Galmés: 23]
...et fallé que **el físico** no puede melezinar a ninguno...

[Galmés: 31]
Esto non vale cosa... [Galmés: 47]

Although *Calila* and *Engaños* are unique in favouring the V–S order, many of the factors which tended to favour anteposition or postposition of the subject in Old Spanish are just as important in *Calila* and *Engaños* as in other Old Spanish works.[4] When the direct object precedes the verb, the subject is usually postposed (10 out of 14 examples in *Calila*), but with a following direct object, the S–V order predominates (237 out of 294 examples in *Calila*, 65 out of 89 examples in *Engaños*); with a preceding subject complement, the subject follows in 43 out of the 62 examples in *Calila*, but with a

---

[4] For fuller details, see England [1979], chapter 3.

following subject complement, the subject precedes the
verb in 199 of the 227 examples in *Calila*, and in 30 of the
36 examples in *Engaños*.

Two factors distinguish the patterns of subject position
in *Calila* and *Engaños* from those found in works composed originally in Castilian such as *El conde Lucanor*.
The first is the position of the subject with the verb *dezir*,
which in *Calila* has an anteposed subject 37 times, and a
postposed subject 685 times, and in *Engaños* has an
anteposed subject 53 times, and a postposed subject 108
times. Many passages in both works have a highly
repetitive ordering of *dixo*-subject-direct speech:

> E dixo **otro**: 'Non creades que el feziese tal cosa'. Dixo **otro**:
> 'Pesquisese la verdat que saber conocer los omnes fuerte cosa es'.
> Dixo **otro**: 'Las poridades non se saben...'.
>
> [*Calila*, 5197-5200]

> E dixo **el alcalle**: –Pues derecho te pide.
> E dixo **el omne** que lo non queria sacar...
> E dixo **el ynfante**: –Señor, non te di este enxenplo sinon porque
> sepas las artes del mundo.
> E dixo **el rey**: –¿Commo fue eso?
> E dixo **el ynfante**: –Oy dezir de una muger...
>
> [*Engaños*, 1459-68]

In this construction, the translators appear to have
retained the word order of the Arabic originals.

The second factor concerns the likelihood of thematic
subjects to follow the verb in *Calila* and *Engaños*. This
can be seen most clearly with subjects which have as the
head-word a noun qualified by *este*, which in *Calila* follow the verb in 13 of the 46 examples (28%); in *Lucanor*,
such subjects are postposed in only 5 of the 71 examples
(7%), and no other Old Spanish text has a proportion of

postposed thematic subjects nearly as high as *Calila*.[5] The
following examples illustrate the difference:

...**esto** les duró un tiempo...	[*Lucanor*, 88.31]
...e duro **esto** un tiempo...	[*Calila*, 2346]

Et **esto** me faze estar en grand reçelo.	[*Lucanor*, 88.9]
.. et fázele **esto** furtar e rrobar.	[*Calila*, 3069]

...**este homne** vos quiere engañar...	[*Lucanor*, 78.13]
...nos ha engañados e enartados **este traydor**	[*Calila*, 3667]

Although it would be difficult to quantify the differences,
examples such as the following show that postposed
thematic subjects in *Calila* and *Engaños* do not appear to
represent a marked order:

...e el palomo non lo quiso creer e començola de picar e de ferirla
de los onbros e de las alas atanto que la mato; e paro mientes **el
palomo** al trigo...

[*Engaños*, 914-6]

...pidote por merçed que me libres deste diablo e de sus
conpañeros. E cayo **el diablo** detras...

[*Engaños*, 520-2]

....e el gato myro la rred e vio que non quedava de tajar de la rred
salvo un lazo, e tyro rrezio e quebrole e fuese fuyendo; e subiose **el
gato** sobre un arvol...

[*Calila*, 4334-7]

Dixo el ximio sarnoso: 'Sy podiere ser, fazlo, ca me faras en ello
gran merçed, e averas por ello buen galardon de Dios'. E fuese **el
ximio**...

[*Calila*, 882-4]

---

[5] See England [1979], chapter 3.

The most obvious explanation of the large number of postposed thematic subjects is that they reflect the predominance of the order V-S in Classical Arabic.

2 *Castigos e documentos para bien vivir*

Castigos, which draws on a variety of sources, is an original Castilian prose work, and shows a clear preference for subject anteposition (59%). Whilst preceding direct objects and subject complements tend to coincide with subject postposition (79% with direct objects, 87% with subject complements), a following direct object or subject complement coincides usually with subject anteposition (77% with direct objects, 86% with subject complements); in other words the dominant orders are S-V-O and S-V-C, with O-V-S and C-V-S dominant in the smaller number of examples with preceding objects or complements.

The nature of the subject is also important in *Castigos*; there is a very strong tendency for thematic subjects to precede the verb, and there are many extreme cases of this in long passages in which the same thematic subject is repeated frequently as a means of conveying the didacticism forcefully:

Por el buen esfuerço tomaras amistad con Dios... **esfuerço bueno de coraçon** te fara que la vida lazrada... te semeja que es muy buena. **Esfuerço bueno de coraçon** te fara que non desesperes de la merçed de Dios... **Esfuerço bueno de coraçon** te fara que mates con tus manos al que te quisiere matar. **Esfuerço bueno de coraçon** te fara que las cuytas e los pesares que te vinieren que non se apoderen sobre ti... **Esfuerço bueno de coraçon** te fara que siruas bien al sennor con que visquieres... **Esfuerço bueno de coraçon** te fara que te auentures a muerte por escapar della a tu sennor o a tu amigo. **Esfuerço bueno de coraçon** te fara que en vna lid do mataren el cauallo a tu sennor, que le des el tuyo... **Esfuerço bueno de coraçon** te fara que en logar peligroso obres tu tan bien con tus manos por que valas mas... **Esfuerço bueno de**

coraçon te fara que te metas en el castillo de tu sennor e que le defiendas... [171.21–172.12]

Similar examples occur on pages 63, 97-8, 108-11, 134-5, 136-7, 169, and 207.

3 *Libro de los gatos*

Gatos is a translation of a Latin work, the *Fabulae* of Odo of Cheriton, probably made in the fourteenth century.[6] The position of the subject in *Gatos* differs little from usage in the *Fabulae*; table 4 gives the figures for subject position in those stories from Odo's work which occur in *Gatos*.[7]

table 4: position of the subject in the Fabulae

	order S - V		order V - S	
Independent Clauses	305	(56%)	242	(44%)
Dependent Clauses	64	(66%)	33	(34%)
Total	369	(57%)	275	(43%)

These overall figures suggest that the translator adhered closely to the word order of the original as far as subject position is concerned, and this impression is confirmed by a detailed comparison of the two texts. In approxi-

[6] Darbord [1981] uses syntactic evidence to suggest the second half of the fourteenth century as the likely date; his analysis is consistent with the proposed fourteenth-century dating in England [1980:2].

[7] I based my findings on the edition of the *Fabulae* in volume II of Léopold Hervieux, *Les fabulistes latins depuis le siècle d'Auguste jusqu'à la fin du moyen âge* (Paris, 1894); the Castilian and Latin texts can now be found conveniently together in Darbord [n.d.]. None of the extant manuscripts of the *Fabulae* can be considered to have been the one used by the translator.

mately half the expressions (409 in all) in *Fabulae* in which the subject is expressed, the overall sentence structure is retained in the Old Spanish version (i.e. type of clause, expression of subject and verb, vocabulary); in 370 such examples, the subject position is the same in both the Latin and the Spanish, with 20 examples of a Latin S-V order rendered as V-S in Spanish, and 19 examples of a Latin V-S order becoming S-V in Spanish. The principal differences are the following:

3.1 *The influence of the adverb*

In independent clauses containing only the three elements subject, verb, and adverb, the following orders are found:

Gatos		*Fabulae*	
S–V–Adv:	38	S–V–Adv:	13
S–Adv–V:	1	S–Adv–V:	18
Adv - V - S:	44	Adv - V - S:	18
Adv - S - V:	1	Adv - S - V:	9
V - Adv - S:	11	V - Adv - S:	5
V - S - Adv:	15	V - S - Adv:	4

Clear differences between the Latin and the Castilian can be observed from these figures. In *Gatos*, when the adverb precedes the verb, the subject is in postposition in 44 of the 46 examples (96%); in *Fabulae*, the corresponding figure is 40%. When the adverb follows the verb, the subject precedes the verb in *Gatos* in 38 of the 64 examples (59%), and in *Fabulae*, in 13 of the 22 examples (59%). Thus subject position in *Fabulae* does not vary in relation to the position of the adverb, but in *Gatos*, as in other Old Spanish texts, subject postposition is much more likely with a preceding adverb. In some instances, the translator changes the position of the subject:

Et **totum prandium** propter hoc maculatum est.

[Fabulae, XXXV, 7-8]

E por esto fue **el ayantar** menospreçiado...   [*Gatos*, 1313]

The more common strategy, however, is for the adverb to be moved, with the Latin S–Adv–V order rendered into Castilian as S–V–Adv:

Sed **lupus** uelocius currebat.   *[Fabulae, LVIII, 10]*
...mas **la liebre** corria mas ligeramente.   [*Gatos*, 1848]

...et **auca** in tantum ponderauit...   *[Fabulae, XXXVI, 4]*
...mas **el ansar** peso tanto...   [*Gatos*, 1327-8]

3.2 *The direct object*

When the direct object precedes the verb, the orders found are:

Gatos		Fabulae	
O–V–S	6	O–V–S	6
S–O–V	3	S–O–V	40
O–S–V	0	O–S–V	0

Two of the examples of the order S-O-V in Gatos are in proverbs [1401, 1651], translated literally from the Latin [*Fabulae*, XXXVIII, 7, and XLV, 6], and the third example also retains the order of the Latin:

Sed **impii** parum uel nichil gustant...   *[Fabulae, XXXII, 9-10]*
...mas **los malos** poco o nada toman dello.   [*Gatos*, 1215]

Usually, however, it is the direct object which is moved, to give the characteristic Castilian S–V–O order.

3.3 *The nature of the subject and verb*

In general, the same patterns of subject position can be observed in *Fabulae* as in Old Spanish texts; for example, thematic subjects such as nouns modified by *hic* or *iste* usually precede the verb, as do nouns qualified by *este* in Old Spanish, and verbs such as *venire* used in presentative expressions usually have the order V–S:

> Dicitur quod quidam Hereticus...predicauit quod uerus Deus non fecit mundum... Et uenit **una musca**...   [*Fabulae*, XII, 1-5]

> Cuenta que...un ereje...dixo que Dios verdadero non fiçiera todo el mundo... Estonçe vino **una mosca**...   [*Gatos*, 134-40]

One difference which can be observed is with verbs of speech. In introducing direct speech in *Fabulae*, the order V–S is consistent; although this order still predominates in *Gatos*, the translator on several occasions alters this to the S–V order:

Dixit **bufo**:	[*Fabulae*, XIV, 7]
El **bufo** respondio:	[*Gatos*, 160]
Et ait **paterfamilias**:	[*Fabulae*, XXIIIa, 10]
El **señor de las ovejas** dixo:	[*Gatos*, 581]
Et ait **coruus**:	[*Fabulae*, XXIX, 9]
El **cuervo** rrespondio:	[*Gatos*, 1104]

4 *El libro de los exenplos por* A.B.C.

Probably written originally in Latin and translated into Castilian by Clemente Sánchez himself between 1429 and 1438, *ABC* has a stronger preference for the order S–V than any of the other texts analysed. In the main, this does not appear to be the result of basic differences between this and other works; rather, the main tendencies of other works are pushed somewhat further in *ABC*, as is the case with following direct objects coinciding with preceding subjects:

S–V–O:	326	(97%)
V–S–O:	8	
V–O–S:	2	

No other text has such a strong preference for subject anteposition with a following direct object.

One feature unique to *ABC* concerns adverbial phrases which have as their head-word a gerund, with which the following orders occur:

Adv–V–S:	28	(26%)
Adv–S–V:	24	
S–Adv–V:	55	

ABC is the only text in which a preceding gerund increases the likelihood of subject anteposition. The number of examples is sufficiently high for the following to be regarded as characteristic of Clemente Sánchez's prose style:

E faziendo oracion Eliseo, **Dios** abrio los ojos del moço... [1321]

Estonçe **el papa**... dando le Dios esfuerço en el spiritu sancto, fizo un luengo sermón... [864-5]

It is possible that the Latin fondness for this construction influenced Clemente Sánchez, who originally wrote *ABC* in Latin.

ABC also has more examples of extraposition than any other text, as in the following:

Sant Gregorio dizen que tanto hera dado a fazer limosnas... [3358]

Un hombre dizen que rrobo a un monje...   [6014]

...ahunque **algunos** paresçe son contra justiçia.   [6150]

5 *Espéculo de los legos*

Comparison of *Espéculo* and its Latin source, the *Speculum laicorum*, is difficult because the edition of Welter [1914] is a partial one, which omits several *exempla* and large portions of the doctrinal sections. The table below gives the figures for subject position in the sections of the *Speculum laicorum* which correspond to *Espéculo*:

table 5: subject position in the Speculum laicorum

	order S–V		order V–S	
Independent Clauses	160	(57%)	121	(43%)
Dependent Clauses	85	(73%)	32	(27%)
Totals	245	(62%)	153	(38%)

As with *Gatos*, there is an increase in subject postposition in comparison with the Latin original, but the figures for *Espéculo* are undoubtedly distorted by Welter's omissions.[8] Nevertheless, the tendency to increase subject postposition in Castilian can be shown by a close comparison of the Latin and Castilian texts. There are 337 clauses

---

[8] Welter edited out the sources of many of the quotations from *auctores*; the few which remain all have the order V–S:
    ...ut ait **magister sentenciarum**...   [8.1]
The Spanish text has huge numbers of similar expressions, almost all with postposed subjects:
    ...aquello que dize **Salomon**...   [417.27]
    ...commo lo dize **Aristotiles**...   [7.18]
    ...segund lo dize **Plinio**...   [409.5]
These are undoubtedly following the Latin order.

with the subject expressed in which the overall structure is retained in the translation; the position of the subject is the same in both texts 287 times, a Latin S–V is replaced by a Castilian V–S 38 times, and a Latin V–S becomes S–V in Castilian 12 times. No fewer than 8 of the 12 examples of the latter change are with verbs of speech:

Refert **Odo de Seriton**...	[*Speculum*, 56.17]
E aun **Odo de Sericon** dize...	[*Espéculo*, 177.26]

Many of the examples of the Castilian order V–S replacing a Latin S–V contain a preceding adverbial phrase:

Quatuor sunt breviter tangenda...	[*Speculum*, 107.14]
Açerca del temor son de ver **quatro cosas**...	[*Espéculo*, 440.8]

Cui una die **dominus suus** dedit novam tunicam.	[*Speculum*, 11.18]
...e un dia diole **su sennor** una saya nueva...	[*Espéculo*, 27.11]

On other occasions it is the position of the adverbial phrase which moves, the Latin Adv–S–V being replaced in Castilian by S–V–Adv:

Circa Verbum Dei predicandum IV sunt consideranda...	[*Speculum*, 108.20]
Tres cosas son de ver e tratar açerca de la predicaçión de la palabra diuinal...	[*Espéculo*, 446.1]

Also similar to the *Gatos* translation is the way in which a preceding direct object or subject complement tends to coincide with a postposed subject. With the direct object, the orders found are:

Espéculo			*Speculum*		
O–V–S:	33	(87%)	O–V–S:	3	(7%)
S–O–V:	5		S–O–V:	37	
O–S–V:	0		O–S–V	2	

With the subject complement, the orders found are:

Espéculo			*Speculum*		
C–V–S:	45	(90%)	C–V–S:	4	(29%)
S–C–V:	5		S–C–V:	10	
C–S–V:	0		C–S–V:	0	

However, the translator usually adopts the characteristic Castilian order by moving the object or the complement.

Amor vel affectus carnalis tria mala facit...   [*Speculum*, 11.29]
El amor carnal faze tres cosas.   [*Espéculo*, 28.23]

6 Conclusions

Even a brief analysis of this type shows clearly the flexibility of Old Spanish in terms of subject position. There is no demonstrable historical progression, although it should be noted that *Castigos* and *Lucanor*, the two texts composed originally in Castilian, have a preference for the S–V order (59% and 64% respectively). All the writers share many features, such as the anteposition of thematic subjects, the postposition of rhematic subjects, and the tendency for preceding adverbs, objects, and complements to coincide with postposed subjects, whilst following adverbs, objects, and complements tend to occur with anteposed subjects. Nevertheless, all writers retain a considerable degree of flexibility, with similar pairs of examples exhibiting different word orders:

E quando **el obispo** lo vio, ovo grand pavor...   [*ABC*, 1573-4]
E quando lo vio **Sant Feliz**, maravillose muy mucho...   [*ABC*, 10165]

...e quando lo sopo **el egipciano**   [*ABC*, 397]
E quando **el su amigo** lo sopo...   [*ABC*, 406]

This flexibility meant that neither s–v nor v–s truly dominated in Old Spanish, and whilst translators did not normally retain the ov order of Latin, because Old Spanish was clearly a vo language [England, 1980:5-6], it did not go against the character of the language for translators from Arabic to retain a high proportion of v–s constructions. A great deal of this flexibility has been preserved in modern Spanish, and whilst there is evidence that some varieties of Spanish are increasingly favouring the s–v order, other studies suggest that this is far from being generalised.[9]

John England
University of Sheffield

[9] For one variety of Spanish which is becoming strongly S–V, see Silva Corvalán [1982]. Meyer-Hermann [1988:88] finds a high proportion of subject anteposition in the written journalism of *El País* (84%), but only 58% in a sample from Spanish radio.

REFERENCES

ABC = Sánchez, 1961

Calila = Keller & Linker, 1967

Castigos = Rey, 1952

Crabb, Daniel M., 1955
 A Comparative study of Word Order in Old Spanish and Old French Prose, Washington D.C.

Darbord, Bernard, 1981
 '*El libro de los Gatos*: sur la structure allégorique de l'exemple', *Cahiers de Linguistique Hispanique Médiévale*, 6, 81-109.

————, n.d.
 Libro de los gatos, Séminaire d'Etudes Médiévales Hispaniques de l'Université de Paris-XIII, Paris

Engaños = Keller, 1959

England, John, 1979
 'Word Order in Old Spanish Prose of the Thirteenth, Fourteenth, and Fifteenth Centuries', unpublished Ph.D. dissertation, Sheffield University

————, 1980
 'The Position of the Direct Object in Old Spanish', *JHP*, 5, 1-23.

————, forthcoming
 'Subject Position in Old Spanish Prose: *El Conde Lucanor*', *Caligrama*

Espéculo = Mohedano Hernández, 1951

Galmés de Fuentes, Alvaro, 1956
 Influencias sintácticas y estilísticas del árabe en la prosa medieval castellana, Madrid.

Gatos = Keller, 1958

Hottinger, Arnold, 1958
 Kalila und Dimna. Ein Versuch zur Darstellung der arabisch-altspanischen Übersetungskunst, Bern.

Juan Manuel, 1971
 El conde Lucanor (ed. J. M. Blecua), Madrid

Keller, John E., 1958
 (ed.) *El libro de los gatos*, Madrid

————, 1959
 (ed.) *El libro de los engaños*, Chapel Hill

Keller, John E., and Robert White Linker, 1967
 (eds) *El libro de Calila e Digna*, Madrid

Lucanor = Juan Manuel, 1971

Meyer-Hermann, Reinhard, 1988
 '¿Se debe la posposición del sujeto en el español a una influencia
 árabe?', *RFE*, 68, 67-96.

Mohedano Hernández, José María, 1951
 (ed.) *El espéculo de los legos*, Madrid

Pardo Huber, Virginia, 1973
 'El orden de los elementos oracionales en la prosa castellana de los
 siglos XII y XIII', unpublished Ph.D. dissertation, Tulane University.

Rey, Agapito, 1952
 (ed.) *Castigos y documentos para bien vivir ordenados por el rey don
 Sancho IV*, Bloomington

Sánchez, Clemente, 1961
 El libro de los exenplos por a.b.c.. (ed. John E Keller) Madrid

Silva Corvalán, Carmen, 1982
 'SubJect Expression and Placement in Mexican-American Spanish',
 in *Spanish in the United States. Sociolinguistic Aspects*, ed. Jon
 Amestae and Lucía Elías Olivares, Cambridge.

Welter, J-Th., 1914
 *Le Speculum laicorum. Edition d'une collection d'exempla
 composée en Angleterre à la fin du XIIIè siècle*, Paris

Three Alfonsine etymologies

WHEN the *Dictionary of Alfonsine Prose*—the first stage of the Wisconsin *Dictionary of the Old Spanish Language* [DOSL]—is published it will provide many earlier first occurrences than those posited by Corominas–Pascual [1980]. The Alfonsine corpus was selected as the core of DOSL, presenting as it does a homogeneous body of datable texts, many of which had not been previously edited and were therefore unavailable to linguists. The search for first occurrences is, of course, trivial, as Pascual pointed out in the introduction to DCECH [1980: 1, ix, n.1]; what is interesting and useful is that many of Corominas' [and Pascual's] hypotheses will be confirmed or rejected, and that previously-unknown words will come to light which later fell by the evolutionary wayside. It will perhaps whet appetites (soon to be satisfied by publication of the Dictionary) to offer examples from both categories:

PREVIOUSLY UNKNOWN WORDS

*selecho

> *& aun tenemos que de aqui se leuanto el saber de labrar en tierra como ollas & cantaros & lo al que se ende faze. & otrossi los uidrios del **felecho**...*

> [*General Estoria* I, fol. 9v60]

It is obvious that we are not dealing here with ferns [*felecho* < FILICTUM]. Glass is made from silica, so that a perfectly regular evolution from a *SILICEUM would give *selecho*. I know of no other occurrence of this or related forms until the introduction of *silicio* in the nineteenth century [DCECH *silice*]. The obvious explanation is confusion by the scribe of *f* and tall *s*; but it is of course possible to posit confusion at the translation rather than the scribal stage, given the similarity between the base forms SILEX and FILIX. Contamination seems unlikely, however, given the semantic difference between them. The copyists of the other two MSS certainly had no idea of what was intended, B offering *desfecho*, D *fecho* [Solalinde, xx]

FORMS POSITED BY COROMINAS

coxa

> *& otrossi enuiaron le uestidos fechos de bezerros de la mar. & unos gusanos que sacaron desse rio que auien en gordo mas que podrie seer una* **coxa** *de pierna de omne. & por uentura podrie seer que fuessen camarones & era el gosto dellos mas dulce que de todos los otros pesces.*

[*General Estoria* IV, fol. 229v74]

Corominas under the headword *cojo* lists as a derivative '*coja, corva', which he classifies as 'ant. [ya Acad. 1843]', concluding that 'en realidad no existe esta palabra en castellano [note 4: 'Se perdió ahí en fecha preliteraria, aunque es común a todos los romances.'] pues su única fuente es Covarrubias y este lexicógrafo, al afirmar que "*coxo* se dixo de *coja*, que vale 'pierna', *poples*" se refiere a la voz latina *coxa*...' It is clear from the GEIV quotation that the word here means a more substantial part of the limb than the rear of the knee implied by 'corva', and the sense seems to require either 'calf' or 'thigh' (making the shrimps in question rather more than bite-sized!). This confirms Covarrubias against Corominas, because, of course, Latin COXA means 'hip' and POPLES 'back of knee' [Glare] (though Latham [359] includes the thigh in his definition of POPLES for Late Latin), and it seems that the seventeenth-century lexicographer—despite the spelling—was indeed referring to a Romance form. This impression is strengthened by his definition of *coxín*: 'se dixo de coxa porque van sobre el los muslos, y de alli cuxa, lanca en cuxa, quando el hombre de armas no la lleva en el ristre, sino armada al muslo...' [146*ra*]

DOSL has more occurrences from the the Alfonsine corpus: *Lapidario* (4), *Astronomía* (17), *Judizios* (2), and *Estoria de Espanna II* (1), of which only one has the sense 'thigh'; the rest refer to the leg, but to which part is not immediately clear. This evidence contradicts Corominas' assertion that the word disappeared in Spanish in the preliterary period; given Covarrubias' knowledge of it, we may speculate that it remained in use, perhaps dialectally, until the sixteenth century. It is still used with the sense 'thigh' in Modern Galician [Boullón Agrelo: 256].

yenque

> *Otrossi el maestro ferrero que sie cerca la yenque asmando la obra del fierro. el bafo del fuego quema las carnes del. & a contienda en el calor de la fragua.*

> [*General Estoria* IV, fol. 271v19]

The difficulties of deriving *yunque* from INCŪDEM have been described by Corominas–Pascual [1980-91:6, 22-4]. They posit a shift of stress in a 'lat. vg. *ĬNCŬDE', giving *incue*, followed by metathesis of the *u* to provide *iunque*.

They give as evidence a recorded form *inque* (which they suppose to have been pronounced *incue*) in a medieval translation of the Bible cited by Scio, which they date as approximately contemporaneous with Alfonso X, and offer VĬDŬA > *viuda* in support. However, both stressed and unstressed *i* might have been expected to give *e* in Castilian, and there is no record other than in our text of such a form. This could be explained quite simply from ĬNCŪDE: an early shift of stress to the initial syllable would have provoked the fall of U in hiatus [Lloyd 191], and the initial palatal would have resulted from the introduction of a glide to prevent hiatus when the word was preceded by the feminine article.

ĬNCŪDEM > *ĬNCŬDE' > [enkue] > [enke] > [jenke]

All explanations of *yunque* have to posit a shift of stress from the second to the first syllable at some stage in the development from ĬNCŪDEM. This Alfonsine form is the only one to show the *e* that would have been expected from Latin initial I, and it seems that Rosenblat's proposal of a derivation *encúe > *éncue > íncue* was the best explanation, despite Corominas-Pascual's rejection [6, 24] on the grounds that such a late shift of stress would have been impossible. All that is required is for the stress-shift to have taken place earlier, allowing the U in hiatus to fall. Another, perhaps parallel, development would have retained the U, either as a vowel or a semi-vowel, which would then have been available for metathesis under the Corominas-Pascual hypothesis.

David Mackenzie
University of Birmingham

REFERENCES

Boullón Agrelo, A. I., *etc.*, 1988
  Diccionario normativo galego-castelán, Vigo
Corominas, J., & J. A. Pascual, 1980-91
  Diccionario crítico etimológico e hispánico, Madrid
Covarrubias, S. de, 1609, 1927
  Tesoro de la lengua castellana, o española, Madrid, New York
DCECH = Corominas & Pascual
General Estoria = Kasten & Nitti
Glare, P. G. W., 1968-82
  Oxford Latin Dictionary, Oxford
Kasten, L. A., & J. J. Nitti (eds), 1978
  Concordances and texts of the Royal Scriptorium manuscripts of Alfonso X, Madison
Latham, R. E., 1965
  Revised Medieval Latin Word-List, London
Lloyd, P. M., 1986
  From Latin to Spanish, Baltimore

El moro te jugara mal [*Cid* 3319]:
rough justice for an Infante?

I N the third *Cantar* of the *Poema de Mio Cid* the man of few words, Pedro Bermúdez, is stung into verbal action: during the Court scene he taunts the Infante Fernán González by reminding him of his earlier cowardice in battle during the siege of Valencia:

> Pedist las feridas primeras al Canpeador leal,
> vist un moro, fústel' ensayar,
> antes fuxiste que a [é]l te allegasses.
> Si yo non uviás, el moro te jugara mal.
>
> [*Cid* 3317-19[1]]

The general sense of the last of these four lines is clear from the context: no good would have come to the Infante had Pedro Bermúdez not happened to turn up as he fled from his Moorish adversary. The explanatory footnotes and translations of recent editors loosely reflect this: 'si yo no llegase, mal te hubiera burlado el moro' [Menéndez Pidal 1913], 'Si yo no te hubiese ayudado el moro te habría jugado una mala partida' [Lacarra 1983], 'If I had not come to the rescue, the Moor would have given you a rough time of it' [Smith 1972], 'If I had not gone to your aid, that Moor would have got the better of you' [Michael-Hamilton-Perry 1975], 'Si no hubiese acudido en tu ayuda, las hubieras pasado negras con el moro' [Michael 1976]. Smith and Michael-Hamilton-Perry deduce the sense from the context: their judgement is that *jugar mal* has the appearance of an idiom meaning 'to get the better of', 'to give a rough time to'. This looks

---

[1]Quotations from the *Poema de Mio Cid* are from Michael [1976].

an attractive idea, but neither editor brings forward internal evidence from the *Cid* or external evidence from other medieval works in support of his interpretation. Menéndez Pidal, as indicated by his vocabulary to the three-volume edition of the *Cantar de Mio Cid* [1908-11: II, 724], interprets *jugar* as a transitive verb, with the sense *burlar* 'to trick', and takes the second hemistich in the sense 'the Moor would have played a dirty trick on you'; María Eugenia Lacarra echoes this. There is a problem of logic here: in this unreal condition the Moor might well have been prepared to inflict physical damage on the fleeing Infante, but why, in such circumstances, would he have wished to trick or deceive his adversary?

Menéndez Pidal does cross-refer to line 3249 of the *Cid* and line 485b of Berceo's *Vida de Santo Domingo* as corroborative evidence for his reading of *jugar* as a reflex of Latin JOCARI and transitive verb (I return to these examples below), and this view is repeated by Corominas, who cites Menéndez Pidal's two examples (*Cid* 3249 and *S.Dom.* 485b), confirms the etymology and offers 'bromear' as a definition, with the parenthetical note that this was a 'sentido que en el castellano arcaico evolucionó en el de "burlar, engañar", en los citados pasajes de *Cid* y *S.Dom*.' [1980-83: III, 535]. Corominas thus repeats Menéndez Pidal, with the same evidence, while Smith and Michael, working independently of each other, take a divergent line without formal justification and without drawing specific attention to what they are doing. A reexamination of the form *jugar*, in the wider context of its usage in Old Spanish, raises some queries about the Pidal–Corominas interpretation, and reveals that Smith-Michael, possibly without quite realizing why, may have come much closer to the mark.

In each of the following examples, taken from texts of the twelfth and thirteenth centuries, *jugar* (on two occasions *juggar*) appears in the sense 'to judge':

1 *Sobre esto pendraron e moujeron pleito, e fueron ante don Diago; e iugo don Diago que eitassen sortes los canonges.*

Document of Santo Domingo de la Calzada, 1199 [Menéndez Pidal 1919: 80.8; Gifford & Hodcroft 1959:12.7]

2   *que es senior de todo el mundo,*
      asi cumo el cilo es redondo;
      de todas gentes senior sera
      i todo seglo iugara.

Auto de los Reyes Magos [Menéndez Pidal 1965:18.43; Gifford & Hodcroft 1959:15.43]

3 *Ca no iugue yo saber entre uos alguna cosa fueras Ihesu Christo, e este crucifigado.*

El Nuevo Testamento [Montgomery and Baldwin 1970: 272.7]. The Vulgate text is: 'Non enim judicavi me scire aliquit inter vos nisi Jesum Cristum' [I Corinthians: 2.2].

4 *E en cabo de* III *dias , cate.l la mano. e si la mano.l fallaren quemada, quemen a ella o suffra la pena cuemo es iugada.*

Fuero de Baeza [Roudil 1962:268d]

5 *De cabo mando que qual quiere que en la presón del querelloso querrá entrar por deudo[r] manjfiesto, fasta tres !X días pague el deudo, o sea padre o muger o fijo que en la presón jaçrá jugado.*

Fuero de Teruel [Gorosch 1950:203.2]

6 Del judez et los alcaldes que non *jugguen* a otros si non aquellos que a ellos uernan

Fuero de Teruel, MS B [Gorosch 1950:72.1]

7 De exceptione rei iudicate. De exceptión de cosa *iugada*.

Vidal Mayor [Tilander 1956:8.1]

8 Item, que la justicia dAragon *juge* todos los pleytos que uenieren a la cort.

Document of Huesca, 1283 [Navarro 1957: 55.10]

9 ca el enuiara este libro al papa Beneyto, et el papa nol entendio como deuiera et *iugaral* por malo.

Primera crónica general [Menéndez Pidal 1955: 302a.41]

10 Ca si por linage daquel logar *iuggo* e mando Dios que diessen esta onrra a alguno dend, mas derechero so yo de auer lo, ca so desse linage que Moysen.

General estoria [Solalinde 1930: 640b.17]

In all of these cases, the context demonstrates beyond reasonable doubt the existence of an Old Spanish verb *jugar* as a reflex of Latin JUDICARE, 'to judge'. Its treatment by editors ranges from that of Montgomery and Baldwin [1970:574], who believe the *Nuevo Testamento* form *iugue* to be an 'error', to that of Gifford and Hodcroft [1959], who accurately define the *iugo* of the Santo Domingo de la Calzada document as 'juzgó' [276] and who, although their text reproduces the *iugura* reading of the Menéndez Pidal [1900] *Auto de los Reyes*

Magos edition, correctly note that the MS reads *iugara* and provide an accurate definition: 'juzgara' [276][1].

Corominas [1980-83:III, 536], lists all but one of the known Old Spanish descendants of JUDICARE: *judgar, juzgar, jutgar, jubgar, julgar, jurgar* (the last two most typical of Western dialect areas). Not surprisingly, however, in view of its relative rarity, the form *jugar* escapes his lexicographer's net. The ten examples just quoted, from ten different Old Spanish sources, must be sufficient to make us discount the possibility of scribal aberration and take the form seriously. It is also noticeable that the *jugar* forms appear in texts whose language is most characteristic of central or Eastern dialect areas of the Peninsula.

Menéndez Pidal [1952:163] himself provides a phonetic explanation for the *jugar* form without actually citing an example of its existence: 'En grupos de dental y gutural la primera se hace continua *o desaparece* [my italics], y la segunda permanece oclusiva, pero convertida en sonora la sorda. Así, TꞋC o DꞋC da ant. *dg*, mod. *zg*:[2] portaticu, ant. *portadgo*, mod. *portazgo*; pedicu (por pedica), *piezgo*; judicare, ant. *judgar*, moderno *juzgar*. Son de origen leonés (en este dialecto se dice *portalgo, mayoralgo, julgar* etc.) los casos de conversión de la primera en *l*'. He gives no examples of the disappearance of the first element in combinations where dental and velar come together as a

---

[1]Pestana [1965: 43] prints *iugura*, following Menéndez Pidal [1900] and Gifford and Hodcroft [1959], also noting that the MS form is *iugara*, which he correctly identifies as the third person of the future indicative of O.Sp. *jugar* < JUDICARE [100-01].

[2] Menéndez Pidal gives the impression that this was a phonetic development. The frequency of forms spelled *zg* in reliable medieval Spanish manuscripts (for examples see Corominas [1980-83: III, 536-37]) suggests the more likely explanation that the graph *z* of these forms represents a dental affricate characteristic of the semi-learned *juez* (< JUDICE) and *judiçio, juiço, juizo, juizio* (< JUDICIU).

result of the late fall of an unstressed vowel, but with
JUDICARE > *jugar* (*juggar*) before us this omission can
now be made good[1]:

JUDICARE
   (Western dialects) > *julgar, jurgar*
   (Central dialects) > *judgar* > (a) *jutgar, jubgar*
                                    (b) *juzgar*
   (Central, Eastern dialects) > *jugar, juggar*

Alongside *jugar* < JUDICARE, the homophone *jugar* (or
jogar)[2] < JOCARI coexisted in Old Spanish, and not
surprisingly gave rise to some confusion in the medieval
period, eventually solved by the standardization of the
form *juzgar* for the first and *jugar* for the second. The
problem of differentiating between the homophones is
illustrated by the two examples [*Cid* 3249 and *S.Dom.* 485b]
cited by Menéndez Pidal in support of his interpretation
of 'el moro te jugara mal'.

The first of these occurs at the beginning of the Court
scene, when Alfonso's two judges rule that the Infantes
de Carrión, in financial difficulties, must borrow as much
as they can towards the two thousand marks they owe
the Cid, and repay him in cash or kind:

> Sobre los dozientos marcos   que tenié el rrey Alfonso,
> pagaron los ifantes   al que en buen ora nasco,
> enpréstanles de lo ageno,   que non les cumple lo suyo,
> mal escapan iogados,   sabed, d'esta razón.
>> [*Cid* 3246-49]

---

[1] The substantive *iuge* (< JUDICE) demonstrates the same phonetic
development; it is the preferred form in *Fueros de Aragon*, where it
occurs on eight occasions, alongside four examples of *iudge* and one of
iutge [Tilander 1937:443].

[2] See Corominas [1980-83: III, 535} for a summary of rival explanations
of the *o/u* alternation in this verb.

The difficulty of interpreting the *jogar mal* of *Cid* 3249 is again illustrated by editors' responses: Menéndez Pidal [1913] and Smith [1972] do not comment, Michael-Hamilton-Perry [1975] translate very freely 'The tables were certainly turned against them that day', and Michael [1976] offers 'sabed que salieron muy escarnecidos de este asunto'. But since the poet is commenting directly on the effect upon the Infantes of the juridical decisions of the Counts Henry and Raymond of Burgundy, as transmitted by the latter (*Cid* 3237), it would seem that although either interpretation could make sense Menéndez Pidal's proposal (supported this time by Michael) of 'severely mocked' sits less easily in the context than the alternative possibility, 'severely judged'.

Menéndez Pidal's second proposal for *jogar* in the sense 'burlar' comes from Berceo's *Vida de Santo Domingo de Silos*, in a context where St Dominic has dealt with a group of recalcitrant pilgrims who, having divested themselves of their clothing, come to him with demands for apparel of higher quality. St Dominic has their own discarded garments gathered up and redistributed to them in random fashion, much to their confusion and discomfiture, causing the poet to remark:

> ¡Qui pudo veer nunqua   cuerpo tan palaciano!
> ¡Nin que tan bien podiesse   jogar a su cristiano!
>
> [*S. Dom.* 485a,b]

Dutton [1978: 280] defines *jogar* as 'burlar'. Teresa Labarta de Chaves [1972: 485n, 228], following Lanchetas [1900], translates *jogar* into Modern Spanish as 'alegrar', but there is little justification for this nonce meaning, even allowing for the usual *lectio difficilior* arguments, since *jogar* is not documented elsewhere in Old Spanish in the sense 'amuse', 'entertain', and since the meanings 'burlar' and 'juzgar' both make sense in the hemistich. Again, the context offers some help in the delicate task of interpretation. Would Berceo be more likely to praise St Dominic for making fun of the misguided penitents or for coming up with a wise judgement in dealing with a tricky situation? Either reading could be argued (and it is noticeable that the difficulties increase when one is dealing with *jugar/jogar* alone rather than the idiom *jugar mal*) but the balance of probabilities appears to lie with the second of the interpretations. This could well be another example of *jogar* 'to judge', in a context where Berceo is enquiring, rhetorically, 'Whenever did you come across ... a man so well able to exercise jurisdiction over his fellow men?'.

One final example of the use of *jugar mal* in Old Spanish should help to put the two debateable lines in the *Poema de Mio Cid* into perspective. In the *Libro de Alexandre*, the first battle between Alexander and Darius involves Philotas and Maceas, a Persian, and a situation and grammatical construction (the unreal condition) crop up which are virtually identical to that in the *Poema de Mio Cid*:

> Ovo y al jnfante Aȳuelos a matar,
> cauallero de presçio sy lo oyestes contar;
> mas presto fue Filotas por luego lo vengar,
> oujeral mal jugado syl podiese alcançar.
>
> [*Alex.* 1018: MS *P*]

Philotas is eager for retribution here, and not concerned with making fun of his enemy; this interpretation is fully borne out by the copyist of MS *O*, whose version of the last line is:

> ouieral mal julgado sel podies alcançar.

Sas [1976: 330] arbitrarily and, as we have seen, wrongly, dismisses the *P* reading, *jugado*, as an 'errata por judgado', although he does get the sense right; Nelson [1979: 386], reconstructing the text, opts for *jugado* on the rather mysterious grounds that *O* '*julgado* desentona con muchas otras expresiones de connotación irónica', when a comparison with *Cid* 3319 would have provided much more convincing justification for his choice. Neither, however, quite appreciates that we are faced with two established Old Spanish phonetic variations on the same verb and that the verb, confirmed by the copyist of *O*, is a reflex of Latin JUDICARE. The poet is expressing his opinion that 'Had Philotas been able to catch up with the Infante, he would have visited a terrible judgement upon him'.

My aim here has been to review a semantic field a little wider than Menéndez Pidal was able to take into account in the light of the evidence available in the first decade of this century, and to draw attention to the problems of interpretation. It is highly likely that since *jugar* < JUDICARE and *jugar* < JOCARI were homophones in Old Spanish, the average Castilian would be in a poor position to distinguish which of the two he was using in a set phrase like *jugar mal*, and that the more the form *judgar* (later *juzgar*) became the accepted standard for the first, and *jugar* for the second, the more the speaker would unconsciously assume, via a kind of popular etymology, that the *jugar* of the phrase *jugar mal* was a reflex of the verb JOCARI. The contamination may well have depended more upon the medieval sense of *jugar* (< JOCARI) 'to wield a weapon, to strike a blow' than on the hypothetical 'to make fun of' proposed by Menéndez Pidal and supported by Corominas, but unsubstantiated by a closer examination of the cases which they cite.

When line 3319 of the *Cid* is reread in the context of *Alex.* 1018 and in its own immediate textual context, there is a case to be made that at the beginning of the thirteenth century both the *Cid* and the *Alexandre* poets were still aware of the etymology of the phrase which they use, and that the second part of Pedro Bermúdez's reflection, 'Si yo non uvias, el moro te jugara mal' should be interpreted as an example of the construction *jugar mal*, 'to visit severe judgement upon', or more loosely 'to deal severely with', possibly contaminated with a vague notion of 'would deal severe blows'. Of the renderings of modern editors, those which most effectively capture the sense and the style are the versions of Ian Michael and Colin Smith: 'Si yo no hubiese acudido en tu ayuda, las hubieras pasado negras con el moro' {Michael] and 'If I had not come to the rescue, the Moor would have given you a rough time of it' [Smith]. The textual evidence is that Pedro Bermúdez is predicting rough justice for an Infante.[1]

Ian Macpherson
University of Durham

[1] I should like to express my gratitude to both editors of this volume for their interest in and constructive comments on an earlier draft, and to Dr Manuel Seco, of the *Real Academia Española* and Dr John Nitti, of the Seminary of Medieval Hispanic Studies in Madison, Wisconsin, for their generosity in providing access to the working files of both institutions. Although Professor Michael has reservations about some of my arguments, the final product has benefited a great deal from his encouragement, patience, energy and skill, and he is of course exonerated from complicity in the detail of my conclusions.

REFERENCES

Corominas, J., & J. A. Pascual, 1980-91
  Diccionario crítico etimológico castellano e hispánico, 6 vols, Madrid
Dutton, B., 1978
  (ed.) Gonzalo de Berceo *La vida de Santo Domingo de Silos*. (Obras completas, vol. 4) London
Gifford, D. J., & F. W. Hodcroft, 1959
  Textos lingüísticos del medioevo español, Oxford
Gorosch, M., 1950
  El fuero de Teruel, Stockholm (Leges Hispanicae Medii Aevi, 1)
Labarta de Chaves, T., 1972
  (ed.) Gonzalo de Berceo *Vida de Santo Domingo de Silos*. Madrid
Lacarra, M. E., 1988
  (ed.) *Poema de Mio Cid*. Madrid
Menénez Pidal, R., 1900
  'Disputa del alma y el cuerpo y Auto de los Reyes Magos', *RABM*, 4: 449-62.
————., 1908-11
  (ed.) *Cantar de Mio Cid*. Madrid
————., 1913
  (ed.) *Poema de Mio Cid*. Madrid
————., 1952
  Manual de gramática histórica española. (9th ed.) Madrid
————., Solalinde, A. G.., Muñoz Cortés, M. & Gómez Pérez, J., 1955
  (eds.) *Primera crónica general de España*, 2 vols., Madrid.
————., 1965
  Crestomatía del español medieval, acabada y revisada por Rafael Lapesa y María Soledad de Andrés, 2 vols., Madrid
————., 1919
  Documentos lingüísticos de España. I. Reino de Castilla, Madrid
Michael, I. D. L., Hamilton, R. & Perry, J., 1975
  The Poem of the Cid. A new critical edition of the Spanish text by Ian Michael. Together with a new prose translation by Rita Hamilton and Janet Perry, Manchester & New York
Michael, I. D. L., 1976[1], 1987[5]
  (ed.) *Poema de Mío Cid*. Madrid

Montgomery, T. & Baldwin, S. W., 1970
  (eds) *El Nuevo Testamento. Version castellana de hacia 1260,* (Anejos del BRAE, XXII) Madrid
Navarro, T., 1957
  Documentos lingüísticos del Alto Aragón, New York
Nelson, D. A., 1979
  (ed.) *El libro de Alixandre,* Madrid
Pestana, S., 1965
  (ed.) *Auto de los Reyes Magos,* Lisbon
Roudil, J. M. V., 1962
  (ed.) *El fuero de Baeza,* The Hague
Sas, L. F., 1976
  Vocabulario del 'Libro de Alexandre', Madrid
Smith, C. C., 1972
  (ed.) *Poema de Mio Cid,* Oxford
——————, 1976
  (ed.) *Poema de mio Cid,* Madrid
Solalinde, A. G., 1930
  (ed.) Alfonso X el Sabio, *General Estoria, 1ª. parte,* Madrid
Tilander, G., 1937
  (ed.) *Los fueros de Aragón,* Lund.
——————, 1956
  (ed.) *Vidal Mayor,* 3 vols., Lund.

Old Spanish *lixo, lixoso*
versus *limpio, lindo, lisonja*

*A study of phonosymbolism's share
in lexical transmission*

1 THERE is scarcely any need for demonstrating, in searching detail, the fact that phonosymbolism, also called sound symbolism, over the last century or so, has developed into something of a problem child, or *Sorgenkind*, among students of historical linguistics. Stray appeals to it have been periodically rejected by stern disciplinarians on account of their irremediable subjectivity, a quality which, being tantamount to unverifiability, is rumored to tend to lower the status of diachronic linguistics among or even alongside the strict sciences.

To some extent this difficulty, or misunderstanding, may have hinged on the fact that the agency of phonosymbolism, as a rule, has been invoked by scholars of liberal persuasion in reference to ultimate word origins which, almost by definition, are clouded in darkness. There may thus be some wisdom in, at least temporarily, changing the perspective and experimenting with the assumption of phonosymbolic causation in the context of the extinction, rather than the birth, of lexical units—a phase of lexical growth, as a rule, more open to close inspection. If positive or negative effects of phonosymbolism are seen, or are suspected to have acted, as terminal factors, then the phenomenon would stand in competition with instances of desirable or harmful homonymy; with the impact of taboo; with the repudiation of morphological troublemakers; and with similar forces and reactions thereto already better known and thus less hesitantly introduced into our arithmetic.

There exist several varieties of phonosymbolism, some of them dubbed 'expressivity', others 'onomatopoeia'. The kind here introduced is of a relative rather than absolute character. The special feature here isolated, not yet investigated on a wide scale, may have operated in just a few languages and/or over limited periods of time.[1]

Those analysts who agree to posit some such pressure simply assume that, if in a given language—perhaps accidentally—several conspicuous lexical items semantically tied together share certain sharply profiled features of form (stress, number and shape of syllables, certain vowels and/or consonants either in isolation or in recurrent combination), then an unintegrated word related to that group by its meaning, but clashing with the salient configuration of the other items, may gradually be squeezed out on account of its eccentricity, especially if sufficient near-synonyms are readily available to the speakers to serve as substitutes.

2 The example here chosen by way of illustration is OSp. *lixo* 'dirt', a word at present listed only by a few monolingual dictionaries aiming at completeness of coverage and, if so, invariably dubbed as an archaism.[2] In medieval

---

[1] A stimulating modern-day statement on how phonosymbolism is supposed to work will be found in Hinton, Nicholls, and Ohala's joint Introduction to their eagerly-awaited book. That same miscellany is to contain an essay from my own pen [Malkiel Forthcoming 1]; for additional completed pieces of mine still unavailable, see the References [Forthcoming 2 to 5]. I prefer to use the tag 'phonosymbolism' rather than 'sound symbolism' (cf. German 'Lautsymbolik' and similar labels in Scandinavian languages), because it exempts me from having to worry about 'unsound symbolism'.

[2] Scattered references to *lixo* and its principal offshoots are already found in Renaissance dictionaries, whether mono- or bi-lingual. I have here made ample use of the statements in the revised 20th edn.

texts, the word was by no means rare and was, moreover, accompanied by the adjective *lixoso* 'dirty' and by the latter's adverbial satellite *lixosamente* (and variants). Members of this word-family appear in the writings of prominent representatives of early- and mid-fourteenth-century literature, including such masters of poetry and prose as Juan Ruiz and Don Juan Manuel, respectively; also, scattered remnants of its use have been faithfully preserved in spontaneous dialect speech of certain regions, especially Galicia. These details will yet come up for more explicit, if parenthetic, mention. What matters more to us is the circumstance that *lixo* /lišo/, the undisputed center of the word-family at issue, to this day has remained, all efforts to the contrary notwithstanding, a word of unknown ancestry. We shall yet briefly survey some lame attempts so far made at etymologizing it; but distinctly heavier emphasis will be placed here on identifying the reasons for its rather sudden disappearance, at least from Standard Spanish.

3 As near-equivalents of 'dirt' (hence also of OSp. *lixo*) Spanish has traditionally made use of such words as *barro* 'mud, clay, earthenware' (*barr-oso* 'muddy', *barr-*

[1984:833] of the Madrid Academy's dictionary. On the side of information, as against interpretation, Vol. 3 of J. Corominas' original venture [1956:90-94] continues to lend good services. On certain peculiarities of the usage of Juan Ruiz and Don Juan Manuel I have fruitfully consulted the respective vocabularies by H. B. Richardson [1930:137] and F. Huerta Tejadas [1956:103]. For quick orientation on Galician preferences I have relied on L. Carré Alvarellos [1933: 362b] beside J. S. Crespo Pozo [1963:601, s.v. *suciedad*]; the latter source, more explicit about geographic distribution, places *lix-ume* 'cosa sucia' in Lámpara and identifies, in the string of synonyms, *roña*, lit. 'scab, mange; sticky dirt', upon which C. López-Morillas' fine study has projected fresh light [1974:488-96]. For my glosses, I have chiefly relied on E. B. Williams' dictionary.

ero 'mudhole', *em-barr-ar* 'to splash with mud, smear');
cieno 'mud, slime, silt' (*cién-aga* 'marsh, moor, mudhole', *cien-oso* or *cen-ag-oso* 'muddy, slimy, silty', *en-
cen-ag-arse* 'to wallow in, get into, the mud'); *fango*
'mud, mire' (*fang-oso* 'muddy, miry', 'soft and sticky',
fang-al/-ar 'quagmire, mudhole', *en-fang-ar* 'to muddy,
cover with mud', refl. 'to sink, be sunk in mud'); *lodo*
'mud' (*lod-oso* 'muddy', *en-lod-ar* 'to soil or plaster or
seal with mud'; *lod-az-ar* 'to bemire'; *en-lod-adura*,
-amiento 'muddying, muddiness'); *mugre* 'dirt, filth'
(*mugr-iento* and, less commonly, *-oso* 'filthy', *en-mugr-
ecer* 'to dirty'); *polvo* 'dust', '[loosely floating] powder', as
against *pólvora* '[assembled] powder (as in gunpowder)';
the adjectives *polv-or-iento* and, less frequently, *polv-or-
oso* function as off-shoots of both nouns; *em-polv-ar*,
-orar, *-orizar* 'to cover with dust, powder'); *tollo*
'quagmire'/ *tolla* 'soggy marsh' (*a-toll-arse* 'to get stuck
in the mud or the mudhole', *a-toll-adero* 'mudhole',
figurative 'blind alley, dead end, obstruction').

This is, beyond question, a list woefully incomplete,
quite aside from having been, on purpose, confined to
representing modern-day Standard Spanish usage.
However, the forms actually culled, in random fashion,
from a corpus deliberately selected on account of its
smallness have here been cited without any exception,[3]

---

[3] As a check on the accuracy of my thinking, here and farther down,
readers may want to collate the list here offered with a sample of
gleanings from dialect speech, such as those put on display by Crespo
Pozo. If one discounts *morr-iña* as an inconclusive suffixal derivative,
one encounters again a clear-cut majority of items with *a* or *o/u* as their
nuclear vowels (*mafa, sarro,* plus the kernel of *carraña; cotra, lorda,
roña,* plus the hard core of *turrualho*), with *guiña* and *rela* alone acting
as the carriers of front-vowels in the same position. The long-baffling
development of SŪCIDU 'juicy' into OSp. *suzio,* Ptg. *sujo* 'dirty' now also
becomes more readily understandable. In the Judeo-Spanish of Balkan
countries, *lodo* appears to predominate [Crews, 1935:306a].

beyond the omission of wholly atypical *cenizas* 'ashes' (*ceni-ciento/-zoso* 'ashen, ashy', *cenic-ero* 'ashpan, ashtray', *ceniz-al* 'ashpit', the phytonym *cenic-illa*, plus *en-ceniz-ar* 'to cover with ashes'). The original outcome of the rhizotonic primitive CINIS, -ERIS (as faithfully preserved in Fr. *cendre*—cf. English *cinder* 'a partially or mostly burned piece of coal or wood', *Cinderella*—, It. *cenere*) collapsed in Spanish,[4] yielding ground to a suffixal substitute. If one, then, agrees to concentrate on the other local members of the chosen semantic group, one makes this discovery: *barro, cieno, fango, lodo, mugre, polvo*, plus *tollo/tolla* each seem to act as nominal centers of a moderately large lexical family. The nouns happen to be preponderantly masculine; they are consistently bisyllabic and paroxytonic; they end, with a single exception, in -*o* rather than in -*e* or in a consonant and, particularly important for the purpose of the demonstration here undertaken, they characteristically have, as a nuclear vowel, an *a* (twice), an *o* (thrice), an *u* (once), or else the diphthong *ie*, with *mugre* thus emerging, from application of the chosen criteria, as the least typical constituent of the entire congeries.

Once these measuring rods have become available to us, how does *lixo*'s candidacy for survival into modern Spanish stack up, in comparison with the chances of its rivals? *Lixo* boasted the apposite grammatical category; the 'right' number of syllables; the desirable gender; the favored stress pattern; the ideal final vowel. But its heavily accented nuclear vowel was incompatible with the kernels of its near-synonyms. As a matter of fact, it represented the ultimate in incompatibility with the majority rule: Had the word under investigation been

---

[4] Perhaps because speakers could not agree on which was more suitable: **cendre* or **cerne*, given the infelicity of **cenre*.

*lexo /lešo/, it might have clashed far less shockingly with *barro, fango, lodo*, etc. than did *lixo*, which presented the more extreme of the two front vowels available to the speakers of Old Spanish.

But, a skeptic may at this juncture be tempted to interject, if this unorthodox method of analysis is at all valid, why was *lixo*, in the first place, allowed to spring into existence within the framework of Spanish lexis?[5] To rebut this perfectly reasonable objection, the advocate of the thesis here defended must be in a position to demonstrate more than just the structural/semantic atypicality of the word here placed under a microscope lens. A certain crucial change must have been taking place within the confines of medieval Spanish—a shift which before long made a word fashioned like *lixo* and, at the same time, endowed with the meaning 'mud, dirt' highly undesirable to speakers and writers alike. This newly-suspected unknown was, as now remains to be shown, the acquisition, by the segment *li-* (especially *lim-/lin-*), of a neatly profiled phonosymbolic connotation

---

[5] On the etymologies of OSp. *lixo* and *lixa/lixar* strange and mutually contradictory opinions have been voiced. These cannot be examined here circumstantially. Here are a few randomly chosen examples. Thus, W. Meyer-Lübke—commenting, in the two versions of his etymological dictionary [1911-20, 1930-35: *5189], on one particularly infelicitous passage in E. G. Parodi's unsatisfactory inquiry into Hispanic etymology—simply declared, by way of concluding the entry L̆UTUM: 'Span. *lijo* 'Schmutz', galiz. *lijar, lujar* 'beschmutzen' gehört nicht hierher'. Corominas, loc. cit., adopted an attitude more aggressive, but scarcely more persuasive: 'Del mismo origen incierto que el port. *lixo* 'basura', probablemente del latín arcaico LIXA 'agua de lejía' ('líquido asqueroso'); pero como este vocablo parece haber tenido *i* breve, que habría dado *e* romance, quizás hubo confusión fonética y semántica con LĪXA 'servidor de un ejército, cantinero', que en la baja época toma el sentido de 'vil' y 'lujurioso'. Etc.

utterly incompatible with some such meaning as 'dirt, mud'.

4 To gain clearer insight into the situation, let us summarize a few Hispanic word histories examined elsewhere in more painstaking detail:

a Viewed superficially, French and Provençal *pur*, Italian (Tuscan) *puro*, and Spanish as well as Portuguese *puro* all three seem to represent roughly comparable adaptations of ancestral PŪRUS 'clean, pure'. But the reality happens to be far more complex: Whereas in Gallo- and Italo-Romance the respective descendants of the Latin adjective at issue indeed have inherited the full scale of its meanings and functions, the humblest and the loftiest alike, the medieval record of *puro* was entirely different in most sections of the Iberian peninsula, where the basic word for 'clean' was consistently *limpio* (in the Center) or *limp(h)o* (in the West), while *puro* and its suffixal offshoots (e.g., the abstracts *puridad* and *pureza*) either boasted angelic overtones or developed very special secondary meanings, such as 'secret, confidence'.[6] While further inspection of the record of Hispanic *puro* must be postponed until some suitable occasion, *limp(i)o* is of direct relevance to us here, descending as it does from parental LIMPIDUS, lit. 'translucent'—a slightly bizarre formation right at the start when measured by Latin standards, since the -IDUS adjective here, for once, counter to expectation, lacked a companion verb in -ĒRE. Some force must have driven such an initially disadvantaged qualifier to considerable prominence in provincial spoken Latin. Could it have been the phonic suggestiveness of the stressed syllable LIM- ?

b Spanish *lisonja* 'flattery', along with its satellites *lisonjero* 'flatterer', 'flattering, pleasing', *lisonj-ear* 'to flatter', 'to please, delight', and *lisonj-eador* 'flatterer', 'flattering',

---

[6] Through haplology, the phrase *dezir por puridad* gave rise to *dezir poridad*, a point A. Castro years ago completely missed. See Malkiel [Forthcoming 4].

clearly go back to Gallo-Romance, as do their Italian counterparts *lusinga, lusinghiero, lusingare* (plus *lusingheria*
'flattery' and *lusinghevole* 'flattering, tempting, alluring').
The Old French form (*losange*), surviving in modern *louange*
'praise', and especially its Old Provençal equivalent *lauzenja, -ga* (known for having developed the meaning 'dif-
famation, gossip, calumny, slander'), which functioned as
centers of important word-families, and also acted as key-
words in conspicuous literary genres, have been firmly established as lexical units of Germanic descent and have also been
persuasively credited with having undergone the influence—
both formal and semantic—of certain Latin words, such as
LAUS, -DIS, 'praise' and the corresponding verb LAUDĀRE; yet
numerous episodes of the transmission process still elude us.[7]
What matters most to the palaeo-Hispanist is the rapid (as a
matter of fact, almost instantaneous) transmutation of
losange/lauzenja into, first, *lesonja*, reliably attested to by
manuscripts, and, next, *lisonja*—the form destined to have
survived; indeed, to have flourished.

The shift *lauzenja > lesonja* embodies an interchange of
vowels, which lends itself only to very tentative explanations: Did words structured like *mejor, peor, menor, redondo*
outweigh those patterned like the infinitives *comer, correr,
poner*? Did *esponja* 'sponge', which is not devoid of figurative
meaning, provide a scheme? Could association with French
mensonge 'lie' have served as a model?[8]

More readily amenable to analysis is the next gambit, the
shift from *lesonja*, var. *lejonja*, to *lisonja*. Here the hypothesis
of association with Spanish/Portugese *liso*—a word whose
ancestry has not yet been firmly established, but whose deep

---

[7] Years ago, I tried to piece together this particular word biography,
without yet fully appreciating the weight of the phonosymbolic factor,
but stressing the possible connection between *losenja > le-, li-sonja* and
(a)limosna 'alms' [1978: 195-205].

[8] This is the more plausible as OFr. *mensonge*, not unlike It. *menzogna*
to this day, was once a feminine. For details see Malkiel [1952-53: 121-
72].

roots in Spanish lexis are no longer subject to doubt—seems tenable. Without disavowing its validity, however, one can ask himself whether the general phonosymbolic potency of the *li(m)-* segment cannot be assumed to have strongly favored, indeed predetermined, such a development along the two axes of form and meaning.

c Over the centuries, *lindo* has been, in etymological terms, one of the most controversial Spanish words, and one endowed with a large scale of nuances, especially in overseas varieties of the language (fundamentally: 'pretty'). All sorts of starting points have been proposed for it, including Germanic bases—a possibility practically ruled out at the current stage of the debate. In the twentieth century, the range of serious possibilities has been narrowed down to two rivals, namely LIMPIDU 'transparently clear' (a choice hampered by separate existence of *limpio* as the direct outcome) and LĒGITIMU, developed in the last analysis from (obl. case) LĒGE 'law'. The last influential and determined advocate for the former conjecture was Menéndez Pidal; the spokesman for the latter educated guess, more successful in the long run, was Cuervo, except that its eventual recognition was long delayed by its champions' failure to give proper account of the elusive -IT- segment.[9]

The clinching argument among the supporters of the LĒGITIMU thesis was the discovery of the intermediate stage *líd-imo, -emo* (especially common in Old Portuguese). The contraction of proparoxytonic *lídemo* into bisyllabic, paroxytonic *lindo* (with co-occurrent metathesis within the nuclear consonant cluster) in preliterary Castilian involves no insuperable difficulty for the analyst. What does baffle the most benevolent observer is the fact—not yet fully accounted for—that the qualifier, repeatedly used for 'true, authentic, legitimate' (in reference to a child or a believer) throughout the thirteenth century should thereafter with striking speed have developed into a typical designation of the attribute of an 'exquisitely pretty, charming' young woman, e.g., an adoles-

---

[9] For a more circumstantial account of the various conjectures see my piece [Forthcoming 5].

cent princess, as portrayed or hinted at by contributors to the *cancioneros*. The argument that a king's or an aristocrat's legitimate daughters, far more elaborately groomed and clothed than were his bastard children, could have provided he real-life situation justifying such a bizarre semantic shift somehow seems to be too tenuous to account, all by itself, for the bold leap from 'legitimate' (ca. 1250) to 'delicate, nicely-dressed, enchanting, bewitching' (ca. 1350. If, in this predicament, we care to remind ourselves of our earlier hypothesis that the segment *li-* (especially its subclass *lim-/lin-*) exuded a certain phonosymbolic power for the Folk Latin–Romance speech community, from late Antiquity until the Middle Ages, then the saltatory semantic development of *lindo* loses most of its aberrancy. To avoid a grievous misunderstanding: no one claims that LÉGITIMUS, from the start, had phonosymbolic potentialities. Only the shift from LÉGITIMU to *lindo*, under the jurisdiction of a set of strictly phonological 'rules', produced the one condition needed for phonosymbolism to have asserted itself.

d Space happens to be unavailable here for any discussion, in comparable detail, of the trajectories of such Spanish words as *lidiça, ligero, limosna, liso, liviano*. Such examination would have lent support to the points here made apropos of *limpio, lisonja,* and *lindo*.

Not every medieval Spanish word that displayed a *li(m)/li(n)-* segment was inexorably drawn into the vortex of phonosymbolic transmutations of meanings, as a rule meliorative. Words endowed with a 'neutral' content, whatever their provenience, were left alone by the speech community and by its writers: witness the reassuringly quiet evolution of the noun *lista* 'roll, list', the adjective *listo* 'ready', and the verbs *lisiar* 'to wound', *listar* 'to stripe'. 'Semilearned' words (such as *alimento* 'element' and *alimaño* 'animal', both dear to Don Juan Manuel, as well as *libro* and *ligión*) were also left alone; so were phytonyms, witness *limón, lino, lirio* and the

dendronym *a-lis-o* 'alder'. Certain words were just
inherently unexciting, such as *linde* 'boundary' < LĪMITE;
but one may be in doubt about *lirón* 'dormouse' < *GLĪR-
IŌNE, on account of the part that rodent is allowed to play
in Spanish folklore, and about *liña* 'generational line' <
LĪNEA, flanked by the Gallicism *lin-aje* and the corresponding adjective *lin-aj-udo*, of mixed ancestry. Yet, a
lexical item calling up memories unpleasant in every
respect, such as *lixo* 'mud, dirt', had no business surviving in this general climate of flattery and melioration.[10]

5 Can one cite or devise some alternative way of
accounting for the rapid decay and well-nigh total extinction of *lixo*, except here and there on the level of dialect
speech? Firm believers in the pervasive applicability of
the 'clash-of-homonyms theory' can be expected to have
their say in this matter. Folk ichthyology, e.g., informs us
that there existed in Old Spanish *lyxa* as the designation,
primarily, of the 'dogfish' [Ruiz, quatrain 1109a] and,
secondarily, of its hard skin used for cleaning, as sand
paper and for metal-polishing, cf. modern *lija*, Portuguese *lixa* and note the corresponding verbs *lijar, lixar*,
which may have had their share of sporadic contacts with
alisar, from *liso* 'smooth' (as S. de Covarrubias, in 1611,
was perhaps the first to suspect). Yet, one fails to see how
lixa/lixar, of dubious background, could have very
seriously interfered with the continued use of our *lixo*, to
the point of undermining its survival, since 'to smooth'
and 'to soil' do not stand in polar opposition to each
other; moreover, one family is pre-eminently nominal,
and the other, except on the fish market, chiefly verbal.
Even so, assuming a measure of confusion was apt to

---

[10] *Lin-aje* and its offshoots can be best judged in light of S.
Fleischmann's revised dissertation [1977] and of critical reactions to it.

arise, speakers were free to resort to solutions other than the straight elimination of *lixo*. Thus, in Galician, where *lixo* is firmly entrenched ('polvo', 'mota', 'partícula insignificante', 'barredura'), some speakers tend to replace *lixar* 'manchar, ensuciar' either by *lix-ugar* or, even more radically, by *luxar*, thus endowing the verb with the—phonosymbolically pregnant—vowel of *ludre* and *zurro*.[11] Another verb *lijar*, flanked by the noun *lijadura*—their flowering is restricted to the Santander zone—matches Castilian *lisiar* 'to bruise, hurt' (beside the noun *lisión*), extracted from LAESU, the past participle of LAEDERE 'to injure', being, all told, less common at present than its near-synonym *lastimar*. Again, it is difficult to imagine any unbearable conflict between this verb, confined to a small area, and its previously mentioned homonyms.

One thus detects no real incompatibility between the classic 'conflict-of-homonyms theory' and the appeal to phonosymbolism as a driving force behind the retention vs. rejection of individual words. The loss of a word whose shape—either through ambiguity or through unsuitable orchestration—refuses to announce effectively its semantic load remains a strong possibility under any set of circumstances, even though speakers are free to remedy the awkward situation by refashioning the hazardous lexical item, making it in the process less unwelcome.

Yakov Malkiel
University of California, Berkeley

[11] On the score of its configuration, Galician *lodre* is reminiscent of Spanish *podre* 'rotten' and *mugre* 'dirt', the latter a product of MŪCŌRE 'mould' (the expected companion of MŪCĒRE 'to be mouldy'), marked by a stress shift which invites separate study.

REFERENCES

Academia Española, Real, 1984
  Diccionario de la lengua española. Rev. 20th ed. Madrid
Carré Alvarellos, L., 1933
  Diccionario galego-castelán e vocabulario castelán-galego. Rev. 2nd ed. La Coruña
Corominas, J., 1984-87
  Diccionario crítico-etimológico de la lengua castellana. 4 vols. Madrid & Bern
Covarrubias, S. de, 1611
  Tesoro de la lengua castellana o española. Madrid. Ed. Martín de Riquer, Barcelona, 1943
Crespo Pozo, J. S., 1963
  Contribución a un vocabulario castellano-gallego (con indicación de fuentes). Madrid
Crews, C. M., 1935
  Recherches sur le judéo-espagnol dans les pays balkaniques. Paris
Fleischmann, S., 1977
  Cultural and linguistic factors in word formation. An integrated approach to the development of the suffix -AGE. Berkeley
Hinton, L., J. Nichols, & J. Ohala, eds. Forthcoming
  Transactions of the Berkeley Sound Symbolism Conference, February 1986
Huerta Tejadas, F., 1956
  Vocabulario de las obras de Don Juan Manuel (1282-1348), Madrid. Reprinted from installments in Vols. 34-36 (1954-56) of the BRAE
López-Morillas, C., 1974
  'A midway report on an etymological crux', *RPh* 27: 488-96
Malkiel, Y., 1952-53
  'Ancient Hispanic *vera(s)* and *mentira(s)*; a study in lexical polarization', *RPh*, 6: 121-72
————, 1978
  'Ancien espagnol *losenja/lisonja* 'flatterie' et *(a)limos(i)na* 'aumône'; en marge du rayonnement transpyrénéen d'un provençalisme littéraire, *Hommage à Jean Séguy* 2:195-205 (=*Via Domitia* 20-21)
————, Forthcoming 1
  'Regular sound development, phonosymbolic orchestration, disambiguation of homonyms'. See under Hinton et al.

————, Forthcoming 2

Diachronic problems in phonosymbolism = Edita and inedita, 1979-1988, Vol. 1. Amsterdam

————, Forthcoming 3

'Phonosymbolism in diachrony: the case of /r/ > /R/ in Hispano-Romance', *Development and diversity: language variation across time and space = Testimonial Volume for C.-J. Bailey*. Dallas: Summer Institute of Linguistics Publications, 93

————, Forthcoming 4

'The secret of the etymology of Old Spanish *poridad*'. To appear in *Studies in Honor of Samuel G. Armistead*, edd. E. M. Gerli & H. Sharrer

————, Forthcoming 5

'El origen de *lindo* y su entronque con el resto del léxico'. To appear in: *Lingüística* (Anuario de la Asociación de Lingüística y Filología de América Latina), ed. M. Humberto López) 2:2 (1990)

Meyer-Lübke, W., 1911-20

Romanisches etymologisches Wörterbuch. Heidelberg. Rev. 3rd edn., 1930-35

Richardson, H. B., 1930

An etymological vocabulary of the Libro de buen amor *by Juan Ruiz.* New Haven

Williams, E. B., 1955

Spanish & English dictionary/Diccionario inglés y español. New York

Final nasals in the
Galician–Portuguese *cancioneiros*

1 Phonological innovation in Portuguese: the final nasals

ONE of the best known and least understood developments in Portuguese historical phonology is the change (or series of changes) by which the final nasal vowels -[ã] and -[õ] merged with the diphthong -[ãu] (itself the product of the contraction of the sequence -[ão]), giving the following diachronic correspondences:

Old Portuguese	Modern Portuguese	
-ão	mão	
-ã	can	-ão [ẽũ]
-õ	razon	
-õ < õe	servidon	

There is still a lack of consensus as to the precise nature, origins or chronology of this development. Phonetic explanations, positing a dipththongisation or diphthongisations of [ã] to [ãu] and [õ] to [õu] and analogical explanations invoking the influence of the suffixes usually represented by these endings, have been busily competing or combining since the beginning of the century.[1] The situation is exacerbated, however, by the absence of any serious attempt to document any of the hypothesised stages of the change and provide a basic chronology.

---

[1] For recent attempts to make sense of these changes, see Carvalho 1988, Lorenzo 1988, Sampson 1983, Schaffer 1983.

2 Documentation

The documentary evidence for the change (either completed or in progress) can take one of the following forms:

1 *evolved forms*
    a   etymological   -ã   written -ão
    b   etymological   -õ   written -ã
    c   etymological   -õ   written -ão

2 *neutralised or hypercorrect forms*
    a   etymological   -ão   written -ã
    b   etymological   -ão   written -õ
    c   etymological   -ã   written -õ

3 *analogical forms presupposing the change*
    plurals in -ões for singular in -ão/ã

It should not be forgotten that the order of appearance of forms from types 1 and 2 could be indicative of the order in which the endings -[ã] and -[õ] were affected. Traditional phonetic theories, in which -[ã] diphthongises directly to -[ãu] while the diphthongisation of -[õ] results in -[õu] which only later merges with [ãu], predict that type 1a and 2a forms would precede other types.

Documentation of all these types is readily available for the fifteenth century, which stands as an uncontested *terminus ad quem* [Williams 1938, Sampson 1983]. Various attempts have been made to assign an earlier date to the change, but none has been conclusive.

Cintra [1963] recorded forms of types 1b and 2a,c in non-literary documents of 1309 from the South of Portugal:

Silves 1309

    tabaliã (coexisting with unevolved *tabaliõ, tabeliõ* 'notary')
    dayõ (coexisting with etymological *dayã* 'Dean')

Albufeira 1309

> *mhã* (etym. *mão* 'hand')
> *taballiã* (coexisting with *taballiõ*)

but his data are either wrong or dubious. Examination of the original manuscripts[2] confirms only one of the transcriptions, *mhã*, which appears in notarial formulae in a somewhat corrupt document, and is likely to be a garbled form of the alternative spelling *mãho*.[3]

Tilander's claim [1959] that evolved forms are found in the 13th-century is based on a generalised mis-dating of sources, examples being attributed to the date of composition of documents which only exist as later copies or translations. Sampson's claim [1983] to have identified forms of type 1b in a late fourteenth-century text is similarly questionable.[4]

The AOPT corpus of medieval documents [Parkinson 1983] has only one clear set of evolved forms before the fifteenth century. These are unstressed final -ã replacing final -õ, in 3rd person plural preterite forms.[5] Even here

---

[2] Cintra was working from transcriptions published around 1900, whose linguistic value is now less secure [Parkinson 1983].

[3] Cintra's source texts also contain mangled forms such as *moo* [ANTT Convento de Chelas no. 38, 1266] and *mhãa* for *mão* and *caa* [Albufeira 1309] for *cão*. The common notarial formula *(com) mha mão* '(by) my hand' could also have been a cause of confusion. The form *tabaliã* is not necessarily indicative of the evolution of the final nasals, but seems to develop by analogy with *escrivam* in the fourteenth century [Louro 1952, Parkinson 1979].

[4] The text in question is the *Crónica da Fundação do Mosteiro de São Vicente* (or more precisely, a short extract in Roberts [1956]). The attribution to the end of the 14th century is a deduction from Roberts' order, the same text being placed in the 15th century by Nunes [1906]; the manuscript (ANTT 1780) is a seventeenth-century copy [Dornelas 1940:158].

[5] e.g. *uirã* (AOPT 66 = ANTT, Ferreira d'Ave no 51, 1270), *forã* (AOPT 67 = ANTT Ferreira d'Ave 53, 1270) for expected *uirõ, forõ*

there is room for doubt, as the forms may reflect a confusion of the preterite -*rõ* and pluperfect -*rã* endings. Sporadic examples of type 1b are reported in many fourteenth-century documents, [Williams 1938] but in many cases it turns out that the form is mis-transcribed or the document is a fifteenth-century copy.[6]

3 Documentary evidence from the *Cancioneiros*

Williams [1938] attributed the change of -[ã] to -[ão] to the 13th century on the strength of a single rhyme, that of *foam* (Ar. *folan*, Sp. *fulano* 'unnamed person') with *vão*.

> per boa fe ben guisado chegou aqui don Foan
> pero non veo no maio por no chegar en vão
>
> [CBN 1444, CV 1055][7]

The implication is that etymological -[ã] has become identical with -[ãu]. (Note that the second part of the process, -[õ] > -[ãu] is explicitly excluded.) Louro [1952] added another Arabism from the *Cantigas de Santa Maria*.[8] The form *albardan* 'rogue' appears rhyming with *can* (and eight other -*an* endings) in CSM 401:

> outrossi que me guardes | d'ome torp' alvardan
> e d'ome que assaca | que é peor que can
>
> [401.68-9]

---

[6] Typical examples from Marques [1944] (a collection much used for philological study) are: doc. 139 *companhia* read as *companham* (<*companhom*); doc. 26 *doaçam* (<*doaçom*) attributed to 1294, in a 15th-century copy of chancery records.

[7] Lapa [1970] replaces the unanimous MSS readings *foam* with *foão* in his critical edition. Lapa's collection contains another example of the same rhyme—*foão* rhyming with *mão* and *loução*—in an unequivocally feminine rhyme, in no 216 (CBN 1502) where the MS reading is *foão*.

[8] All quotations from the CSM are from Mettmann 1986-9.

and rhyming with *verão/chão/vilão* in CSM 406.

> Ben vennas maio con bõo verão
> e nos roguemos a Virgen de chão
> que nos defenda d'ome mui vilão
> e d'atrevud' e de torp' alvardão
>
> [406.48-51]

In addition, there is a form which has ecaped the attention of scholars, in CSM 192, of the form *cão* (=*can* 'dog') rhyming with a sequence of *-ão* endings:

> E disse: 'Pagão
> sse queres guarir
> do demo de chão
> t' ás a departir
> e do falsso, vão
> mui louco, vilão
> Mafomete cão
> que te non valer
> pode, e cristão
> te faz e irmão
> nosso, e loução
> sei e sen temer'.
>
> [192.98-109]

The form *cão* has to be *can* used as a term of abuse; there seems to be no reasonable interpretation involving *cão* < CANU 'whitehaired'.

Taken at face value these rhymes would seem to justify Williams' contention that there was a diphthongisation of -[ã] by the end of the 13th century. A simple consideration of metrics dispels this illusion. In each case, the apparently evolved form cannot be a diphthong but must be bisyllabic, as the metrical scheme of each poem requires a feminine rhyme at the relevant point:[9]

CV 1055   15'a   15'a   15'B
  (rhymes *-ado, -ão, -oste, -oso*)

CSM 406   10'a   10'a   10'a   10'a   4'B
  (rhymes *-ia, -ude, -ade, -ezas* etc.)

CSM 192	10'A	10B	10'A	10B	5'c	5d
5'c	5d	5'c	5'c	5'c	5b	5'c
5'c	5'c	5b				

Metrical evidence is also relevant to a second significant point. The merger of the nasal endings by phonetic means (i.e. diphthongisation) could not have been complete until the original bisyllabic ending -[ão] has itself contracted to form a diphthong. There is very little evidence for such a contraction in the *Cancioneiros* in general and none at all in the *Cantigas de Santa Maria*.[10] My own observations on the *Cantigas de Escarnho* [Lapa 1970] reveal one clear case of monosyllabic *-ões* and one of *-ãa*:

os zevrões foron buscar/Rodrigo polo matar (heptasyllables)
[Lapa 258]

des que veo nunca s'a el chegou
nen quer chegar se d'el certã non é (decasyllables)
[Lapa 102]

---

[9] These formulae follow the conventions of Tavani 1967 .
[10] There has been no specific study of this aspect of medieval metrics, where the emphasis has been on interverbal contractions [Cunha 1961]. Rubecamp [1934], the only systematic study of the CSM to date, finds no evidence of contraction of *ão, ãa* or *õe*. A review of the data in the light of more recent editions is clearly in order.

The only cases of monosyllabic -*ão* involve the by now familiar form *foão*:

Diss'oj' el-Rei - Pois Don Foão mais val (decasyllable)
[Lapa 113]

Se vos, Don Foão dizedes (heptasyllable, feminine rhyme)
[Lapa 120]

in which -*ão* could be interpreted variously as contracted -[ão], diphthongised -[ã] or an MS error for *foan*. Lapa himself hesitates, noting that the author of both pieces is the 14th-century Stevam da Guarda: 'Aqui *Foão* que deveria contar por três sílabas, já vale por duas. Hesitamos en alterar a forma para *Foan*, por se tratar de um trovador do século XIV' [1970:192].

4 Interpretation

The evidence of the *Cancioneiros* is a very weak indication of a merger of -[ã] and -[ão] in the 13th century. Non-literary documents, on the other hand, indicate some merger of -[ã] and -[õ], without confusion of them and -[ão], which should lead us to be cautious in giving too much weight to the poetic evidence.

There is a further reason for caution in the case of the evidence from the *Cantigas de Santa Maria*. The language of the *Cantigas de Santa Maria* is Galician-Portuguese, the poetic *lingua franca* used at the Court of Alfonso X. Insofar as it represents a definable dialect, it is Galician rather than Portuguese. (Two of the *Cantigas* cited are among the small group which are unequivocally attributed to Alfonso X himself [Mettmann 1986:19].) It would be very surprising if this literary language had undergone changes which did not take place in Galician. The changes in the final nasal vowels are in fact one of the phonological innovations which most clearly distinguish Portuguese from Galician [Lorenzo 1988] and Central/Southern Portuguese from Northern Portuguese [Cintra 1963]. The whole of Maia's corpus of Galician and Northern Portuguese documents from the 13th to the 16th century [Maia 1986] yields only three non-etymological forms, all of type 2: *escriuõ* in a Galician document of 1499, and *pom* (=*pam*), *Vayrom* from Portuguese documents of 1448, 1472 (indicative, according to Maia of an extension of -[õ] rather than the Southern Portuguese development). If *cão*, *foão* and *albardão* are not the evolved forms they were thought to be, what are they?

A closer look at the attested examples of *foão* in the *Cantigas d'escarnho* makes it clear that *foã* and *foão* are a doublet, alternative forms of the same word. We have unequivocal cases of bisyllabic *foã*, in both rhyming and line-internal positions, and equally unequivocal cases of trisyllabic *foão*:

Foã

   a Ja lhi nunca pediran
       O Castel' a Don Foan   [Lapa 61.1-2]

   b don Foan disse que partir queria
       quanto lhe deron e o que avia   [Lapa 216.1-2]

Foão

   c Chegou aqui Don Foão e veo mui ben guisado
       pero non veo ao maio por non chegar endoado
                        [Lapa 393.1-2]

   d Don Foão que eu sei que a preço de livão
       vedes que fez ena guerra daquesto sõo certão
                        [Lapa 60.1-2]

> *e*   e quer andar ja custos' e loução
>   e dixi-lh'eu :- esso ai Don Foão   [Lapa 216.10-11]

> *f*   per boa fe ben guisado chegou aqui Don Foão
>   pero non veo no maio por non chegar en vão
>   [Lapa 393.4-5]

The two forms appear not only in separate works by the same poet (examples *a,d*) but even in the same poem (examples *b,e*). Both Portuguese and Galician poets use the doublet—examples *a,e* are from the Portuguese Pero Barroso, while *c* and *e* are from the Galician Johan Garcia de Guilhade [Ferrari et. al. 1982].

The doublet *foa/foão* is not an isolated one. The forms *vilan/vilão, ermitan/ermitão* and *Stevam/Stevão*[11] are attested in the *Cancioneiros*; Tilander [1959] documents the doublet *ortolam/ortolão*. There is a corresponding alternation in Castilian (where the situation is confused by widespread apocope) between *-an* and *-ano*. Louro's claim that the *-ã* ending was perceived as an importation (French and Arabic) and was thus supplemented or replaced by hispanic forms in *-ão* cannot be the whole story: *-ã* seems to have had as much vitality as *-ão* as an agentive suffix in Galician-Portuguese. Apart from *foam* (where the Romanized form could be a Castilianism) and *cão*, the doublets seem to occur where the ending is or

---

[11] Clear evidence of a bisyllabic ending comes from the line
     Don Estevão achei noutro dia
     mui sanhudo depos um seu om' ir   [Lapa 73.1-2]
in which the whole name requires four syllables. Other readings are less secure, as a 3-syllable form could be *Estevam* or *Stevão* [cf Lapa 1970 no. 79]. The usual form in non-literary documents is *Stevam*.

can be interpreted as a suffix,[12] which points to a morphologically based alternation of -*ã* and -*ão*.

5 Conclusion

It is quite clear that the apparently evolved forms in the *Cantigas de Santa Maria* are not evidence for the change in Portuguese nasals. They are nevertheless indicative of one of the conditions which influenced that change. Louro [1952] and Tilander [1959] emphasized the role of doublets in promoting a merger of -[ã] and -[ão], in addition to the phonetic forces (diphthongisation of -[ã], reduction of -[ão] to a diphthong) which eroded their distinctiveness. The evidence of the *Cancioneiros* shows that the creation of doublets was productive, and was used to effect by poets among whom metrical virtuosity was an end in itself. The form *cão* is important because it marks the point at which the creation of doublets broke its morphological bounds, and allowed the creation of a doublet for a form where -*ã* was not remotely suffixal and where there was no possibility of double transmission. It is no coincidence that this should be in a poem of considerable power and using an extremely demanding rhyme scheme.[13]

Stephen Parkinson
University of Oxford

[12] *Stevam* would be divided *Stev-am* on the basis of the patronymic *Stev-es* and the apocopated form *Steve* as in *Steveanes* (= *Stevam Eanes*).

[13] See Parkinson [forthcoming] for the function of such rhyme-schemes in the style of the CSM.

REFERENCES

Carvalho, J. Brandão de , 1988
'Nasalité et structure synchronique en portugais et en galicien: approche non-linéaire et panchronique d'un problème phonologique', *Verba*, 15, 237-63.

Cintra, L.F.L., 1963
'Observations sur l'orthographie et la langue de quelques textes non-littéraires galiciens-portugais de la seconde moitié du XIIIe siècle', *Revue de Linguistique Romane*, 27, 59-77.

Cunha, C. F. da, 1961
Estudos de poética trovadoresca, Rio de Janeiro.

Dornelas A., 1940
'Crónica da fundação do mosteiro de S. Vicente de Lisboa', *Anais da Academia Portuguesa de Historia*, 1st ser., vol 2, 147-96.

Ferrari, A. et al., 1982
'Geografia da lírica galego-portuguesa', *in* D. Kremer & R. Lorenzo (eds) *Tradición, actualidade e futuro do galego. Actas do Coloquio de Treveris*, Santiago de Compostela.

Lorenzo, R., 1988
'Consideracións sobre as vocais nasais e o ditongo -ão en portugués', *in* D. Kremer (ed) *Homenagem a Joseph M. Piel por ocasião do seu 85º aniversário*, Tübingen.

Lapa, M. Rodrigues, 1970
Cantigas d'Escarnho e de Maldizer dos cancioneiros medievais galego-portugueses, Vigo, 2nd ed.

Maia, C. de Azevedo, 1986
História do Galego-Português, Coimbra.

Marques, J. M. da Silva, 1944
Descobrimentos Portugueses. Documentos para a sua história I, Lisbon.

Mettmann, W (ed.), 1986-89
Alfonso X el Sabio. Cantigas de Santa María, 3 vols, Madrid.

Nunes, J. J., 1906
Crestomatia Arcaica, Coimbra.

Parkinson, S. R.[1976-79
'Os tabeliães, o seu título e os seus documentos', *Boletim de Filologia*, 25, 185-212.

Parkinson, S. R., 1983

'Um arquivo computorizado de textos medievais portugueses', *Boletim de Filologia*, 28, 241-52.

————., forthcoming

'Miragres de Maldizer? Dysphemism in the Cantigas de Santa Maria', *Bulletin of the Cantigueiros de Santa Maria*, 5.

Roberts, K. J., 1956

An Anthology of Old Portuguese, Lisbon.

Rubecamp, R., 1932

'A linguagem das Cantigas de Santa Maria', *Boletim de Filologia*, 1, 273-356.

————., 1933-4

'A linguagem das Cantigas de Santa Maria', *Boletim de Filologia*, 2, 141-52.

Sampson, R., 1983

'The origin of Portuguese *-ão*', *Zeitschrift für Romanische Philologie*, 99, 34-68.

Schaffer, M.E., 1983

'Old Portuguese *-dõe/-dom*, Modern Portuguese *-dão*, and the evolution of Portuguese *-ão*' in Harry L. Kirby (ed.) *The Third Louisiana Conference on Hispanic Languages and Literatures, 'La Chispa' '82*, Louisiana State U.P., 256-72.

Tavani, G., 1967

Repertorio Metrico della lirica galego-portoghese, Rome.

Tilander, G., 1959

'Porque *-am, -o m* se tornaram *-ão* em Português?', *Revista de Portugal*, 24, 292-303.

Williams, E. B., 1938

From Latin to Portuguese, Philadelphia.

Class-changing aspects of
three Spanish augmentative suffixes

THE affective suffixes of Spanish—diminutives, augmentatives and pejoratives—occupy a singular position in the derivational morphology of the language. They have attracted considerable and sustained attention chiefly on account of their semantic and stylistic ramifications. They are also set apart from most other derivational suffixes by an obvious factor which bridges the semantic and structural aspects: namely that their function is essentially a qualifying or 'adjectival' one. For example, *niñito, asuntillo, egoistón, bromazo* still convey the same recognisable semantic information as the forms *niño, asunto, egoísta, broma*, though it is clear that a nuance—which may be one of size but which is more frequently emotional or affective—has been added in each case. Even where the suffixes are used lexically to create 'new' words, as in *platillo* 'saucer' from *plato* 'plate', *sillón* 'arm chair' from *silla* 'chair', it is arguable that a simple transfer of name, often metaphorical, has taken place which is based essentially on the qualifying (usually literally diminutive or augmentative) function of the suffix: a saucer is called *platillo* because it resembles a small plate; among the features distinguishing a *sillón* from a *silla*, one basic one is size.

It follows from this that the vast majority of diminutive and augmentative suffixes are used in a homogeneous or class-maintaining way.[1] The derived form will

---

[1] For a general discussion of the classificatory questions involved, including a summary of the positions of Lewicka [1960], Togeby [1965], Robins [1967] and von Wartburg [1969], see Pattison [1975:3-8]. A more up-to-date treatment is to be found in Lang [1990:20, 91-92, 97]; I was

normally belong to the same form-class as the simplex. The purpose of this essay is to point to three cases, all of suffixes traditionally called 'augmentative', where this is not so in all cases. The suffixes *-ón*, *-azo* and *-udo* are all, in some more or less significant classes of word, used in a heterogeneous or class-changing way, to the point that it is hard to accept the traditional nomenclature of augmentative as truly applicable. These facts have all been noted elsewhere, but it is my purpose to bring together considerations often overlooked in standard treatments of the subject and to suggest that earlier discussion of these suffixes has often centred disproportionately on semantic and stylistic nuances to the relative neglect of important morphological factors.

The suffix *-ón* is normally regarded as the leading, the most versatile of the augmentative suffixes, and an analysis of its functions has tended to concentrate on this versatility from the semantic point of view: words in *-ón* may be pejorative (*egoistón*), though often with an attenuative nuance (*sinvergonzón*, *perezosón* are arguably pejorative in a less downright way than the simple forms *sinvergüenza*, *perezoso*); Gooch has very aptly drawn attention to the tendency of *-ón* to stress favourably, unfavourably, or neutrally according to the meaning of the root words: '*memorión*—'phenomenal memory'; *novelón*—'tediously long novel' (an exceptionally big memory is, of course, considered a desirable thing, while an exceptionally long novel is, as a rule, not)'. [1967:11]

This suffix, however, has two uses which ought to be separated from these homogeneous augmentative

---

able to consult this useful recent work only when this essay was in a late stage of drafting, and references to it are therefore less coherent and complete than I should have liked.

examples. The first, which is perhaps more marginal, is mentioned by Gooch [1967:11] who also devotes one of his lists to what he calls 'action or result of action'. These are words such as *empujón, atracón, apagón*, etc. [Gooch, 1967:181-83]. If Gooch's analysis is correct, this is just such an example of heterogeneous or class-changing derivation as is my focus of attention here: for if the simplex forms of the three words cited are in fact the verbal stems of *empujar, atracar, apagar*, then the suffix is being used in a way reminiscent of, e.g., *-ada* (*entrada*) or *-miento* (*llamamiento*). His list comprises forty-three words, but of these it is notable that approximately half correspond not only to verbs but also to nominal forms in *-o, -a*, or *-e* which are also straightforward verbal action nouns.[2] These include a number of extremely common pairs such as *empuje/-ón, paro/-ón, rasgo/-ón, tiro/-ón*, and it is surely legitimate to see these as straightforward cases of a normal augmentative use of *-ón*. The pattern then established of *empuje/empujar/empujón*, etc., could then have spread to other cases (on the whole rarer) such as *abollar/abollón, resbalar/resbalón* by a simple process of analogy.[3] Whatever the process, we can here clearly recognise that modern Spanish has adopted *-ón* as an

---

[2] The following forms correspond to verbal nouns as well as verbs: *apretón, atracón, bajón, chamuscón, chapuzón, desgarrón, empujón, envión, limpión, parón, pellizcón, pescozón, planchón, plantón, rasgón, remojón, repentón, revolcón, socavón, sofocón, tirón, tropezón, valsón*. Compare the following, where no simpler verbal noun exists: *abollón, acelerón, achuchón, apagón, bofetón, borrón, chafarrinón, desconchón, empellón, estirón, estrujón, lametón, madrugón, pisotón, resbalón, reventón, sopetón, tiritón, vacilón*. One further word in Gooch's list, *moratón*, has no verbal connection.

[3] See Malkiel [1959:256-57] and Pena [1980:221-25]. The association between *-ón* and violent action has long been realised: see Alonso [1961:164], citing earlier views of Spitzer and García de Diego.

action-forming suffix, albeit in a limited number of unambiguous cases.

Less straightforward is another use of *-ón* to form not action-nouns but agent-nouns. These are exemplified by words such as *acusón*, *llorón*, *respondón*, which are all patently words also formed on verbal stems signifying a person much given to that action.[4] Gooch does not give a single list of the words characterised morphologically in this way, but three of his lists are relevant, those entitled 'Noun–Masculine (Persons)', 'Adjective' and 'Noun–Feminine' [1967:159-62;165-71;192-93]. These yield a total of 185 distinct forms, of which just over a third (sixty-three) are agent-nouns of the type under discussion.[5] In a handful of cases there are formal complexities, usually involving an infix *-il-* (*comilón*, *dormilón*, *perdilón*, *rompilón*), but occasionally *-al-* (*trepalón*), *-ic-* (*lloricón*) or *-uc-* (*besucón*).[6]

Clearly, these are not straightforward agent-nouns; *acusón* is not, like *acusador*, 'accuser' but 'habitual accuser' or, to place the word in its normal childish register 'tell-tale'; the same is true of *llorón* 'cry-baby', *respondón* 'cheeky (person)', and a high proportion of other cases. In short, one notes both a specialisation of register—essentially to that of the school and childhood—and a nuance of characteristic behaviour, of doing something regularly or to excess.

A case which neatly encompasses both types of heterogeneous derivation so far discussed is *limpión*. As Sylvia

---

[4] Again, this use has often been commented on; see, for instance, Alonso [1961:164 n.4]. It has origins in Latin [Pena 1980:220]: see also Monge [1978:162].

[5] The relevant forms, which Lang [1990:114] calls 'augmentative adjectives', are listed in section I of the Appendix.

[6] The formal question is discussed by Faitelson-Weiser [1980:149 n.231, 178] who sees it as 'protection du thème d'infinitif'.

Faitelson-Weiser [1980:160-61] makes clear, this word is in fact a case of double derivation from *limpiar*: in the sense 'wipe, quick clean' (*dar un limpión a algo*) it is an action-noun analogous to *apagón*; in the sense (which Faitelson-Weiser perhaps misleadingly calls adjectival) 'cleaner, houseproud person, one given to cleaning' it is an agent-noun like *acusón*.

These, then, are some further morphological ramifications of the suffix *-ón*. They should not, however, be made over-complex. Just as I have argued that, e.g., *empujón* can adequately be explained as deriving from *empuje*, so I would argue that to see *tapón* and *plantón* as examples of post-verbal derivation is unnecessary. These cases are also discussed by Faitelson-Weiser, who argues that the first is analogous to words like *buscón*, *gritón*, *matón* [1980:154ff.] while *plantón* 'seedling' is from *plantar* and denotes a patient rather than an agent, not dissimilar from *pelón*, 'hairless or close-cropped', from *pelar*, which again would stand in a passive rather than an agential relationship to the verbal root. Both *tapón* and *plantón* can in fact equally well be seen as post-nominal (i.e., homogeneous) derivation, from *tapa* and *planta* respectively, that is, as examples of the diminutive use of *-ón* (cf. *montón*, possibly *ratón*). *Pelón* is arguably more problematical. If it is from *pelar* then it might indeed be seen as a rare case of passive use of *-ón*; the reflexive use of *pelarse* could explain this apparently anomalous use; alternatively, it could be post-nominal on *pelo*, expressing a metonymic relationship (cf. *barrigón*), though clearly with a strongly ironic content in this case.

The second 'augmentative' suffix to be discussed is *-azo*. This may be added to nominal simplexes to denote a blow, literal or metaphorical, with that thing. Although this is not strictly speaking a case of heterogeneous or class-changing derivation (since both simplex and derived forms are nouns) it is none the less apparent that the function of the suffix in, e.g., *hachazo* is morphologically and semantically different from that which it fulfils in, e.g., *animalazo*, *bromazo*, or *exitazo*. Put simply, these three forms refer to the same underlying concepts as the forms *animal*, *broma*, *éxito*, while *hachazo* is not a larger form of *hacha*. Gooch lists ninety-four forms of this type [1967:204-09], most of which are transparent in meaning and lead to no points of special interest (e.g., *balazo*, *botellazo*, *codazo*, *ladrillazo*, etc.).[7] Occasionally the meaning is metaphorical rather than physical: *flechazo* can refer to Cupid's dart, *planchazo* to a great disappointment, *telefonazo* (cf. French *coup de téléphone*) to a telephone call. Still less frequently, the idea is of a blow on rather than with the simplex form: both *pianazo* and *teclazo* refer to keystrokes (the latter on any kind of keyboard, the former obviously only the one of the instrument in question), and *espaldarazo* is normally a blow on the back (sometimes metaphorically, as with English 'accolade').

Faitelson-Weiser claims to see a post-verbal derivational pattern in -*azo* in forms like *pinchazo* (*pinchar*), *chupetazo* (*chupetear*), etc. [1980:173]. However, on a purely synchronic level that seems both unnecessary and anomalous in many cases, given the existence of, e.g., *pincho* 'pointed stick', *chupete* 'dummy'. One case which does, however, appear anomalous is *quemazo* (cited by Faitelson-Weiser, though not in any dictionary I

---

[7] The relevant forms from Gooch are listed in section II of the Appendix; his list contains one further word, *batacazo* 'thump, heavy fall', which appears to be a 'mirage' word as far as this suffix is concerned. Corominas saw it as probably onomatopeic, and there seems to be no obvious simplex, verbal or nominal, to which it can be related. On -*azo* in general, see also Lang [1990:112-14].

have consulted).[8] Even if one admits the possibility of such heterogeneous derivation with *-azo*, this comes as no real surprise in the light of Yakov Malkiel's exhaustive and ingenious investigations into the origins of the suffixal use in question. His 1959 article demonstrated that the use of *-azo* to signify a blow appears to have distinct etymological origins from the more straight-forward post-nominal augmentative *-azo* in e.g., *animalazo, bromazo, exitazo*. He designated the blow-suffix *-azo²*, *-azo¹* being the unremarkable augmentative which is a reflex of Latin -ACEU. In Malkiel's view, *-azo²* is related to Latin -ATIO, the nominative form of the suffix which we know best as *-zón/-ción* in Spanish [Malkiel, 1959:193-258, esp. 251-57]. A post-verbal origin therefore goes some way towards explaining both the anomalous **quemazo* and indeed the whole semantic peculiarity of the *-azo* words under discussion. It must, however, be made plain that the importance of this suffix in the derivational system is to have created the capacity for the formation of 'post-verbals' where no verb is necessary or indeed in existence. On simplexes like *hacha, botella, ladrillo*, *-azo* forms can arise signifying in effect the action of the non-existent verbs **hachar, *botellar, *ladrillar*.

The final suffix to be discussed in this essay is *-udo*. This is added to nominal simplexes to form noun/adjectives, as in *barbudo (barba), orejudo (oreja), velludo (vello)*. Gooch's list of such forms [1967:232-36] comprises

---

[8] It might be argued that *quemazón* postulates an underlying **quemazo*, but it is in fact a standard late mediaeval post-verbal on *quemar*: see Pena [1980:150] and on *-zón* in general Pattison [1975:93]. If *quemazo* does exist, it may be a case of back-formation. On the extreme scarcity of *-azo + -ón*, see Monge [1978:164 n.14].

sixty-six forms,[9] the great majority of which refer to physical characteristics, like those already cited. Non-physical characteristics may, however, be referred to, as in *caprichudo* 'headstrong' (*capricho*) and *pacienzudo* 'long-suffering' (*paciencia*); *cabezudo* (*cabeza*) may refer either to the physical size of the head or to stubbornness.

In all these cases, however, the primary morphological point is that a common noun has been transformed into a noun/adjective signifying 'one who possesses the physical or metaphorical characteristic'. In that, *-udo* parallels *-ado/-ido*, also adjective-forming suffixes of similar nature: cf. *barbado*, 'bearded', *vellido*, 'downy'. The distinguishing feature of *-udo*, and the reason why it is generally considered an augmentative, is that it signifies the possession of the feature in question in abundance or in a large size.[10]

These three suffixes, then, *-ón*, *-azo* and *-udo*, can properly be considered as augmentatives, but in each case that is only a part of their function, and to concentrate on that aspect of their semantic role is to ignore important morphological considerations. There may indeed be senses in which an augmentative nuance shows through: *llorón* means not one who cries but one who does so habitually or to excess; a *frenazo* is a violent application of brakes; a man who is *barbudo* has a more luxuriant beard than one who is only *barbado*. This should not, however,

---

[9] The relevant forms are listed in section III of the Appendix; one other form contained in Gooch's list is excluded from this figure: *menudo* (Lat. MINUTUS) 'small' is not recognisably a derived form in Romance.

[10] Wuest [1948:1283-93] lists 129 forms and comes to the conclusion that 'the pejorative sense seems to predominate, with an emphasis on physical grotesqueness' [p. 1293]. Lang rightly states that *-udo* 'is fundamentally different from the other suffixes grouped...under the augmentative heading since it is strongly class-changing, producing adjectives on noun bases' [1990:116]. I would add only that the same can often be said of *-ón* and *-azo*.

blind us to the fact that these suffixes are functioning in a way which has links at least as close to, say, *-dor*, *-ada*, and *-ado*, as to the affective area. They are, in short, a part of the larger system of class-changing or heterogeneous derivation so vital to the development of the lexical system of the language.

D. G. Pattison
Magdalen College, Oxford

APPENDIX

Word lists from Gooch 1967

I *-ón* suffix

abusón	*dormilón*	*mirón*	*remolón*
acusón	*empollón*	*mordelón*	*replicón*
adulón	*escamón*	*pagón*	*respondón*
aprovechón	*faltón*	*pegón*	*retozón*
bailón	*fisgón*	*peleón*	*reventón*
besucón	*fregona*	*perdilón*	*rompilón*
burlón	*gruñón*	*pidón*	*saltón*
cagón	*ligón*	*practicón*	*sisona*
comilón	*logrón*	*preguntón*	*sobón*
contestón	*lloricón*	*protestón*	*soplón*
copión	*llorón*	*refunfuñón*	*tardón*
criticón	*machacón*	*regalón*	*temblón*
chillón	*mamón*	*regañón*	*tragón*
chupón	*mandón*	*regatón*	*tumbón*
derrochón	*matón*	*remachón*	*zumbón*
destrozón	*meón*	*remendón*	

II -*azo* suffix

abanicazo
aldabonazo
aletazo
alfilerazo
almohadillazo
arañazo
balazo
bancazo
baquetazo
barquinazo
bastonazo
bayonetazo
bocinazo
boñigazo
botellazo
braguetazo
brochazo
cabezazo
cacharrazo
campanillazo
cantazo
cañazo
cañonazo

capotazo
carpetazo
castañazo
codazo
coletazo
cordonazo
cristazo
cuartelazo
culatazo
chinarrazo
chinazo
derechazo
encontronazo
escobazo
escopetazo
espaldarazo
esquinazo
estacazo
flechazo
fogonazo
frenazo
garrotazo
golletazo

guantazo
guarrazo
hachazo
ladrillazo
latigazo
lengüetazo
linternazo
manotazo
martillazo
mazazo
metrallazo
navajazo
paletazo
palmetazo
patinazo
pianazo
picotazo
pinchazo
planchazo
plumazo
porrazo
portazo
pucherazo
puñetazo

puyazo
ramalazo
rasponazo
regletazo
rodillazo
sablazo
sartenazo
taconazo
taponazo
teclazo
telefonazo
tijeretazo
timbrazo
topetazo
trallazo
trancazo
trastazo
trompazo
varetazo
ventanazo
vergajazo
vistazo
zarpazo
zurdazo.

III *-udo* suffix

barbudo
barrigudo
bezudo
bigotudo
cabelludo
cabezudo
cachazudo
cachetudo
campanudo
caprichudo
carrilludo
cejudo
ceñudo
cogotudo
cojonudo
complejudo
concienzudo

conchudo
confianzudo
copudo
corajudo
cornudo
dentudo
embadanudo
fachudo
forzudo
ganchudo
geniudo
greñudo
hocicudo
huesudo
juanetudo
lanudo
linajudo

macanudo
machotudo
melenudo
membrudo
mofletudo
morrocotudo
morrudo
narigudo
nervudo
orejudo
pacienzudo
pantorilludo
panzudo
patilludo
peludo
pellejudo
pestañudo

picudo
pistonudo
rabudo
repolludo
sañudo
sesudo
talentudo
talludo
tesonudo
testarudo
tozudo
tripudo
velludo
ventrudo
zancudo.

REFERENCES

Alonso, A., 1961
  'Noción, emoción, acción y fantasía en los diminutivos', in *Estudios lingüísticos: temas españoles*, pp. 161-189, Madrid.
Faitelson-Weiser, S.,1980
  Les Suffixes quantificateurs de l'espagnol, Paris.
Gooch, A., 1967
  Diminutive, augmentative and pejorative suffixes in modern Spanish: a guide to their use and meaning, Oxford.
Lang, M. F., 1990
  Spanish word formation: productive derivational morphology in the modern lexis, London & New York
Lewicka, H., 1960
  La Langue et le style du théâtre comique français des XVe et XVIe siécles: La Dérivation, Warsaw & Paris.
Malkiel, Y., 1959
  'The two sources of the Hispanic suffix *-azo, -aço'*, *Language*, 35, 193-258.
Moliner, M., 1966
  Diccionario de uso del español, Madrid.
Monge, F., 1978
  '-ción, -sión, -zón, y -ón: función y forma en los sufijos' in *Estudios ofrecidos a Emilio Alarcos Llorach*, II, Oviedo.
Pattison, D. G., 1975
  Early Spanish suffixes: a functional study of the principal nominal suffixes of Spanish up to 1300, Oxford.
Pena, J., 1980
  La derivación en español, Santiago de Compostela.
Robins, R. H., 1967
  General linguistics: an introductory survey, 4th edn, London.
Togeby, K., 1965
  Structure immanente de la langue française, Paris.
von Wartburg, W.,1969
  Problems and methods in linguistics, trans., Oxford.
Wuest, A., 1948
  'The Spanish suffix *-udo'*, *PMLA*, 63, 1283-93.

Neutralization of voice in Spanish and the outcome of the Old Spanish sibilants

A case of phonological change rooted in morphology

1 THE notion that phonological change can have its origins in morphological conditions is one that has previously been appealed to in historical linguistics. In the case of the history of Spanish, the phonological work of Malkiel has with some frequency been angled in this direction [see, for example, Malkiel 1968, 1969, 1970, 1971, 1974, 1980]. What the present paper seeks to show is that the well-known devoicing of the Old Spanish sibilant phonemes /dᶻ/, /z/, /ʒ/, finally established in the standard language in the sixteenth century, owes its origins to patterns of noun morphology in the medieval language.

2 It is highly likely that, as happens in the modern language, there was no case in Old Spanish of syllable-final phonemic contrast based solely upon the distinctive feature of voice. It is well-known that in modern Spanish (in all regions) the phonemic opposition p/b, t/d and k/g (e.g. *pala/bala, nata/nada, rascar/rasgar*) are neutralized when these phonemes occur in the syllabic coda and that the same articulation (more precisely, the same range of articulations) is accorded to syllable-final units spelled *p, t, c* as to those spelled *b, d, g*, respectively: *óp[tico = ob[tener, at[leta = ad[mirar, ac[to = ag[nóstico* [Alarcos 1965:184, Navarro 1961:83, 96, 138]. Of course, in the modern language it is not possible to have a clear view of this neutralization in word-final position, because five of the six phonemes concerned (/p/, /b/, /t/, /k/, /g/) do not occur in this position in the native

vocabulary, but only in recent loans (e.g. *clip, club, vermut, coñac, zigzag*). However, it would seem that insofar as the final consonants of these words are maintained (which is not always the case), they are subject to the same neutralization of voice (/p/ with /b/, /t/ with /d/, /k/ with /g/) as their internal syllable-final counterparts.

3 The evidence for similar neutralization of voice in Old Spanish consists of free alternation, in syllable-final position, between the graphs *p, t, c* and *b, d, g*. Since the phonology of Old Spanish allowed the phonemes concerned to appear in word-final position (at least until the thirteenth century), it is possible to check for such spelling alternation in a reverse glossary of the language. Using the concordances of the Madison Alfonsine corpus [Kasten and Nitti 1978], it becomes clear that the final graph (*p* or *b, t* or *d, c* or *g*) is for the most part determined by the spelling of related forms in which the phoneme concerned is syllable-initial (where voice remains phonologically pertinent). Thus, to plural *prínçipes* corresponds singular *princep/prínçep/princip* (419 occurrences), with only a single instance of *princeb*. Similarly, the forms *grandes, grandeza*, etc., are responsible for the fact that cases of *grand* outnumber cases of *grant* by 4947 to 910, and the plural *mercedes* determines the greater frequency of the spelling *merced* (372 tokens) than the spelling *mercet* (127). On the other hand, forms like *adelantar* account for the numerical superiority of *(a)delant* (1172 cases) over *(a)deland* (16 cases). However, the appearance of *p* rather than *b* (or *vice versa*) or of *t* rather than *d* (or *vice versa*) does not reflect any phonemic contrast (or indeed any systematic phonetic difference), any more than the modern alternation between syllable-final *p* or *b, t* or *d* (in *apto*,

abyecto, atmósfera, admirar, etc.) indicates phonemic or phonetic contrast.

Word-final *c* and *g* are relatively rare in the Alfonsine corpus, so that it is correspondingly difficult to judge whether neutralization of voice takes place between the phonemes normally indicated by these graphs. There is a single relevant case: the name *Rabiçag* is six times spelled thus, but once appears as *Rabiçac*, giving some evidence (albeit slight) that the velars are subject to similar treatment to that observable between the voiced and voiceless labials and dentals.

Particularly interesting in the present context are the Old Spanish descendants of CIVITĀTE. We find 1450 tokens with final *d* (*cibdad, çibdad*), against 995 with *t*, despite the fact that plural *cibdades* would lend strong pressure towards forms with final *d*. Even more revealing is the fact that, of the tokens with final *t*, 360 are spelled *ciptat* or *çiptat*, giving clear indication of the failure of the p/b voice-contrast in internal syllable-final position.

If further evidence is needed, it can be seen in the alternation of final consonants in morphologically invariable words, such as personal names. *Cid/Çid* appears 1258 times, but on three occasions is spelled *Çit*, while the dominant spelling *Mahomat* (221 tokens) alternates with *Mahomad* (10).

A further case of neutralization of the distinctive feature of voice occurs in Old Spanish in the case of the f/β contrast. Where final /e/ was lost after /β/ (< -B-, -V-), the newly-final consonant is sometimes spelled -*f*. The following table gives comparative data from the Alfonsine corpus, indicating the frequency of forms spelled -*f* and those spelled -*ve*/-*ue*:

af	10	*aue*	105	'bird'	
bref	2	*breue*	14	'short'	
dizenuef, dizi-	5	*dizenueue, dizi-*	40	'nineteen'	
grief	1	*grieue*	100	'serious'[1]	
naf	56	*naue*	94	'ship'	
nief	7	*nieve*	19	'snow'	
nuef	11	*nueve*	302	'nine'	
nuf	15	*nuue*	58	'cloud'	

Although there are no forms corresponding to these but spelled with final *-u/v,*[2] and although the precise phonetic value associated with *-f* is difficult to determine,[3] we can conclude that the sounds represented in these words by *f* and *u* are in complementary distribution (and do not represent contrasting phonemes). Clear evidence of neutralization of voice between *f* and *u /v* is provided by the form *almoxerif(es)* 'tax-collector(s)'; the singular form (23 tokens) ends with the same graph as *af, grief, nuf,* etc., although the underlying phonemes are evidently in contrast (as can be seen from the contrasting graphs of the plurals *almoxerifes* vs *aues, nuues,* etc.).

4 Neutralization of voice in Old Spanish was not limited to the pairs of consonants so far examined, but was extended to the dental, alveolar and palatal fricatives and affricates (the sibilants). Leaving aside the palatal affricate (spelled *ch*), it is clear that in thirteenth-century

[1] From *GRĚVIS (which also leaves descendants in French, Occitan, etc.), an analogical modification of GRAVIS based on LĚVIS. The Alfonsine corpus also shows 32 tokens of *graue*.

[2] Such a spelling is impossible at the medieval stage, where final *-u* could only indicate an off-glide.

[3] Since the *-u* of *naue* probably represents the voiced bilabial fricative [β] in thirteenth-century Spanish, it is likely that its alternant *f* represents the voiceless bilabial fricative [θ], the phone also represented by *f* in words of the type *fuente, frente,* For details, see Penny 1972, 1990.

Alfonsine Spanish, the sibilants were organized into three pairs which in syllable-initial position were spelled *c/ç/sc/sç* vs *z*, *ss* vs *s*, *x* vs *i/j/g*, and that the distinctive feature which separated the members of each pair was the feature [voice]. It is equally well known that this spelling-contrast (and the phonemic contrast it reflects) was neutralized when, for morphological or other reasons, the consonants concerned came to occupy syllable-final position. This neutralization can be illustrated by comparing the plural forms of certain nouns with their singulars in the Alfonsine corpus. In the following table, the first column shows forms in which the sibilants are syllable-initial and the second column gives the corresponding singular forms, in which (at least when a pause follows or when the following word begins with a consonant) the sibilant is in syllable-final position.

uozes / vozes / bozes	*uoz / voz / boz*	'voices'
foces / foçes	*foz*	'sickle(s)'
pazes	*paz*	'peace'
pe(s)ces / pesçes	*pez*[4]	'fish'
meses	*mes*	'month(s)'
miesses	*mies*	'ripe corn'
linages/linnages	*linax*	'lineage'
carcaxes	*carcax*	'quiver(s)'

5 Although Alfonsine spelling reveals in this way the existence of phonemic neutralization of sibilants, it does

---

[4] Although the Alfonsine corpus contains no example of word-final *ss* or consonantal *i/j*, the graph *ç* does occur (with low frequency) in word-final position. Such spellings (e.g. *cruç, paç, peç, rayç, vegeç*) are heavily concentrated in the second half of the *Estoria de España* and examples from other texts amount to no more than a tiny handful. In every case of a word spelled with final *ç*, such spellings are heavily outnumbered by the more usual spelling in *-z*.

not, of course, immediately reveal the phonetic value(s) to be attached to each graph; in particular, the spelling system does not indicate whether syllable-final *z, s* and *x* represented voiceless or voiced sounds.

It might be thought that, since medieval *z* and *s* were often associated with voiced articulations (as in *dezir* 'to say', *casa* 'house'), they also indicate voiced sounds in the syllabic coda (*paz, pez, mes, mies*, etc.). It might similarly be assumed that, since *x* is associated with voiceless articulation in syllable-initial position (e.g. *caxa* 'box'), it also represented a voiceless sound in syllable-final position, but the reality must have been more complex. Judging by the rules of voice-assimilation in the modern language (for which see Navarro 1961:94-5, 108), it is highly likely that the medieval sibilants adopted the voice-quality of the following syllable-initial consonant (where this existed, either in the same word as the sibilant or at the beginning of the following word).

It is more difficult to reach conclusions about the voice-quality of the Old Spanish word-final sibilants when followed by a word with vocalic onset. In the modern language, such phonemes are realised with voiceless articulations, but those varieties of Romance most closely related to Castilian which have preserved the voiced/ voiceless contrast in their sibilant sub-systems (Catalan, Portuguese, Judaeo-Spanish) show voiced phones under these conditions (for example, J S *maz o menos*, where *z* indicates [z]). Since the medieval Castilian sibilant sub-system was similar in other regards (apart from absence of *seseo*) to that of Catalan, Portuguese and Judaeo-Spanish, it is likely that the similarity extended to having voiced word-final sibilants before a word-initial vowel.

Most difficult of all (and most important of all from the point of view of the present article) is an assessment of the voice-quality of word-final sibilants when followed by a pause, since the voice-quality which surfaces under these conditions (which include the 'citation' shape of the word concerned, that which occurs when the word is articulated in isolation from others) is likely to reflect the voice-quality of the underlying (archi-)phoneme.[5] There is little internal medieval evidence that can be brought to bear on this problem, and no modern Spanish analogues (since the modern language lacks the voiced sibilant phonemes, which, if they existed, might enter into neutralization with their voiceless counterparts). The closest analogues available are again Catalan, Portuguese and Judaeo-Spanish:[6] in these languages, there is neutralization of word-final pre-pausal sibilants in favour of the voiceless member of each pair. It is therefore likely that the final unit of Old Spanish words terminating in a sibilant and pronounced in isolation was voiceless.[7]

6 Although the medieval Spanish sibilant sub-system is usually described (no doubt correctly) as showing phonemic voice-contrasts (between /tˢ/ and /dᶻ/, /s/ and /z/, /ʃ/ and /ʒ/), it nevertheless appears to be the case that the functional load of these contrasts was extremely

---

[5] For the notion of the archiphoneme, the unit which combines those features which remain pertinent in positions of neutralization, see Alarcos 1965: 49-51.

[6] For Catalan, see Dinnsen 1977.

[7] This conclusion is reached by Alonso [1969:157-74]. Evidence from modern languages such as German suggests that neutralization of voice in word-final position is likely to have been associated with voiceless realization. Thus *bunt* 'variegated' and *Bund* 'band' are both realized in isolation with final [t].

low. Minimal pairs identified for Old Spanish which rest on these oppositions can be listed as follows:[8]

deçir	'to descend'	*dezir*	'to say'
faça	'to strip'	*faza*	'towards'
façes	'bundles'	*fazes*	'you make'
foçes	'sickles'	*fozes*	'throats, ravines'
cosso	'enclosure'	*coso*	'I sew'
espesso	'thick'	*espeso*	'spent'
osso	'bear'	*oso*	'bear'
coxo	'lame; he cooked'	*cojo*	'I grasp'
fixo	'fixed'	*fijo*	'son'
puxar	'to strive, push'	*pujar*	'to rise, raise'

Although this list is probably not exhaustive (an exhaustive list cannot be created for past stages of a language), it probably represents a major portion of the minimal pairs based on this contrast in medieval Spanish. It can also be noted that few of these cases are genuine minimal pairs; that is, only in some of these instances could a proposition containing one of these words be changed into a new proposition by replacing the word concerned by its counterpart in the list above. Only *deçir/dezir*, *foçes/foçes*, *espesso/espeso*, *puxar/pujar* qualify as genuine minimal pairs on this narrower definition, since the members of other pairs belong to different word-classes and are not therefore commutable.

It should also be noted that the voice-contrast between pairs of Old Spanish sibilants was probably restricted to word-internal intervocalic position (like the r/r̄ contrast of the modern language). In word-initial position, /z/ did not occur, /dᶻ/ was of very low frequency, and /ʒ/

---

[8] We can never be sure of the complete list of minimal pairs before the modern period, but it is unlikely to exceed the number given here by more than a small margin.

probably absent from Castilian until its introduction via Gallo-Romance loans.[9]

This extremely low functional yield of voice contrast between the Old Spanish sibilants implies lack of resistance to its elimination from the Old Spanish phonemic system.[10]

7 We can now turn to the reason which arguably under-lies the elimination of voice-contrast between the pairs of Old Spanish sibilants. Given that before a pause both /t^s/ and /d^z/ were realized as [t^s], that /s/ and /z/ were realized as [s], and /ʃ/ and /ʒ/ as [ʃ] (see section 5), and given lack of resistance to elimination of the sibilant voice-contrast [section 6], we can conclude that a process of morphological levelling would lead to generalization of voiceless realizations of sibilants in the plurals of nouns and adjectives ending in z, so that forms of the type *paz/pazes* (traditionally with voiceless [t^s] in the singular, but [d^z] in the plural) were entirely assimilated to forms of the type *pez/peçes* (where [t^s] traditionally occurred in both singular and plural). In the case of the alveolar sibilants, the change envisaged here implies that the type *mes/meses* (traditionally with [z] before the plural morpheme) came to have the same voiceless [s] in this position as the type *mies/miesses* had always had.

---

[9] For the absence of initial /ʒ/ from early Old Spanish, see Penny [1988].

[10] It is true that in some languages a voice-contrast has been maintained between consonant phonemes despite its low functional yield in the pairs concerned. This is arguably the case with English θ/ð and ʃ/ʒ. However, voice-contrast between these English fricatives is no doubt sustained (at least in part) by the existence of voice-contrast between other pairs of fricatives (f/v, s/z). In the case of Old Spanish, there were no pairs of fricative or affricate phonemes, outside the sibilant sub-system, which were contrasted solely by the distinctive feature of voice.

It is harder to exemplifiy this remodelling in the case of the palatal sibilants, because of the relative rarity of final [ʃ] resulting from loss of /-e/ after /ʃ/. Occasional medieval examples of *linax*[11] (vs. *linage*), etc., allow us to conclude that *linax/linages* came to coincide in its morphological patterning with *carcax/carcaxes, açedrex/açedrexes* 'chess', producing voiceless articulations in the remodelled plural *linages* (and in the unapocopated singular *linage*).[12]

8 Since the voice-contrast between the members of each pair of sibilants was limited to the onset of internal syllables (section 6), its neutralization (in favour of voiceless realizations) in the final syllables of nouns and adjectives must have established a substantial precedent for its neutralization in other phonological and morphological circumstances. Such increasing neutralization (and eventual total merger) of each pair of phonemes was, as we have seen, only very weakly restrained by the need to maintain contrast between minimal pairs (section 6), and it is this merger which has been so well documented by others [notably by Alonso 1967, 1969].

---

[11] Cases of final *-x* are not attested in the Alfonsine corpus, but occur elsewhere in the medieval period; e.g. *barnax* (a variant of *bernage*), *CMC* 3325.

[12] The process under consideration here may have received support from a similar process occurring in Old Spanish verbal endings. A voiceless realization (respectively [tˢ], [s], [ʃ]) of the final phoneme of such frequent (apocopated) 3rd sing. pres. ind. (and sing. imperative) forms as *faz* [*fazer*] 'he does/do!', *cos* [*coser*] 'he sews/sew!', would give rise to phonetic identity between the stem-consonant of such forms and that of *crez* [*cre(s)cer*] 'he grows', *tos* [*tosser*] 'he coughs/cough!', thus perhaps encouraging the use of the voiceless phones in those forms of *fazer, coser*, etc., in which the sibilant was not word-final.

9 It is well known that the merger of the voiced sibilants with their voiceless counterparts (revealed by rhyme, misspelling and comments by contemporaries) is at first characteristic only of Old Castile and is radiated from there to other parts of the Peninsula [Lapesa 1980:371]. The change may be ancient in the north, but was evidently resisted in the centre and south, at least until the sixteenth century, and in remote peripheral regions until the twentieth [see Espinosa 1935]. The spellings adopted by Antonio de Nebrija [see, for example, Nebrija 1516] in essence continue those of the Alfonsine corpus, maintaining a rigid distinction between voiceless and voiced sibilants, using *c/ç, ss, x* for the first and *z, s, j/ g* for the second. However, a little-noticed feature of Nebrija's recommended forms is that he does not use the traditional spelling of words like *coz, hoz* (earlier *foz), haz* (earlier *faz), pez, mies*. That is, he rejects final *z* and *s* in the case of morphemes whose final sibilant is voiceless when followed by a bound morpheme beginning with a vowel (i.e. in plural and derived forms such as *coces, cocear, hoces, hocino, haces, hacina, peces, pecina, miesses*), prescribing *coce, hace, hoce, pece, miesse.*[13] Since all of these forms appear in earlier texts without a final vowel, we can conclude that Nebrija's forms (also found in other late fifteenth- and sixteenth-century writers) reflect a phonological change (addition of /e/) rooted in the same morphological conditions as those which caused the devoicing of sibilants, but with the opposite outcome: phonological differentiation of singular forms (where no phonetic difference previously

---

[13] However, Nebrija also uses the form *pece* in the sense 'pitch, tar' < PICE 'id.', in which case the expected consonant is voiced. Lack of a plural form **pezes.* in the case of this mass-noun perhaps helps to explain Nebrija's confusion.

existed) on the basis of the pattern of vowels and consonants observable in the corresponding plurals:

Old Spanish			Nebrija		
pazes	*paz*	>	*pazes*	*paz*	'peace'
faces	*faz*	>	*haces*	**hace**	'bundle'
meses	*mes*	>	*meses*	*mes*	'month'
miesses	*mies*	>	*miesses*	**miesse**	'ripe corn'

10 Spelling evidence is notoriously treacherous, and must always be judged in the context of the general competence of the writer concerned. In the case of Nebrija, we can be certain that there is a reasonably close fit between graphs and phonemes, but this is far from being the case with all writers at all times. The spelling of the Alfonsine corpus is usually held to provide a reasonable representation of the phonology of thirteenth-century educated Toledo usage, so that departures from 'standard' spelling carry some wieght as evidence of phonological variation and change. In this context, it is interesting to note that in a small proportion of cases in the corpus a spelling -*ces*/*çes* or -*ses* is used, in the plural of nouns and adjectives, where etymology (and the spelling elsewhere in the corpus) leads us to expect -*zes* or -*sses*. The cases concerned, each of which appears once in the corpus, are the following: *cruçes*, *preces*, *rafeces* and *mieses*. Further enquiry is evidently needed, but these cases may represent the first reliable evidence that neutralization of voice had been carried, in nouns and adjectives, from word-final to intervocalic position, as a result of the morphological levelling process described above.

Ralph Penny
Queen Mary & Westfield College, London

REFERENCES

Alarcos Llorach, E., 1965
   Fonología española, Madrid

Alonso, A., 1967
   De la pronunciación medieval a la moderna en español, vol. 2, Madrid

Dinnsen, D. A., 1977
   'A functional explanation of dialect difference', *Language Sciences*, 46:1-7

Espinosa, *hijo*, A. M., 1935
   Archaismos dialectales: la conservación de la 's' y 'z' sonoras en Cáceres y Salamanca, Madrid

Kasten. L. A., and J. J. Nitti, eds., 1978
   Concordances and texts of the Royal Scriptorium manuscripts of Alfonso X, el sabio, Madison., Microfiches

Malkiel, Y., 1968
   'The inflexional paradigm as an occasional determinant of sound change', in *Directions for historical linguistics: a symposium*, edd. W. P. Lehmenn and Y Malkiel, Austin, 23-64

————., 1969
   'Sound changes rooted in morphological conditions: the case of OSp. /sk/ changing to /θk/', *Romance Philology*, 23:188-200

————., 1970
   Le Nivellement morphologique comme point de départ d'une "loi phonétique": la monophthongaison occasionnelle de *ie* et *ue* en ancien espagnol', in *Mélanges de langue et de littérature du Moyen Âge et de la Renaissance offerts à Jean Frappier*, Paris, 701-35

————., 1971
   'Derivational transparency as an occasional co-determinant of sound-change: a new causal ingredient in the distribution of -ç- and -z- in ancient Hispano-Romance [I', *RPh*, 25: 1-52

————., 1976
   'Multi-conditioned sound-change and the impact of morphology on phonology', *L*, 52:757-78

————., 1980
   'Points of abutment of morphology on phonology: the case of archaic Spanish *esti(e)do* "stood"', *RPh*, 34:206-09

Lapesa, R., 1980

    Historia de la lengua española, 8th ed., Madrid

Navarro Tomás, T., 1961

    Manual de pronunciación española, 10th ed., Madrid

Nebrija, A. de., 1516

    Vocabulario de romance en latín, ed. G. J. Macdonald, Madrid

Penny, R. J., 1972

    'The re-emergence of /f/ as a phoneme of Castilian', *ZRP,* 88:463-82

———— [1988

    'The Old Spanish graphs 'i', 'j', 'g' and 'y' and the development of Latin G ^{e,i}- and J-', *BHS,* 65:337-51

———— [1990

    'Labio-dental /f/, aspiration and /h/-dropping in Spanish: the evolving phonemic values of the graphs *f* and *h*', in *Cultures in contact in Medieval Spain: historical and literary essays presented to L.P. Harvey,* edd. D. Hook and B. Taylor, London, 157-82

Language conflict or language symbiosis?

Contact of other Romance varieties with Castilian

IN offering a tribute to Fred Hodcroft on the occasion of his retirement from Oxford, I bear in mind his long-standing interest in Spanish dialectology, and especially in the Eastern dialects of Spain. His own field-work has been mainly concerned with Aragonese, and we have together regularly attended classes in Catalan, ably conducted in Oxford by Miquel Ruiz Lacruz. It seems appropriate therefore to dedicate to him a survey of some of the current sociolinguistic problems of contact and bilingualism associated with Spain, though not exclusively the East.

These are not new problems: in the Iberian peninsula there must have been contact between Latin and pre-Roman languages, between Latin and Romance varieties, and between both Latin and Romance and Arabic and Hebrew. Still today there is contact, and conflict, between Spanish and Basque, and, in America, between Spanish and native American languages, and between Spanish and English. I, however, wish to concentrate on contact of Castilian with other Romance varieties, in tune with a volume of studies soon to appear on Romance-Romance contact and conflict [Posner–Green, forthcoming]. This volume includes comprehensive surveys of bilingualism between Castilian and Catalan (by Miquel Strubell i Trueta), and Galician (by Henrique Monteagudo and Antón Santamarina), as well as of Spanish-based creoles (by Armin Schwegler and John Lipski), of Uruguayan *fronterizo* (by Fritz Hensey) and of American Spanish-Italian interlects (by Giovanni Meo-Zilio). A theoretical introduction by the editors also covers the history of studies on bilingualism and conflict, as well as specifically Spanish and Portuguese themes. Here, therefore, I shall fill in gaps, with reference to issues that might interest Fred.

'Conflict' is a notion that, in the Spanish linguistic context, became important during the Franco era, and was developed especially by Valencian activists [Aracil 1965, Ninyoles 1969]. It has more recently become a centre of interest in sociolinguistics [Nelde 1987], developing the now-classic ideas on language contact and language loyalty advanced by Weinreich [1953]. 'Language conflict' can refer to two separate, but not unrelated, things—one is the conflict of allegiance felt by a bilingual speaker, the other in the competition between neighbouring communities that habitually use different languages, especially if one is felt to be subordinate to the other. If the two languages are very similar, as with all Romance varieties, both sorts of conflict can be intense: in the former case the speaker is confused about which language he is at present using, and 'mixes' them indiscriminately; in the latter, one of the languages can be 'dialectalized', and treated as a substandard form of the other [Posner–Green, forthcoming]. Where one language is a national language, and the other a regional language, 'asymmetrical bilingualism' is imposed, with speakers of the latter being obliged to acquire the national language, without any corresponding obligation imposed on the national language speaker. Whether in fact bilingualism is advantageous to the intellectual development of a speaker is debatable: Moya–Lago [1977] discusses the Spanish problems from the social and medical point of view. It will be recalled that Fascist ideology despised bilinguals in the same way as those of mixed race, as in some sense 'impure', 'disloyal', or, at any rate, 'marginal' [Weinreich 1953]. More rationally, there are fears that bilingualism can result in a sort of 'semilingualism', when the speaker is fully competent in neither language, or 'schizoglossia' where the bilingual is anxious about the non-native-like features of his speech [Baetens–Beardmore 1986]. Psychological studies are inconclusive about the disadvantages of bilingualism [Albert–Obler 1978]. It seems that other parameters, such as inherent intelligence, social environment or the conditions in which the languages are acquired, are more important than the fact of bilingualism itself.

One fear often expressed is that imposed bilingualism will inevitabily lead to the 'death' of the submerged language, and the culture of which it is the vehicle, by way of 'shift' to the more prestigious language. Fashionable 'ecological' approaches to language seek ways of avoiding minority language attrition and death [Mackey 1985]: the greater the linguistic distance between the two languages, the less the risk, but it is believed that it has most chance of survival where the language is a symbol of community identity [Woolard 1989], and where efforts are made to fit it for all the functions of modern society (status planning or *normalización*) and to codify it for educational purposes (corpus planning or *normativización*). These are the strategies adopted for minority languages in Spain, against the opposition of more traditional dialectologists and linguists. The strategies can be successful only if the minority languages can be associated with a delimited territory, in which they are protected and promoted.

The 1978 Spanish constitution attempts to repair some of the damage done by Franco's 'España, una' linguistic policies. However it maintains the belief that became accepted in the nineteenth century, that a political unit requires a common language in order to preserve cohesion and to facilitate intercommunication: 'El castellano es la lengua oficial del Estado'. The use of 'Castilian', rather than 'Spanish', as the name of the official language is controversial [Salvador 1987], but shows recognition that Castilian is not the only language of Spain, and, moreover, indicates a desire to continue linguistic links with Latin America, where 'Castilian' is usually preferred to 'Spanish', which has territorial connotations. However, some ambiguity arises because the language of Castile is not wholly identical with the standard language [Mozos 1984]. Note that the term used for the political unit is 'state', not 'nation', which is usually preferred in Latin America: the Catalan slogan of 'a nation, but not a state', is relevant here (for the link between language and nation-state, see Posner–Green [forthcoming]). The term 'official' is understood as indicating validity in all legal and administrative exchanges. The gloss

> Todos los españoles tienen el deber de conocerla y el derecho de usarla

limits the rights of co-official languages that may be used in the *Comunidades Autónomas*—Basque, Catalan and Galician—imposing bilingualism on minority language speakers but not on mother-tongue Castilian speakers. The Constitution goes on

> La riqueza de las distintas modalidades lingüísticas de Espana es un patrimonio cultural que será objeto de especial respeto y protección.

This is a catch-all provision which avoids the controversial distinction between language and dialect, and signals a desire for linguistic benevolence and tolerance, in contrast to Franco's policies. It leaves open, however, the question of what degree of 'official protection' should be accorded to 'modalities' that are not designated in the

Statutes of the Autonomous Regions as co-official languages. Here I shall consider some of the most disputed varieties and their past and present status, beginning with Aragonese, as Fred Hodcroft's favoured stamping-ground.

Aragonese

The Community Statute in Aragon echoes the constitution

Las diversas modalidades lingüísticas de Aragón gozarán de protección...

The use of the plural makes no commitment about the existence of a distinctive Aragonese variety, but takes into account the use within the political unit of Pyrenean local dialects (*altoaragoneses*) and a Catalan-speaking Eastern fringe. The language question arouses bitter controversy between rival academic groupings. Some [Conte *et al.* 1977] who wish to defend the Aragonese varieties against extinction by developing a regional *koiné* that will embrace both the interlects—Castilianized or Catalanized Aragonese or Aragonese-tinged Castilian or Catalan—used in most of the region, and the isolated and shrinking local dialects of mountain villages (Mott [1989] is a detailed study of the (Catalano-)Aragonese dialect and folklore of an isolated village of 400 inhabitants in the 70s and 80s, a dialect unlikely to survive much longer). Others [Alvar 1986, Monge 1989] retain affection for old rural uses but insist that the language of culture and political activity in Aragon should be Castilian, which began to displace Aragonese in the sixteenth century.

One argument for the separate identity of Aragonese is based on its historical development direct from Latin, parallel to, rather than by way of, Castilian. Blasco Ferrer [1989] argues that, apart from their disputed Gallo-Romance lineage, Catalan and Aragonese stand together, from a typological point of view, against Castilian, sharing syntactic and pragmatic features with French and Occitan. Another argument is that it is the mother-tongue, in some form or other, of a substantial population: estimates of the number of Aragonese speakers depend greatly on what linguistic criteria are applied, and range between 10,000 and 60,000. Development of a standard Aragonese *koiné* would give spoken varieties the support of a written norm that could be taught in schools, thus halting their attrition, degradation and eventual loss. Opponents of this view insist that there never has been an Aragonese language, merely *hablas aragonesas,* and that these ceased to be vehicles of culture long before the time of the Catholic Monarchs. They claim that the move to establish a unified Aragonese is an exaggerated reaction by the political left to the humiliation and injustice caused by Franco's linguistic policies. They tend to make light of the fear of the death of the dialects, pointing out that they have survived so far and that, with the protection of the Constitution, they are not in great danger. However, none can deny that the territory in which Aragonese varieties are spoken has shrunk drastically since the sixteenth century, and that the Civil War dealt a near-fatal blow to some previously flourishing local dialects.

At present the prestige of Castilian, as the language of education and social advancement, means that Aragonese varieties are treated as inferior, so that users suffer from linguistic insecurity and conflict of loyalty. As Castilian and Aragonese are linguistically very close, and mutually intelligible, the latter is felt to be merely an uncultured variant of the former. Apart from regional pronunciation and vocabulary, more generalized Aragonese features include the Catalan-like retention of the 'adverbial pronouns' *ne* and *y* and morphological peculiarities like the use of *-oron* as the third-plural ending of the preterite. However, little is known about the language consciousness of speakers, and many predict the demise of Aragonese as a separate entity. This is, of course, quite different from the Catalan situation today, even though it would seem that Catalan was reduced in the nineteenth century to a state similar to that of Aragonese at present: its revival by the deliberate action of cultural and linguistic activists now appears to be complete (see Miquel Strubell i Trueta's contribution to Posner–Green [forthcoming]). The Southern Catalan variety, spoken in Valencia, is not quite so healthy, though it is certainly in a more vigorous state than Aragonese.

Valencian

The Valencian Statute states:

> Los dos idiomas oficiales de la Comunidad Autónoma son el valenciano y el castellano

but the bilingual policy does not solve all problems. Repopulation of the region from the thirteenth century means that there has always been juxtaposition, and interaction, of different linguistic groupings. The east was settled mainly by Catalan speakers, whereas in the west two varieties of Castilian are found: Aragonese-based *xurro* and Castilian-based *murciano*. It is unknown how far these interacted with the language of the local Mudéjar population about whose usage there is some controversy, the traditional view [Galmés de Fuentes 1986] being that they spoke a Romance variety (which the

Jews certainly did). On the other hand evidence is adduced to suggest that, unlike the Jews, the *mudéjares* spoke a variety of Arabic and not the conservative Romance usually called Mozarabic, after the name used for Christians under Arabic rule, most of whom had fled or had been expelled by the time of the Valencian crusade [Burns 1984]. Both camps agree however that interaction between the invaders and the farmers who remained *in situ* may mean that the local substratum language was of prime importance in differentiating Valencian from other varieties of Catalan. Until the fifteenth century Valencia enjoyed considerable prestige, but the union of the Castilian and Aragonese crowns diminished its importance, and, since that period, close links between Valencian and the Catalan spoken further North have been broken. In the fifteenth century the name *valencià* for the language began to be preferred to more traditional *llemosí* and *romanç*, or to *català*, though *aljamía* was frequent, especially in references to Moriscos [Ferrando Francés 1980]. The expulsion of the Moriscos left the way open for further immigration, at first from Majorca, and in more recent times from all parts of Spain, especially Andalusia and Castile, with a consequent increase in the linguistic complexity of the region. By the time of the mid-nineteenth-century *Renaixença* Castilianization had succeeded in virtually eliminating the Valencian written language even from local parish records [Vila Moreno 1983].

Today about half the population speaks Valencian. Although the written forms of Valencian and Catalan are very similar, there is resistance to linking them [Salvador 1987, Ferrando Francés 1988]. In the North the *tortosino* variety is the most widely used and the most like Catalan, though there are some salient differences, like the use of the definite article *el* rather than *lo*. *Apitxat* has converged more towards standard Castilian, whereas *alcantino* has been in close interaction with *murciano* since the seventeenth century [Colomina i Castanyer 1985, Casanova 1988] and has been largely displaced from some regions [Montoya Abad 1986]. The sociolinguistic history of Valencian is very different from that of Barcelona Catalan, long the preferred language of a prosperous and independent-minded middle class. Valencian, on the other hand, was more like other minority languages in being associated with less privileged social groups. Now, however, the standing of the language in the estimation of its speakers has risen [Gómez Molina 1986, Byrne 1989]. The 1983 'Llei d'ús i ensenyament del valencià', which encouraged teaching of the language in schools, has done much to promote and revive the use of spoken varieties [Ferrando Francés 1988]. Some purists, however, object to the normalized language adopted for educational and administrative purposes, as distorting the living usage of mother-tongue speakers [Cremades Marco 1982]. As in Catalunya, bilingualism is required of Valencian speakers, but not of their Castilian neighbours—a situation that is a source of resentment and conflict, and one that seems to be particularly resented [Aracil 1966]. I shall omit from this survey any discussion of Murcian and Andalucian, which are usually considered to be, not wholly uncontroversially, Castilian varieties (see Posner–Green [forthcoming]) and turn to the varieties of Western Spain.

Leonese

The extreme West of the peninsula is occupied by Galician-Portuguese varieties, which are extensively discussed in Posner–Green [forthcoming]. Wedged between these and Castilian, with in the North an almost unbroken dialect continuum, from West to East, is

Leonese, as the varieties of the region are labelled in classic philological works [Lang 1982]. It is better, however, to draw a distinction between Asturias, the home ground of these varieties, and the reconquered and repopulated Leonese and Extremaduran regions, where what was probably already a diluted dialect type has been penetrated by Castilian and Portuguese features on the respective sides of the frontier. Castilian, we are told [Lloyd 1987:178-180], was originally an innovating and dynamic variety of Leonese, spoken by enterprising and daring settlers implanted in the depopulated no-man's-land between Christians and Moors, possibly intermingled with Basques and refugees from the South. The language eventually elbowed out its rival Christian neighbours, as its speakers swept South, 'equating their private brand of Castilian with prestigious standard Spanish' [Malkiel 1988]. We recall that the term *España(s)* seems to have been originally used for the land south of the fastnesses (*La Montaña*) never occupied by the Moors [Moya–Lago 1977].

In the Middle Ages, Leonese was the vehicle for a number of important texts, but the union of the Leonese and Castilian crowns (1230) meant that it eventually lost its most prestigious functions, and bit by bit gave way to Castilian, with which it was probably always mutually intelligible. By the time of the Golden Age, the *sayagués* variety represented the stereotype of peasant speech. Today Leonese has lost all its territory in Zamora and Salamanca provinces, though *rasgos leoneses* [Llorente Maldonaldo 1986] colour the Castilian of the region, more so in the West than the East. Very few localities preserve any degree of bilingualism: for instance, in San Martín de Castañeda, a Sanabrian Leonese variety is in diglossic relationship with a regional version of the official language. Elsewhere the two varieties have converged, with Leonese features persisting more in isolated communities. A sociolinguistic study of Valladolid [Williams 1987] shows that, in that large town well to the east of the former Leonese region, some Leonese phonological features are associated with lower-class speech, but that among young adults there is more individual than group variation, presumably because 'covert prestige' factors are at work. Consciousness of Leonese as a distinct variety seems to be fairly high within the region, but low outside [Pérez Alonso 1979]. There seems, however, to be little support for the revival of the language in what remains largely a backward and underpopulated agricultural area.

Asturian

Further north in Asturias, however, controversy rages, and conflict is sometimes even more bitter than in Aragon. The name *bable*, especially in the plural, to designate local varieties arouses mixed feelings, as it is seen by some as depreciative, by others as affectionate. It is probably not a traditional term and seems to date only from the eighteenth century, when Jovellanos and others attempted to promote Asturian. Some prefer the more dignified territorial name of 'Asturian', associated with loyalty to place, as well as to language. The 1981 Statute of Asturias decrees:

> El bable gozará de protección, se promoverá su uso, su difusión en los medios de comunicación y su enseñanza, respetando, en todo caso, las variantes locales y voluntariedad en su aprendizaje.

Castilian remains the only official language and the legal status of Asturian varieties is strictly limited [Tolivar Alas 1989]. Historically Asturias, and its centre Oviedo, was soon eclipsed, when the seat of power moved to León in the tenth century [Cano Gonzales

1987]. During the Middle Ages, the literary language was 'Leonese' (or 'Asturo-Leonese') which began to replace Latin only from the thirteenth century. However, although further south, as we have seen, Castilian has almost ousted the regional language, in Asturias local dialects have shown more resistance, and, because of their intrinsic characteristics, have attracted much attention from dialectologists. One particularly interesting feature of many of the local varieties is the use of a 'neuter'—or rather differentiation between mass and count nouns—that is not paralleled anywhere else in Spain (though some South-Central dialects of Italy have traces of a similar distinction).

At present, Asturian varieties remain the everyday language of most country folk, and in the industrial areas they are still used by many working-class speakers. In 1985 30% of the Asturian population claimed to speak the language fluently, in a diglossic relationship with Castilian, the *falar fino* associated with upper-class usage [D'Andres 1987]. Consciousness of the identity of the language is high, with 72% denying that it is a dialect of Castilian, and 76% recognizing the varieties as some sort of cohesive entity. Controversy, however, exists about the desirability of the establishment of an Asturian *koiné* [Neira 1982]. The Academia de la Llingua Asturiana, founded in 1981, is militantly in favour of normalization of the language and the introduction of co-official status. The question is politically sensitive in the extreme, and linguists can contribute only by pointing parallels elsewhere [Muljačić 1988].

Apart from fine, traditional dialect descriptions like those of Penny [1969, 1978], there is little in the way of sociolinguistic work on the region. In his study of the *montañés* variety spoken in Ucieda, a village of some 600 inhabitants in Santander province, Holmquist [1988] shows that this transitional variety still evokes language loyalty, though the sense of identity is rather low: it is described in terms like 'hablar mal' or 'casteyanu con la -*u*' (as the use of [u] for Castilian final [o] is regarded as a salient dialect marker), and it functions almost exclusively as a means of identifying people from a very small area. As the population becomes more exogamous, and as the region becomes more popular among weekend visitors, the chances of survival of the dialect diminish. More centrally, information about attitudes and usage appears to be scant in Asturias, although it seems clear that a substantial body of opinion views the demand for some degree of recognition of Asturian usage as legitimate.

Given the governmental view that Spain should have an official language that must be used throughout the state, how can conflict be resolved for those Spaniards whose mother-tongue is not Castilian? The 'territorial principle' espoused by Switzerland cannot be reconciled with the acceptance of a single language for the whole country. In Switzerland conflict is also averted by the existence of 'cross-cutting'—by which language groupings do not coincide with religious or political allegiances—and by the fact that speakers of the majority language, German, are willing to acquire another Swiss language, and therefore do not impose asymmetrical bilingualism on the other groupings (though in this respect Romansh speakers are in a subordinate position). These conditions do not hold in Spain.

Is the alternative for the minority languages, therefore, submission and assimilation, or revolt and differentiation? Another possibility is that the official language should recognize, as permitted variants, usages that are regarded as characteristic of the regional Romance varieties. Accommodation and convergence, as well as language mixing, would have to be permitted and not deprecated as substandard. Instead of the fixed, purist norm associated with Academy rulings, it would require a 'polynomic' norm (see Marcellesi [1980]; also Ghja-cumu Thiers' contribution to Posner–Green [forthcoming]), more tolerant of phonological, morphological and lexical variation, and which allows educated speakers from every region equal self-esteem.

It remains to be seen whether indeed this is possible in a Spain which for much of its history has shown little tolerance of deviations from a rigid norm. In present circumstances, admiration is voiced for the *convivencia* that was found in the early post-Reconquista periods: a symbiotic relationship between different faiths, cultures and languages seems to have existed, compared with what later at best was a 'tense stalemate' [Burns 1984], and at worst open conflict. Today there seems to be greater respect than hitherto for non-standard pronunciation. The next stage would appear to be greater tolerance of grammatical and lexical variation, to the point of achieving a sort of 'passive multilingualism' on the part of all educated speakers.

Rebecca Posner
University of Oxford

REFERENCES

Albert, M. L., and L. K. Obler, 1978
  The bilingual brain. Neuropsychological and neurolinguistic aspects of bilingualism, New York-San Francisco-London
Alvar López, M., 1986
  'Modalidades lingüísticas aragonesas' in M. Alvar López, ed., *Lenguas peninsulares y proyección hispánica*, Madrid, 133-42
Aracil, L. V., 1965
  'Conflit linguistique et normalisation linguistique dans l'Europe nouvelle', *reprinted as* 'Conflicte lingüístic i normalització lingüística a l'Europa nova' *in* Aracil [1982] 23-38
  ————., 1966
  'El bilingüisme com a mite' *original in English, reprinted in* Aracil [1982] 39-58
  ————., 1982
  Papers de sociolingüística, Barcelona
Baetens Beardsmore, H., 1986
  Bilingualism: basic principles, Clevedon, Avon
Blasco-Ferrer, E., 1989
  'Tipología y clasificación: el caso contradictorio del catalán y del aragonés' *in* Holtus *et al.*, 179-86
Burns, R. I., 1984
  Muslims, Christians, and Jews in the crusader kingdom of Valencia, Cambridge
Byrne, A., 1989
  'A sociolinguistic study of Valencian: its usage and status' *M. A. thesis, National University of Ireland*
Cano Gonzales, A. M., 1987
  'Averamientu a la hestoria de la llingua asturiana' in *Informe so la llingua asturiana* Oviedo, 11-23 [*French version*, 65-77]
Casanova, E., 1988
  'El valenciano dentro del diasistema lingüístico catalán' *in* Juárez Blanquer [1988] 13-24
Colomina i Castanyer, J., 1985
  L'alacantí: un estudi sobre la variació lingüística, Alicante
Conte, A., *et al.*, 1977
  El aragonés: identidad y problemática de una lengua, Zaragoza

Cremades Marco, F. de B., 1982
La llengua valenciana en perill, Valencia
D'Andres, R., 1987
'La situación social de la llingua asturiana' in *Informe so la llingua asturiana* Oviedo, 25-44 [French version, 79-94]
Ferrando Francés, A., 1980
Consciencia idiomàtica i nacional dels valencians, Valencia
Ferrando Francés, A., 1988
'Presente y futuro de la normalización lingüística en el País Valencián' in Juárez Blanquer, 25-34
Galmés de Fuentes, A., ed., 1986
Las lenguas prevalencianas, Alicante
Gómez Molina, J. R., 1986
Estudio sociolingüístico de la comunidad de habla de Sagunto (Valencia), Valencia
Holmquist, J. C., 1988
Language loyalty and linguistic variation: a study in Spanish Cantabria, Dordrecht
Holtus, G., et al., 1989
La Corona de Aragón y las lenguas románicas. Miscelánea de homenaje para Germán Colón, Tübingen
Juárez Blanquer, A., ed., 1988
Las lenguas románicas españolas tras la constitución de 1978, Granada
Lang, J., 1982
Sprache im Raum. Zu den theoretischen Grundlagen der Mundartforschung. Unter Berücksichtigung des Rätoromanischen und Leonesischen, Tubingen
Llorente Maldonaldo de Guevara, A., 1986
'Las hablas vivas de Zamora y Salamanca en la actualidad' in Alvar López, 107-32
Lloyd, P. M., 1987
From Latin to Spanish, Philadelphia
Mackey, W. F., 1985
'La mortalité des langues et le bilinguisme des peuples' in U. Pieper and G. Stickel, eds., *Studia Linguistica Diachronica et Synchronica. Werner Winter sexagenario...ab eius collegis amicis discipulisque oblata*, Berlin–New York, 537-562
Malkiel, Y., 1988
'Spanish language' in J. R. Strayer, ed., *Dictionary of the Middle Ages*, New York

Marcellesi, J.-B., 1980
    'Pour une approche sociolinguistique de la situation du corse',
    Etudes corses 14:133-50
Monge, F., 1989
    '¿Una nueva lengua románica?' *in* Holtus, 275-83
Montoya Abad, B., 1986
    Variació i desplaçament de llengües a Elda i a Oriola durant l'edad
    moderna, Alicante
Mott, B., 1989
    El habla de Gistain, Huesca
Moya, G. and J. Lago, 1977
    Bilingüismo y trastornos del lenguaje en España, Madrid
Muljačić, Z., 1988
    'Le paradoxe élaborationnel et les deux espèces de dialectes dans
    l'étude de la constitution des langues romanes', *Lletres asturianes*
    31:43-56
Neira, J., 1982
    Bables y castellano en Asturias, Madrid
Nelde, P. H., 1987
    'Research on language conflict' *in* U. Ammon, *et al.*, eds.,
    Sociolinguistics–Soziolinguistik, 2 vols, Berlin, 607-12
Ninyoles, R. L., 1969
    Conflicte lingüístic valencià, Valencia
Penny, R. J., 1969
    El habla pasiega: ensayo de dialectología montañesa, London
    —————., 1978
    Estudio estructural del habla de Tudanca, Tübingen
Pérez-Alonso, J., 1979
    'Catalan—an example of the current language struggle in Spain:
    sociopolitical and pedagogical implications', *International Journal*
    of the Sociology of Language 21:109-25
Posner, R., and J. N. Green, forthcoming
    Bilingualism and linguistic conflict in Romance (Trends in
    Romance linguistics and philology, 5), Berlin
Salvador, G., 1987
    Lengua española y lenguas de España, Barcelona
Mozos, S. de los, 1984
    La norma castellana del español, Valladolid
Tolivar Alas, L., 1989
    'Normalización lingüística y Estatuto Asturiano', *Lletres asturianes*
    31:7-24

Vila Moreno, A., 1983

La lengua valenciana en la administración parroquial (siglos XVII a XIX), Valencia

Weinreich, U., 1953

Languages in contact, New York (*repr*. The Hague, 1968)

Williams, L., 1987

Aspectos sociolingüísticos del habla de la ciudad de Valladolid, Valladolid

Woolard, K. A., 1989

'Language convergence and language death as social processes' *in* N. C. Dorian, ed., *Investigating obsolescence. Studies in contraction and death*. Cambridge, 354-67

Spanish adjective negation

0 BY 'adjective negation', I mean in principle negation which has only an adjective or adjectival past participle as its scope. However, superficial 'sentence negation' may in effect be 'adjective negation' if an adjective is the only complement (I shall call this **syntactic adjective negation**). Negation of *es posible*, for example, may be realised as *es imposible* (**prefixal adjective negation**) or *no es posible* (**syntactic adjective negation**). The **antonymic** relation is also frequently recognised as one of effective negation: in a clear case of antonymy of incompatibles, for instance, *muerto* could be said to imply *no vivo*.

Setting aside for the moment syntactic adjective negation and the relation of antonymy, adjective negation proper in both Latin and Spanish is both **synthetic** (i.e. prefixal) and **analytic** in nature. However, a general movement in favour of analytic structures may be perceived: Vulgar Latin shows a striking reduction in the prefixal types available, and Spanish preserves and extends the analytic types available.[1] The aim of this paper is to trace these movements and to call attention to the inclusion within analytic adjective negation types of the uniquely Spanish *sin* + infinitive construction.

[1] Llorens [9] asserts that 'las lenguas románicas prefieren la negación sintáctica, por medio de palabras especiales, por el mayor realce que obtiene la idea de negación, cuando se expresa por términos negativos especiales', citing examples from glosses quoted in Menéndez Pidal. I believe that this conclusion is unwarranted on such a basis, however, since 'syntactic negation' (= my analytic negation) is much more common in the somewhat artificial language of glosses and dictionaries.

1 Synthetic negation in Spanish and its history

The most productive negative prefixes of Latin were IN-, DIS- and DE-, all of which, though they had other meanings as well, were capable of forming polar antonyms: MORTALIS/IMMORTALIS, FACILIS/DIFFICILIS, DECORUS/ DEDECORUS. Of these, IN- must count as the principal, unmarked negative prefix, and it was certainly the most productive: DIS- and DE-, when used with the same roots, carry meanings that are in contrast with simple negation. Brea [1980: 127] points to the triple INCOLOR 'having no colour' / DISCOLOR 'of a different colour' / DECOLOR 'having lost its colour'. It is therefore perhaps remarkable that IN- in its negative meaning survives, by popular route, so tenuously and unrecognizably in Spanish, in such fully lexicalised forms as *enfermo* < INFIRMUS and *enemigo* < INIMICUS. The negatives in IN- which are found in the later medieval and modern stages of the language are all learned borrowings. Even allowing for the lack of textual attestation, which is a considerable problem in dealing with the history of such relatively infrequently occurring elements, the figures are striking: Kasten and Nitti's Alfonsine corpus, for instance, contains only four items in *in-*: *inascendente*, *ineptu(m)*, *infortunado* and *insipida*.

Why IN- should have lost ground so dramatically in Vulgar Latin is not clear. Discussing Spanish *in-*, Gyurko [230], suggests that 'the conflict between the negative affix and homonymous *in-* = 'on': *im-poner*, *in-flamar*, *in-suflar*' is a factor detrimental to its effectiveness as a negative, and the same principle might be applied to the IN- of Latin; but, as will be seen, the DIS- > *des-* prefix, with apparently an even greater functional load, seems to have survived and prospered. Brea [1980: 131] suggests that the extensive use of IN- was a characteristic of the cultured language, especially technical language; but the same is broadly true of Spanish *in-* [Gyurko: 233]. Brea also points out that coinings with IN- were particularly favoured in Christian Latin, from which direction more support for popular survival might have been expected.

Words in IN- seem generally to have been completely lost until learned restitution occurred, if it did. DIS- > *des-* sometimes migrates to roots formerly associated with IN- (*desigual* corresponding to INAEQUALIS, *desenfrenado* to IN(EF)FRENATUS, *desfavorable* to INFAVORABILIS); but in the majority of cases a gap seems to have been left— symptomatic of this is the rendering in Blánquez's Latin-Spanish dictionary of Latin IN- words by analytic negation types (e.g. INACCUSATUS—*no acusado*).

Latin DIS- survived in Spanish as *des-* and enjoyed enormous productivity, so that, as far as can be judged, the situation is the reverse of that with *in-*: this time it is Latin that has the 'lexical gaps' by comparison with Spanish, and so a creation like *desadeudar* can only be rendered back in Latin by paraphrase. But, as we have already noted, *des-* does not simply replace IN-: whilst *des-* is not uncommon with purely adjectival stems (e.g. *desapacible, deshonesto, desigual*), and is even found with noun stems (e.g. *desamor*), it is chiefly restricted to verb stems and verb stems formed on the basis of nouns: hence it is most often associated with adjectival past participles (e.g. *desconocido, desprevenido*). And although all the examples given so far do illustrate the simple negative value of *des-*, its most frequent value (as Latin DIS-) is privative with noun-based stems (e.g. *desbrozado* 'cleared of weeds (*brozas*)', *deshelado* 'thawed out, ridded of ice (*hielo*)'), or reversive with verbal stems (e.g. *desatado* 'untied', *descargado* 'unloaded'). Further adding to the functional load on *des-* is its occasional inheritance of the functions of Latin

EX- (e.g. *desarmar* corresponding to EXARMARE)[2] and possibly DE- (e.g. *desdeñar* coresponding to a postulated DEDIGNARE).[3]

The failure of *des-* to act widely as a simple negative meant that the reintroduction of *in-* adjectives took place without substantial synonymic clash. *In-*, when it does occur in Spanish, has, like Latin IN-, a simple negative value. Hence when the same stem combines with *in-* and *des-*, there is usually a difference in meaning, e.g. *incontaminado* 'uncontaminated' / *descontaminado* 'decontaminated'.[4] Such contrasts can often be obscured by English translation: *deshabitado* and *inhabitado* are both rendered by the García-Pelayo dictionary as 'uninhabited', though the former presupposes a former state of habitation which is not presupposed by the latter. Even so, it appears to be the case that *in-* + stem is more likely to exist where *des-* + stem does not, that is to say, where the semantic nature of the stem denies or makes unlikely a privative or reversive reading, e.g.:

inacentuado/*desacentuado*,
inaveriguado/*desaveriguado*.
incumplido/*descumplido*, etc.

---

[2] See Brea [1976: 324-5] for a more detailed discussion and Neira [317-8] for an interesting but rather feebly substantiated hypothesis concerning the uniting of DIS- and EX- in Castilian *des-*.

[3] DE- as a negative survives only marginally in such examples as *demérito*.

[4] But note *desaprovechado*/*inaprovechado*. Gyurko's list [227 ff.] reveals that generally there is a difference perceived between *des-* and *in-* pairs, or that one is preferred to the other. Those that remain undifferentiated from his list are: *des-/inadvertido*, *des-/inaprovechado*, *des-/incómodo*, *des-/inobediente*. (We found it possible to go further with an informant who accepted only *des-/inaprovechado* from Gyurko's list as being exactly equivalent in meaning, register and frequency.)

With past participle stems, *in-* formations often do not have a corresponding *in-* + verb formation (e.g. *indo mado* 'untamed', but **indomar, inexplotado* 'unexploited', but **inexplotar*), whereas *des-* formations always do. A further property militating against synonymic clash is that *in-* has a much greater productivity with *-ble* suffixed stems than with past participle stems; the productivity of *des-* with *-ble* suffixed stems, whilst not negligible (compare *desagradable, desapacible,* etc.), is restricted.

But even with the reintroduction of *in-* by learned route, the majority of adjectives and adjectival past participles in Spanish do not have synthetic negative forms,[5] and it must be borne in mind that where simple antonymic pairs exist (e.g. *bueno/malo, lento/rápido, caro/barato*), speakers have no need to have recourse to other kinds of negation, synthetic or analytic (indeed, such analytic formations as **no bueno, *poco bueno* are judged unacceptable).

2 Analytic negation in Spanish and its history

The analytic negation formulae available in modern Spanish are:

No + adjective
Poco + adjective
Nada + adjective
Sin + infinitive

[5] In a survey of Spanish equivalences for English adjectives and adjectival past participles in *un-* based on the García-Pelayo dictionary, we found that for the adjectives 3% of the equivalents given were combined with *des-* and 17% with *in-*, and that for adjectival past participles 28% combined with *des-* while 8% were combined with *in-*. Even those which are so recorded in dictionaries are often avoided in neutral register: our informant rejected *estoy inacostumbrado* in favour of *estoy poco acostumbrado* or *no estoy acostumbrado*.

2.1 *No* + adjective

No + adjective or adjectival past participle, a continuation of Latin NON + adjective, is the most transparent in structure, and the most productive in terms of the range of adjectives and past participles with which it may potentially combine (although it is avoided with simple antonyms [Gyurko: 236]). It may even combine with adjectives which display prefixal negation to yield litotes such as *no imposible*.

But *no* + adjective, in some ways the most obvious and satisfactory candidate for a new analytic formula, is limited in usage. First, it belongs to formal register and has much the same value as English *non-*: typical examples are *personal no docente* 'non-teaching staff', *objeto volante no identificado* 'unidentified flying object'. In neutral register, *Traiga una ensalada sin aderezar* would be preferred to *Traiga una ensalada no aderezada* 'Bring a salad without dressing'. *No* + adjective is found extensively in dictionary definitions where there is no synthetic negative adjective expression available. A second, syntactic, restriction is that it is available only attributively, since in predicative use[6] the *no* is always moved to preverbal position and straightforward sentence negation (i.e. syntactic adjective negation) results:

1   **Este objeto volante está no identificado*

      must be expressed as

      este objeto volante no está identificado

---

[6] There appear to be other syntactic restrictions on *no* + adjective as well: note the oddity of *??Dejó la carta no contestada*, where *sin contestar* or, more marginally, *?incontestada*, are strongly preferred.

2.2 *Poco* and *nada* + adjective

The second analytic adjective negation formula, *poco* + adjective, is more problematic.

2.2.1 *Poco* as a negative

First, is *poco* properly a negative at all? Informally, it has usually been considered as such. Foreign translation equivalents are revealing: antonyms for which there are lexical gaps in Spanish are regularly rendered by *poco* + existing adjective structures, e.g. deep/shallow—*profundo/poco profundo*; thick/thin—*denso/poco denso*. And, though we are admittedly on shakier ground here, such native speakers as comment linguistically on the structure see it as negative [e.g. Moliner: 787]. More importantly, the implicational properties of *poco* + adjective certainly suggest its negative nature. *Poco* is in origin a degree adverb, the antonym of *muy*, and it has identical implicational properties to those of *no muy*, as seen in example 2a. We may simultaneously consider the third analytic adjective negation formula, *nada* + adjective, which similarly appears to be equivalent to *muy poco* + adjective, with similar implicational properties, as seen in example 2b. (But note that *nada* in postverbal position requires, as in other circumstances in Spanish, the insertion of *no* preverbally.)

2
  a Both *Es poco difícil saber* and *no es muy difícil saber* imply *no es difícil saber*
  b Both *No es nada difícil saber* and *es muy poco difícil saber* imply *no es difícil saber*

Poco + adjective is to be sharply differentiated from *un poco* + adjective, as well as from *poco* + noun and *poco* +

verb. The implicational properties of *un poco* + adjective are shown in 3:

3   *Es un poco difícil saber* implies *es difícil saber*

Similarly, with a noun, *poco* has a positive meaning as a quantifier:

4   *Pocas personas lo saben* implies *algunas personas lo saben*
        Me queda poca madera implies *me queda alguna madera*

and while negation of *poco* + noun is acceptable [5a], the litotic negation of *poco* + adjective, whilst logically interpretable, is resisted as being too tortuous for normal use:

5

   a   *No es poco trabajo escribir una tesis*
   b   *??No es poco difícil saber*

The value of *poco* with past participles depends on the source of the past participle. If the source is a passive (*ser-* or *estar*-passive), then *poco* has the value it would have with the corresponding verb:

6

   a   *Una canción poco cantada* is *una canción [que es] poco (= pocas veces) cantada*
   b   *Un hombre poco convencido* is *un hombre [que está] poco (= no muy) convencido*

2.2.2 *Poco* as a degree adverbial

The restrictions on *poco* + adjective are problematic to describe and we will do no more than summarise them here.

Poco retains sufficiently the characteristics of a degree adverbial to combine only with gradable adjectives; non-gradables cannot be negated by *poco*: **poco muerto*, **poco cerrado*. Adjectives which are not normally gradable— for example, provenance adjectives [Quirk et al: 265-6]— accept negation with *poco* if they accept qualification by *muy*, e.g. *poco inglés*, *muy inglés*. But *poco* does not enter into a contrastive relation with *muy*:

7

a *No era muy difícil, sino *poco/un poco/medianamente difícil*
b *No era *poco⁷/un poco/medianamente difícil, sino muy difícil*

Although *poco* + adjective has been shown to share the implicational properties of *no muy* + adjective, it is in fact very much more limited in availability, as the judgments in 8 show:

8

a *Esta habitación está poco limpia / no está muy limpia*
b *La superficie es poco lisa / no es muy lisa*
c *El río ?es poco ancho / no es muy ancho*
d *La montaña ?es poco alta / no es muy alta*
e *Este metal *es poco duro / no es muy duro*
f *La suma *es poco pequeña / no es muy pequeña*

Charting the domain of *poco* as opposed to *no(...)muy* is difficult since informant reactions tend not to be clearcut. But the following general restrictions emerge:

i As observed by Gyurko [238], *poco* tends to be used with 'positive' adjectives and avoided with 'negative' ones: thus *poco seguro* but not *?poco peligroso*; *poco*

---

⁷ The ungrammaticality of *poco* in this example would in any case follow from the 'double negative' constraint exemplified in 8.

limpio but not *?poco sucio*. However, the definition of 'positive' appears to rely on the relation between noun and qualifying adjective: the neutral (9a) is rejected whereas (9b), in which cruelty is seen as somehow 'positive', is accepted:

9

  a *?El nuevo amo era poco cruel*
  b *Es poco cruel para ser un tirano*

ii *Poco* is avoided with simple antonymic pairs, as is *no*, whether 'positive' or 'negative'. But again, contexts indicating 'desirability' or 'necessity' may make *poco* possible:

10

  a *Es poco alto para su edad*
  b *?La montaña es poco alta*
  c *La cuerda es poco larga: no alcanza*
  d *?La calle es poco larga*

iii *Poco* is impossible with adjectives indicating extremes [11a] (such adjectives are resistant to gradation and hence to qualification by *muy*). However, once again, contexts can be found to force readings, such as 11b:

11

  a **Mercurio es poco enorme*
  b *El monstruo era poco gigantesco*

2.2.3 The historical development of *poco* and *nada* + adjective

We turn now to the historical development of the *poco* + adjective construction.

The functional antecedent in Classical Latin is PARUM + adjective: the OLD's description of PARUM as 'sometimes almost equiv[alent] to a simple neg[ation]' closely parallels Moliner's [787] description of Spanish *poco*, and to judge by the OLD's list of examples, it would seem that PARUM was similarly restricted to 'positive' adjectives (BLANDUS, LAUTUS, SANUS, VEHEMENS, etc.). It is a nice question as to whether a distinction was made in Latin corresponding to the striking difference we have observed in Spanish between *poco* and *un poco*. On the evidence of Blánquez (entries for PARUM, PAULO and PAULUM), it would seem that with verbs PARUM was generally the equivalent of *poco* and PAULO and PAULUM the equivalents of *un poco*. However, Blánquez has the apparently inconsistent equivalences EPISTOLAE ME PAULUM RECREANT— *las cartas me consuelan poco* (Cicero) versus PAULUM REQUIESCERE—*descansar un poco* (Cicero). As far as adjectives are concerned, PAULO and PAULUM are used, in the Classical language at any rate, only with the comparative forms of adjectives and adverbs, e.g. LIBERIUS PAULO, PAULUM TARDIUS, and therefore always have the value of *un poco*; this restriction eased in later Latin, however, and it may be supposed that PAULO, like MULTO, NIHILO and ALIQUO, came to be used with adjectives in the positive degree [Bassols: 422]. Was there an opposition, then, between PARUM and PAULUM corresponding to *poco/un poco* in this later period?

Looking ahead to a still later stage: since Spanish *poco* and its congeners have a similar use in many Romance languages, it is reasonable to postulate a VL PAUCU which had the value of CL PARUM. PAUCUS in CL was used adjectivally and usually in the plural; no adverbial usage is recorded. We have so far failed to find any VL attestation of PAUCU used adverbially. But instances of PARVI for

PAUCI are found: Bonnet [276] refers to examples in Gregory and the *Peregrinatio*, and Hofmann/Szantyr [206] trace examples as far back as Propertius. PAUCUS is also encountered in the singular [Bonnet: 201; Blaise: 601]. Bearing in mind that PARVUS, to which PARUM is related, was to be universally replaced in the sense of 'little' by new creations presumably of popular origin yielding Spanish *pequeño*, etc., we can see that there must have been considerable movement in the area of PARVUM/ PAUCI, with PARUM and PARVUS eventually falling out of use. The movement may be represented diagrammatically thus:

12

	Adjective	Adverb	Quantifier sg	Quantifier pl
CL	PARVUS	PARUM	PARUM + gen	PAUCI
Sp	*pequeño*	*poco*	*poco*	*pocos*

Bonnet's explanation [276] of the use of PARVI for PAUCI in Gregory may be turned to our purposes here in explaining the expansion of PAUCU:

> *Petit* et *peu* sont des idées qui se touchent; *un peu* se dit *un petit* en plusieurs langues, et en latin même, *paulum*.

Apart from the semantic proximity of the notions of 'little' and 'few',[8] one might also suggest that the anomaly of the existence of PAUCI only in the plural was likely to be resolved by its extension to the singular, especially as a singular quantifier, and that its challenge to PARUM in that function favoured a challenge to PARUM more generally as an adverb. The perplexing

---

[8] Corominas [585] notes *poco* in the sense of *pequeño* in old texts, and notes the similar value of Old Catalan *poc* and Old Occitan *pauc*. See also Löfstedt [338-9].

thing is that such textual evidence as we do have shows the reverse tendency, i.e., the increase of PARVI at the expense of PAUCI; one is tempted to wonder whether this is not a hypercorrection symptomatic of the decline of PARVUS.

The evolution of *nada* + adjective is to be seen in the context of the development of a range of modifiers which, like *poco*, have a pronominal as well as an adverbial function. Spanish has developed *poco, mucho, nada* and *algo* in this way, though *mucho* as an adjective modifier gave way to the reduced form *muy*. *Algo* and *nada* appear to be peculiarly Spanish survivals,[9] though *ALIQUO and *NIHILO as VL adverbs of degree would not be extravagant reconstructions.[10]

2.3 *Sin* + infinitive

The last of the Spanish analytic negation types to be considered, *sin* + infinitive, has a quite different surface appearance from *no, poco* and *nada* + adjective, and is an original Romance creation, as well as apparently being peculiarly Spanish. Perhaps because of this, it has never, to our knowledge, been descriptively related to other adjective negation types.

2.3.1 *Sin* + infinitive as an instance of analytic adjective negation

The adjectival nature of *sin* + infinitive is suggested by a number of factors. First, it is the semantic equivalent of *no* + past participle and *in-* + past participle: the DRAE

---

[9] See Meyer-Lübke [246-7] for discussion of *algo*.
[10] The OLD records NIHIL with adjectives and adverbs in the sense of 'in no respect. not at all', and adverbial uses for ALIQUID, ALIQUO, NIHIL and NIHILUM.

glosses *indomado,* for example, as 'que está sin domesticar'. Secondly, it is used precisely as an equivalent for a past participle which combines with *estar.* The conjoined constructions of 13a suggest that *sin* + infinitive is perceived as being syntactically parallel to a past participle:

13

a *El 80% de la producción hispánica medieval está todavía sin editar o mal editada* (El País, 6.10.87)

b *El edificio... lleva año y medio terminado pero sin ocupar* (El País, 11.11.87)

Thirdly, *sin* + infinitive may take an agent as if it were a past participle:

14

Sus mujeres, oferentes y sin debilitar por la civilización europea (El País, 15.11.87)

Fourthly, it can be used attributively like other adjectival past participles and adjectives: *vigas sin pintar, casitas sin habitar;* and predicatively with verbs which typically have adjectival complements: *permanecer, quedar(se), estar, dejar.* Lastly, the data in 15, based on Bosque [43], shows 'adjectival' rather than 'verbal' placing of the adverb with *sin* + infinitive:

15

a *El todavía sin acabar monumento al Sr. Alcalde*
   (Compare *El todavía inacabado/incompleto monumento al Sr. Alcalde* and *Todavía no han acabado el monumento al Sr. Alcalde*)

b **El sin acabar todavía monumento al Sr. Alcalde*
   (Compare **El inacabado/incompleto todavía monumento al Sr. Alcalde* but *No han acabado todavía el monumento al Sr. Alcalde*)

The adjectival nature of *sin* + infinitive therefore seems clear.

In each of the examples so far considered, the infinitive has a passive value, as in 16a. This must be distinguished from the *sin* + active value infinitive construction, exemplified in 16b, which does indeed have parallels in the other Romance languages:

16

  a *una pared sin pintar = una pared que no está/ha sido pintada*
  b *[Yo] lo hice sin querer = [Yo] lo hice sin que [yo] quisiese*

2.3.2 The history of *sin* + infinitive

Documentary evidence for the history of the *sin* + infinitive construction has so far proved elusive. This could be because there is a resistance to the construction in the written language: Beinhauer [274] regards all such uses of passive value infinitives as more typical of the spoken than of the written language (though that is not a view that appears to be confirmed by present-day native speakers). Boyd-Bowman [865] furnishes two early Latin-American examples: *pieças labradas de piedra con su corredor sin cubrir* and *están sin gratificación y la tierra sin conquistar*; otherwise, the earliest example we have been able to find is in the 1771 RAE Grammar, where *la obra está sin acabar* is cited as an example of the use of *sin*: but the distinctively passive value of the infinitive is either not realised or not pointed out.

To understand the development of *sin* + infinitive, we suggest that two features of Spanish are of particular relevance. The first is that familiar peculiarity of Hispano-Romance, the *ser/estar* distinction. *Sin* + infinitive can be the complement of only a restricted range of verbs, and significantly of *estar* but not *ser*. It will be remembered that *estar* associates with the following complement types (in schematic historical order): *a* locatives, *b* prepositional phrases, *c* past participles, *d* adjectives [Pountain: 155-8]. *Sin* + infinitive falls naturally into this sequence at stage *b* since it is a preposition + verbal noun; as such *sin* with an active value infinitive would have been able to take its place amongst the complements of *estar* from early times. As the range of complements of *estar* extended to past participles with their characteristic passive value, so perhaps *sin* + infinitive was drawn into a passive value usage, as it steadily moved towards a purely adjectival function, demonstrated today by its attributive as well as predicative use. The second, less distinctive, feature of Spanish to which we would call attention is the development of a range of preposition + passive value infinitive structures. Most closely related semantically to *sin* + infinitive is *por* + infinitive (Gili Gaya [233] goes so far as to say that *por* and *sin* are equivalent in these constructions). *Por* + infinitive often appears to fulfil the role of a 'future participle', despite its formal distinctness from the past participle; syntactically, too, it is often contrastively conjoined with the past participle (we noted that this was also a property of *sin* + infinitive):

17　　*los libros vendidos y por vender*

Other preposition + passive value infinitive constructions are exemplified in 18:

18
　　a　*Hay varios problemas a resolver*
　　b　*Muchas cosas que hacer*
　　c　*Es difícil de hacer*
　　d　*Es bueno de comer*
　　e　*Son bastante de admirar*
　　f　*Una manzana a medio consumir*

A in 18a is a popular, but puristically castigated, equivalent to *por. Que* in 18b, though not superficially a preposition, appears to fulfil the same functional role in this construction, although the full sentence constructions involving *que* + infinitive do not unambiguously suggest the passive value of the infinitive in the way that 18a and c-e do, e.g. *Tengo muchas cosas que hacer*, where the subject of *tengo* is also that of *hacer. De* participates in a number of passive value infinitive constructions [18c-e] derived from various underlying sources. In short, *sin* + passive value infinitive is accommodated comfortably in the surface patterns of Spanish.

3 Conclusions

We have suggested in this paper, first, that the fall of Latin IN- (and DE-) as synthetic adjective negators and the tendency for *des-* to be restricted to adjectival past participles, coupled with the heavy functional load on the latter as privative and reversive as well as simple negative, favoured the expression of adjective negation in Romance by analytic rather than synthetic means.

Secondly, turning to patterns of adjective negation in Spanish, we have seen how the development of an alternative, analytic means of negating past participles by *sin* + infinitive might have come to be favoured. Of the synthetic means available, *des-* is most frequently privative or reversive, rather than simply negative, with past participles, and even after restoration, *in-* was principally available with *-able* and *-ible* stems rather than with past participles. Of the analytic means available, apart from the high register *no*, we have seen how the value of *poco* with a past participle is dependent on the corresponding verb and so does not always act as a simple negative. The development of *sin* + infinitive in the particular environment of an *estar* complement may therefore have felicitously fulfilled an area of need. [11]

Christopher J. Pountain
Queens' College, Cambridge

---

[11] I would like to acknowledge the kind hospitality of the Department of Classical and Romance Philology of the University of Oviedo where the main part of this article was prepared.

REFERENCES

Bassols de Climent, M., 1945
   Sintaxis histórica de la lengua latina, Barcelona
Beinhauer, W., 1968
   El español coloquial, 2nd ed., Madrid
Blaise, A., 1954
   Dictionnaire latin-français des auteurs chrétiens, Turnhout
Blánquez Fraile, A., 1985
   Diccionario latino-español español-latino, Barcelona
Bonnet, M., 1890
   Le latin de Grégoire de Tours, Paris
Bosque, I., 1980
   Sobre la negación, Madrid
Boyd-Bowman, P., 1971
   Léxico hispanoamericano del siglo XVI, London
Brea, M., 1976
   'Prefijos formadores de antónimos negativos en español medieval',
   Verba, 3, 319-41
————., 1980
   Antónimos latinos y españoles: estudio del prefijo in-, Santiago de
   Compostela
Corominas, J., & J. A. Pascual, 1980-91
   Diccionario crítico etimológico castellano e hispánico, 6 vols, Madrid
DRAE = Real Academia Española, 1984
   Diccionario de la Lengua Española, 20th ed., Madrid
García-Pelayo, R., et al., 1976
   Diccionario moderno español-inglés English-Spanish, Paris
Gili Gaya, S., 1955
   Curso superior de sintaxis española, 5th ed., Barcelona
Gyurko, L.A., 1971
   'Affixal negation in Spanish', *Romance Philology*, 25, 225-40
Hofmann, J.B., rev. Szantyr, A., 1972
   Lateinische Syntax und Stylistik, Munich

Kasten, L. & J. J. Nitti, 1978
  Concordances and Texts of the Royal Scriptorium Manuscripts of Alfonso X, el Sabio, Madison
Llorens, E.L., 1929
  La negación en español antiguo con referencia a otros idiomas, Revista de Filología Española, Anejo 11., Madrid
Löfstedt, E., 1911
  Philologischer Kommentar zur Peregrinatio Aetheriae: *Untersuchungen zur Geschichte der Lateinischen Sprache*, Uppsala
Menéndez Pidal, R., 1950
  Orígenes de la lengua española, 3rd ed., Madrid
Meyer-Lübke, W., 1974
  Grammaire des langues romanes, Geneva-Marseilles
Moliner, M., 1975
  Diccionario de uso del español, Madrid
Neira, J., 1976
  'El prefijo /des/ en la lengua gallego-portuguesa', *Verba*, 3, 309-18
OLD = Glare, P.G.W., ed., 1977
  Oxford Latin Dictionary, Oxford
Pountain, C.J., 1983
  '*ESSERE/STARE as a Romance phenomenon', in *Studies in the Romance Verb*, ed. N. Vincent and M. Harris, 139-60., London
Quirk, R., et al., 1972
  A Grammar of Contemporary English, London
Sarmiento, R. (ed.), 1984
  Gramática de la lengua castellana, 1771, edición facsímil y apéndice documental, Madrid

Specificity and gender-switching in a contemporary peninsular Spanish diminutive suffix: some diachronic semantic inferences

1 Abstract

In this study I shall be analysing the twin-suffix *-ín/-ina* in contemporary coinings, since it is my belief that a study of the underlying issues involved may well shed new light on the use and growth of the typical Castilian diminutive suffix *-illo/-illa*, together with parallel developments in *-ito/-ita*.

2 Antecedents

Before embarking on an exposition of the tentative hypothesis which is the subject of this study, I shall offer a brief résumé of the current state of play in the status of diminutives (and augmentatives where relevant) in Spanish.

As their names suggest, diminutive and augmentative suffixes indicate first and foremost **size**; or, rather, accepted wisdom has always stated that size is the main function: according to the suffix chosen, the derived form refers therefore to something either bigger or smaller than that usually experienced, described or referred to in the simplex. Whether this function is and always was uppermost will become clearer, I hope, by the end of this paper.

Secondly, these suffixes can indicate **attitude** to the simplex, with traditional studies suggesting amelioration and pejoration as the principal focus, plus attributes such as courtesy, *captatio benevolentiae*, etc.: a (usually) positive attitude to the object or concept in the case of diminutive suffixes and a usually negative one in the case of augmentative suffixes. (The latter may also indicate a **blow** with the simplex but this usage will not be discussed here.) However, as I hope to show, this traditional basically bipartite taxonomy may not always be sufficient.

One consequence of the size/attitude duality is that there may often exist a situation of potential ambiguity when diminutive suffixes are used: *casita* may indicate size (i.e. 'little house') attitude (i.e. 'sweet/charming/cute house') or even an amalgam of the two ('sweet little house'). I shall return to this point later.

Historically, we know that the *-ín/-ina* suffix is of northern origins; that it is still the preferred diminutive suffix in the Asturian region; and that with respect to Hispanic dialectology it is a cognate of Galician *-iño/-iña* and Portuguese *-inho/-inha*. However, I believe that, although the number of simplexes which have developed diminutives ending in *-ín/-ina* in contemporary peninsular Castilian is small, the relative importance of the process far exceeds this numerical paucity; indeed, the process involved may be relevant to the overall patterning of diminutives in diachronic Hispanic dialectology.

Accepted wisdom also tells us that the phonic context of the simplex may well determine which diminutive suffix(es) may not be used in order to avoid cacaphonic combinations (e.g. *callecita*, to avoid **callilla*). Although all diminutive suffixes begin with *-i*, epenthesis may occur in some cases to foster the union between simplex and suffix: *ratoncillo/ratoncito* appears to sound better to Hispanic ears than **ratonillo/ratonito*.[1]

---

[1] I note, but have no rational explanation for, the difference between the forms *fajín* (from *faja*) and *cajetín* (from *caja*), two of the diminutives studied here; one would expect some sort of parallelism (i.e. **fajetín*, or **cajín*). One explanation for the intrusive *-et-* might be

However, there appears to be an important added semantic element at work in the formation of diminutives, in both synchronic and diachronic planes, and the purpose of this paper is to attempt to describe and analyse part of these processes.[2]

3 The data

The following forms merely exemplify the process I am about to analyse, and therefore do not claim to be in any way representative of the 400-odd words ending in *-ín*, and the nearly 1,000 words ending in *-ina*. They are:

maletín briefcase, document-case, special bag containing medical instruments, samples, etc

cajetín special sliding container found mainly as a security device in taxis, in order for cash to be passed between customer and driver

---

the analogy of the *-etería* suffix. In many cases the *-et-* of that suffix is itself analogous on those shops (and the trades on which they are based) the name for which does have an etymological *-et-* (e.g. *bonetero*, then *-onetería*), and then spreads to those in which there is no *-et*, (e.g. *peletero*, thus *peletería*). The *-et-* is also etymological in some words in which the suffix means "group of" (e.g. *cohetería*), and then spreads analogically to other groups (e.g. *pobretería*). Indeed, if vowel harmony is also taken into account (i.e., the extremely common /e+e+ía/ pattern), even the typically Madrilenian 'mistake' of writing and saying *carnecería* can be better explained, rather than being considered as an isolated form, and the result of the always unsatisfactory sporadic change theory. If these considerations might go some way towards explaining the *-et-* of *cajetín* (already found in *cajetilla*), we are still left with the "irregularity" of *fajín*, instead of the expected *fajetín*.

2 I am extremely grateful to my friends, Dr David Pattison, Fellow of Magdalen College, Oxford, and John Wright, Representative, British Council, Bahrein, for their perceptive comments on an earlier draft of this paper, which is dedicated to Suzie Ofner. I should also like to thank José Antonio Guzmán Palacios for valuable bibliographical and documentary assistance.

fajín military sash
botellín bottle of beer containing 25 centilitres
balín pellet
plumín nib
bombín bowler hat
calabacín marrow, courgette
balancín various technical instruments, seesaw
sillín saddle
camarín theatrical dressing-room
listín personal list of telephones and addresses
banderín linesman's flag
taladrina certain kinds of electrical drilling equipment
papelina cigarette paper used for rolling joints, or containing an
   acid-tab, line of cocaine, etc.
chocolatina[3]

A couple of brief general notes on these words may be apposite at this point. Firstly some of these words are doublets of pre-existing diminutives: *cajetilla* 'packet' (esp. of cigarettes), *fajilla* 'address label to send newspapers magazines, etc.', *plumilla* also 'nib', *bombilla*

---

[3] Certain words ending in -*ín*- and -*ina*- patently do not belong to this category. I shall not be dealing here with the following:

a   words like *hollín*, *postín*, and many others in which the ending is etymological [DCELC];

b   forms which are non-postnominal (e.g. *bailarín*, *andarín*, *parlanchín*, etc. which are postverbal);

c   forms which have been in Spanish for centuries (e.g.. *espadín*, *comodín* etc., mainly coined from cognate French and Italian forms);

d   humorous coinings such as *sudorina*, *sobaquina*, *borrachín*, *cagachín*, *escabechina*, etc.);

e   the [sometimes pseudo-] medical coinings which ape the terminology of drugs such as *morfina*, *gammaglobulina*, etc., and which are often pharmaceutical products and brand-names such as *Vaselina*, *Mecromina*, *Bristaciclina* etc., the vast majority of which are borrow-ings from French, German, or English. (One suspects, however, that the product-name *Cunticina,* made by Laboratorios Farmacuticos Rovi, is a Spanish invention).

'electric lightbulb', and *banderilla* as a technical bull-fighting term.

Secondly, some of these forms are based on simplexes which have given rise to a plethora of derivatives, for example, *pluma* gives, apart from *plumín* and *plumilla*, the adjectives *plumado*, and *plumoso*, plus the nouns *plumada*, *plumaje*, *plumazo*, *plumero*, *plumífero*, and *plumón*, *inter alia*. *Caja* is similarly fertile.

4 Synchronic analysis

The (seemingly) diminutive forms ending in *-ín/-ina* have two vital characteristics in common: firstly, their gender is different from that of the simplex from which they derive; and secondly, far from being true diminutives (size and/or attitude), they actually lexicalise a special kind, type or category of the simplex. I shall deal with this latter point first.

A closer look at all these forms reveals that we are, in fact, dealing with a special variety and not merely a smaller and/or nicer variety of the simplex; I refer to this feature as 'specificity'. Each object is indeed smaller than that lexicalised by the simplex but also constitutes a specific kind, and has a different, specialised use from the object described in the simplex.

To take a few examples, *maletín* refers to a briefcase or document-case, and in no way could be described as a small suitcase; likewise, *sillín* is a saddle, especially on a bicycle, and not a small chair; *botellín* is not just a small bottle, but specifically a bottle of beer containing 250 centilitres. And so on throughout the list. It seems quite clear, therefore, that these forms ending in *-ín/-ina* do not refer merely to smaller versions of the object expressed in the simplex.

What is perhaps more interesting is the change of gender referred to above. In every case, the original gender of the simplex has been changed. The two relevant questions here are: Is this change deliberate? What function does it serve?

As far as the first question is concerned, the change could hardly be accidental: examples such as *taladrina*, *papelina* and *chocolatina* show beyond doubt that we are *not* dealing with a standard, non gender-differentiating suffix such as -*ón*;[4] here, the feminine suffix -*ina* has been added to a **masculine** simplex. However, it should be noted that the vast majority of cases shows the opposite tendency: that of changing feminine nouns into masculine ones.

So we may safely conclude that we are dealing with something more than a mere morphological process which continues the simplex's original gender; couched in slightly different terms, since normal diminutive suffixation respects the original gender of the simplex, the process under study here cannot be considered a case of straightforward diminutivisation.

To take the second question, we must now ask what function this gender change might serve, now that it is clear that the change is deliberate. I can offer no ready solution as to how these diminutive formings ending in -*ín*/*ina*[5] came to be used throughout Spain to denote

---

[4] The comparison with the augmentative suffix -*ón* is revealing: postnominal -*ón* is invariable (i.e. there is no feminine noun ending in -*ona* to correspond to the feminine simplex). Here too we see the classical concepts of size and/or attitude—negative in this case (e.g. masculine *nubarrón* and *vozarrón* from feminine *nube* and *voz*). There do exist a fair number of nouns ending in -*ona*, but they are either postverbal, and/or the feminine counterpart of masculine nouns and adjectives ending in -*ón* (e.g. *chillona*, *meona*, *culona*, etc.) and have overwhelmingly negative connotations.

[5] How has this regionalism spread throughout Spain? Mention might be made of forms such as *poquitín*, *momentín*, *secundín*, etc., which are quite widespread throughout peninsular Spain, and normally used

specificity. Perhaps we may speak with some justification of a feeling by non-Asturian native Spanish speakers that the suffix -*ín* is a pre-existing, diminutive suffix, which was 'available' as it were to be put to a new use, especially if, to pre-empt my hypothesis, Spanish always has had a diminutive suffix to connote specificity.

Be that as it may, it should be stressed that the use of the -*ín*/-*ina* suffix *alone* would appear to have been insufficient to denote specificity. Could it be that the change of gender is being used in conjunction with the suffix to indicate a **new** lexeme in which the suffix connotes smaller type, and the change of gender connotes specificity?

5 Diachronic analysis

The stage is now set to attempt to tackle the all-important question. Might the data and phenomena studied in this paper cast any light on past linguistic processes? Or rather, couched in slightly different terms, is it possible to postulate an on-going trend in Spanish suffixation whereby derived diminutive forms become autonomous lexemes? And in the final instance, would such a trend not be in keeping with widely-accepted ideas on the continuing reinforcement of synthetic modes of expression in Spanish?

Those of us who took our first faltering steps in Old Spanish with *Gifford and Hodcroft*, and/or those privileged to have been taught by Fred Hodcroft himself, will recall that one of the Seven Distinguishing Traits of Castilian was the development of the diminutive suffix -*illo*, as a result of the reduction of the standard

---

in an apologetic, *captatio benevolentiae* sort of way (cf. *ahorita* in Mexico). In other words, they are not mere diminutives referring to size, but they are not specific either.

peninsular *-iello*. Other dialects developed other typical suffixes.[6]

As alluded to briefly in 2 above, what appears to have received little comment is the semantic development of many of the earliest 'diminutives' in Castilian. Although what follows must be somewhat speculative, it would seem from the very outset that specificity, which I am now proposing as a third main category of so-called 'diminutive' usages, was possible, and always present *in potentia*.

Just a tiny sample of typical *-illo/a* words in modern Spanish shows us that even in the case of standard diminutivisation (i.e., size and/or attitude), lexicalisation must have taken place very soon after these diminutives had been coined, thus rendering it impossible for the size/attitude use of this suffix to be available without serious danger of ambiguity.

A major problem is that one simply cannot tell in many cases whether lexicalisation took place at the very moment of the first use of the suffix. But it is surely reasonable to postulate, given the current meaning of hundreds of words ending in *-illo/a*, that they were actually coined to mean 'special kind of', rather than '(nice) little', or very soon acquired specific, autonomous, simplex status. In other words, there would appear to be a process of:

[6] Reference has already been made to *-ín/-ina* in Asturias, and *-iño/ -iña* in Galicia. Mention should also be made of *-ico/-ica* in certain areas of Spain (notably Navarra and Murcia) and *passim* in Spanish-speaking Latin America together with the pan-Hispanic *-ito/-ita*. So widespread is the *-(t)ico* diminutive in Costa Rica, for example, that the nick-name for nationals of this country is *ticos*. It is in Latin America where the most exotic combinations of *-ito* and *-ico* are to be found the now defunct Swedish pop-group Abba popularised—in English and Spanish—the song entitled *Chiquitita*.

1 simple diminutive derivation with the meaning of small;
2 optional, subsidiary attitudinal semantic developments;
3 creation of autonomous simplex (specificity).

Examples of this phenomenon abound. It is obvious that *pitillo* can no longer be used to refer either to a small whistle,[7] a nice whistle or a nice little whistle, since by default it would always mean 'ciggie, fag' (GB). The same ambiguity would pertain for forms such as *alfombrilla, casilla, bolsillo, cigarrillo, ventanilla, calzoncillos*, and literally hundreds of others. In each case, the simplex meaning would automatically be assumed. These four co-existing functions of the *-illo/a* suffix (size, attitude, size plus attitude, specificity) must at some stage have put too great a semantic strain on it. Although considerable research would need to be done into dates of first documentation,[8] a working hypothesis might well be that at some stage the *-illo* suffix stopped being able to be used **generatively** to produce *ad hoc* diminutive forms meaning size, attitude, or both, since its primary function was felt to be that of producing brand-new lexemes connoting specificity.

If this is the case, then the problem immediately arises: what suffixes became and are still currently available to fulfill the size/attitude function in Castilian, given the demise, or at least unbearable ambiguity of, *-illo/a*, save

---

[7] Or even as the euphemism for 'penis' in children's languages (from *pito*), which in turn means that *colita*, which carries out this function, is similarly no longer available to mean 'little tail'. In fact, it would be difficult to express 'little tail', 'cute tail', or 'cute little tail' in Spanish using diminutive suffixation, since *colilla* has already been lexicalised to mean 'cigarette-end'. This example shows the kind of semantic pressure that diminutives can and do exert on simplexes.
[8] DCELC is, typically, unhelpful in this area, and dates practically no diminutive suffixal forms, and is not interested in semantic aspects of etymology anyway.

perhaps for some remote rural Castilian areas, which still retain the traditional -*illo* to refer to size and attitude? The answer would seem to be -*ito*, the only universally-used 'pure' diminutive which has taken over the size/attitude function in contemporary Spanish, without acquiring the idea of specificity.

A further corollary is that a new gap appears: given that -*illo/a* itself has become unproductive in all its roles, with the exception referred to above, and that -*ito* has taken over the functions of the generative diminutive size/attitude role, what resources are now available for the specific function?

Before answering this question, perhaps I should state here that I do actually accept the above question as legitimate; that is, I believe that, once a language has realised the potential of a given linguistic process, and exploited it fully (the case of diminutive suffixes in Spanish from the earliest times), it is loath to abandon it. Spanish always has had morphological means of indicating size, attitude, and, as this paper is attempting to show, specialised type. I therefore consider it logical and normal that the language should attempt to seek out new (as far as its standard contemporary possibilities go) formulae or varieties of a long-established process.

The new emergence of -*ín* in standard contemporary peninsular Spanish would tend to bear this hypothesis out: its role appears to be that of filling a morphologico-semantic gap created by the generative demise of -*illo* on the one hand, and the concomitant rise of -*ito* as a pure diminutive on the other.

6 Conclusion

Throughout its history Spanish has shown a remarkable penchant for derivations of all kinds, a trend which has never been stronger than the present day.[9] Specifically it has always favoured diminutive suffixation, which has traditionally been treated from a semantic viewpoint in terms of size and attitude. This paper has tried to show that specificity may also have played a vital role in the development of diminutive suffixes. There appears to be a case for postulating a recurring, morphological-semantic cycle whereby Spanish continues to exploit its derivational possibilities in such a way that semantic gaps are immediately filled by utilising pre-existing morphological patterns: the exploitation of *-ito/a* to fill the role as the new, standard diminutive suffix, and the rise of the hitherto markedly dialectal *-ín/-ina* suffix to continue the little-observed and now defunct role of *illo/a* to denote specificity.

Chris Pratt
Universidad Complutense, Madrid

[9] Urban slang has taken up exploiting the multiple derivational possibilities of the contemporary language. One of the favourites is the *-ata/-ete/-ote* type in the *lenguaje del rollo*, with neologisms such as *cubata*, *bocata*, *polvete*, *salidote*, etc., etc..

Translating without a dictionary: the Englishing by Edward Hellowes of Guevara's *Epístolas familiares*

FERNANDO DE ROJAS was the first Spanish writer translated into English, in 1530, when John Rastell published a free poetic adaptation of acts I-IV of *La Celestina*. Fray Antonio de Guevara (1480?-1545), the Bishop of Mondoñedo, was the second. Guevara's English translators occupy, then, an important place in the history of literary translation, and deserve more attention than they have received, as does Guevara himself. Among these pioneers, Edward Hellowes stands out as a meticulous and skilful practitioner in difficult circumstances.

Guevara was the most popular Spanish writer in England and all over Europe during the sixteenth century, and *The Golden Boke of Marcus Aurelius*, the first translation of Guevara into English, was the text of Spanish origin that went through most English editions in that period. The first was published in 1535, and there were at least twelve more by 1587, when the flow ceased, Guevara's popularity in England having come to an end. Yet Guevara's name does not appear in the *Golden Boke* or in the *Libro áureo de Marco Aurelio* itself, for this was pirated from an early draft of *El relox de príncipes* which he had been unwise enough to entrust to Charles V, and was published without his permission [Guevara 1534 , x^r-x^v]. On the last page of the English translation is the only information given about it:

Thus endeth the volume of Marke Aurelie emperour, otherwise called the golden boke, translated out of Frenche into englysshe by John Bourchier knyghte lorde Barners, deputie

generall of the kynges towne of Caleys and marches of the
same, at the instant desyre of his neuewe syr Francis Bryan
knyght, ended at Caleys the tenth day of Marche, in the
yere of the reygne of our Soueraygne lorde kynge Henrye the
.VIII. the .XXIII.

So not only were the first English readers of this book left
unaware of the author's identity, they were even led to
believe that he was French. It is difficult to explain the
extraordinary success of this translation, for it is clumsy
and inaccurate, and in some places meaningless.

Sir Francis Bryan was the author of the next Guevara
translation, *A Dispraise of the Life of a Courtier, and a
Commendacion of the Life of the Labouryng Man* (1548),
a version of *Menosprecio de corte y alabanza de aldea*.
But Bryan's translation, despite being somewhat better
than his uncle's effort, did not enjoy any great success,
and was only published once more during the sixteenth
century: in 1575, under another, shorter and more positive title, *A Looking Glass for the Court*.

El relox de príncipes, a much-expanded version of the
Libro áureo de Marco Aurelio, was the next book by
Guevara to be translated into English. *The Diall of
Princes* appeared in 1557, nearly thirty years after the
Spanish original, and the new translator was Thomas
North. Another edition of *The Diall of Princes* came out
in 1568, enlarged by the addition of North's translation of
Aviso de privados y doctrina de cortesanos. This new
volume was republished in 1582 and in 1619, the latter
being a version corrected by the playwright and translator
of *Amadis of Gaul*, Anthony Munday. All Munday did,
despite some grand claims on the title-page, was to
modernize the orthography and tamper with the style,
without checking against the Spanish original. He corrected none of North's mistranslations. In spite of these,
North is a better translator than his two predecessors.

The Familiar Epistles, the translation by Edward Hellowes of most of the letters from the first volume of *Epístolas familiares*, was published in 1574 and reissued three times in the next decade. In 1575 a companion volume appeared: *Golden Epistles*, a further selection from *Epístolas familiares*, translated by Sir Geffray Fenton, and reissued in 1577 and 1582. At the end of the seventeenth century the growing interest in the letter as a literary genre stimulated a rare late Guevara translation, *Spanish Letters*, another selection from the *Epístolas*, translated by John Savage and published in 1697.

The success of *The Familiar Epistles* encouraged Hellowes to translate two more of Guevara's books: *Una década de Césares*, which appeared in English in 1577 as *A Chronicle, Conteyning the Lives of Tenne Emperours of Rome*, and *El arte de marear*, *The Art of Navegation*, 1578. But neither of these was republished. Finally, *The Mount of Caluarie*, an English version of *El monte Calvario* prepared by an anonymous translator, was published in two volumes in 1595 and 1597, the first volume being republished in 1618. Altogether there are some thirty English editions of Guevara's works, nearly all of them from the sixteenth century [Thomas 1930].

These sixteenth-century translators faced problems which should make us modern practitioners, with every aid at our disposal, feel ashamed of ourselves if we fail to do our job properly. Castilian was a little-known language in sixteenth-century England outside court circles. Travel to Spain was difficult and hazardous. And it was not possible to consult a Spanish-English dictionary, because there was none worthy of the name. Some polyglot handbooks for traders included both English and Spanish, but these were of little use to the literary translator. The first genuine dictionary of these two languages, *A Dictionary in Spanish, English and Latine*, by Richard

Percyvall, did not appear until 1591. The first Spanish grammars written in English appeared at the same time: *The Spanish Grammar*, by Antonio de Corro, translated by John Thorius (both Oxford men), and *The Spanish Schoolemaster*, by William Stepney, published in 1590 and 1591 respectively. [Martín-Gamero 1961:58-97]

The solution that most of the sixteenth-century English translators of Guevara found to this problem was a simple one, though not one to be recommended. Like John Bourchier, they did not translate from the Spanish but from French translations without, as far as it is possible to tell from an examination of their work, even glancing at the original in order to resolve doubts. The only one who always translated from the Spanish was Edward Hellowes. Among the others, Thomas North alone seems to have known any Spanish: in *The Diall of Princes* there are some direct translations of letters that had not appeared in the French version. Textual comparison makes it clear, however, that North retranslated the rest of *The Diall of Princes* from the French, as stated on the title-page, and that his knowledge of Spanish did not dispose him any more than the other translators to consult the original when in difficulties.

Bourchier, Bryan, North, Hellowes and Fenton had nothing to say in their prologues and dedications about the theoretical aspects of their work. But Guevara's French translators were a little more forthcoming. René Berthault de la Grise states in 1531 in the dedication of *Le Livre doré de Marc Aurèle*:

Toutefois considerant les profonds & vertueux enseignemens, pour la crainte de desuoyer de si haut style, me suis determiné en ceste translation au plus pres que i'ay peu du tout suyure le Castillan, à fin que ceux qui se voudront esbatre à lire l'oeuure, accommodans l'Espagnol au François, y prennent plus de goust: leur laissant la gloire de ce qu'ils y pourront adoucir, amender, corriger & mieux faire.

De la Grise here identifies the central problem of literary translation, discussed again and again during previous and subsequent centuries: whether the translator owes his first allegiance to the author and his language, or to the readers and theirs. In other words, whether he should write an exact, literal translation, even though this gives rise to an awkward, unnatural style, or a free translation in idiomatic prose, even though this betrays the original author and what he wrote [Rutherford 1989]. It is often taken for granted nowadays that the latter position is the only respectable one, but literal translation has had its distinguished supporters and de la Grise was one of them. What he says is that it is up to his readers, if they wish, to convert his deliberately Hispanized French into something they find more acceptable, for it is not Guevara's translator's job to gain himself glory in this way but to convey the most precise idea he can of what Guevara wrote, and to be a guide for those Frenchmen who wish to read the Spanish text.

There were objections to this manner of translating. To the non-translator it could seem all too easy. In a pseudonymous letter of 1548 which parodies the attitudes of an old soldier with literary pretensions, 'el capitán Salazar' blusters:

Don Jerónimo de Urrea, ¿no ha ganado fama de noble escritor, y aún, según dicen, muchos dineros (que importa más), por haber traducido a *Orlando el Furioso*, poniendo solamente de su casa, a donde el autor decía *cavalieri, caballeros*, y a donde el otro decía *arme*, ponía él *armas*, y donde *amori, amores*? Pues deste arte yo me haría más libros que Matusalén y aun más que hizo el de Mondoñedo. [Paz y Melia 1890:89]

There are more serious difficulties about literal transla‐
tion. Another of Guevara's French translators, Antoine
Allaigre, warns the reader in 1542 in the prologue to his
version of *Menosprecio de corte y alabanza de aldea*:

> S'il te semble que ie n'aye obserué si diligement la Loy, &
> proprieté de bien traduire, comme beaucoup d'autres, qui en
> font profession, ie te prie entre autres choses penser, que la
> phrase du Castillan est trop plus copieuse, que la Françoise,
> & la liaison bien fort differente. Donq si prens mescontente‐
> ment en quelque periode mal sonant, ou tronqué, sache, que ie
> me suis asseruy, iusques à faire conscience, de ne vouloir rien
> perdre de l'intention de l'Auteur.

When Allaigre refers to 'la phrase du Castillan' it is
possible that he is thinking more of 'la phrase du
Castillan de Guevara', but his point is still a valid one:
since the structures of any two languages are different,
any exact translation must be ill-sounding. In spite of
this, Allaigre declares his support for the position
established by de la Grise.

This difficulty gave rise to objections to the French
translation of *Marco Aurelio*, according to de la Grise in
the prologue to his translation (1540) of *El relox de
príncipes*, where he continues to defend his position.
Readers have attacked his work, he says,

> disans que ung translateur ne doit si serrement suyure les
> motz, & qu'il suffit donner pour les poix les sentences les
> adoul-cissant de leur rudesse ainsi que ont faict noz
> predecesseurs.

If this account is accurate, de la Grise's detractors had
merely repeated what Guevara himself had written on
the subject of translation. Guevara had claimed that
Marco Aurelio and *El relox de príncipes* were not his
original compositions but his translations of Greek and

Latin texts, the seriousness of which claim can be judged from the delightful absurdity of:

> Los que dizen que yo solo compuse esta dotrina: por cierto yo les agradezco lo que dizen: aun que no la intencion con que lo dizen: porque a ser verdad que tantas y tan graues sentencias aya yo puesto de mi cabeça: una famosa estatua me pusieran los antiguos en roma. [Guevara 1534: x^r]

In the *Relox* we also find the following words:

> Heme aprouechado enesta escriptura que es humana delo que muchas vezes los doctores se aprouechan enla diuina: en no traduzir palabra de palabra: sino sentencia de sentencia: porque los interpretes no estamos obligados dar por medida las palabras: sino que abasta dar por peso las sentencias... No se engañe el lector en pensar que lo uno y lo otro es del auctor: porque dado caso que el estilo del romance es mio: yo confiesso que todo lo mas que se dize es ageno. Como los historiadores y doctores de que me aprouechaua eran muchos: y la doctrina que escriuia no mas de vna: no quiero negar que quitaua algunas cosas inutiles & insipidas: y entretexeria otras muy suaues y prouechosas: por manera que es menester muy delicado juyzio para hazer que lo que en vna lengua era escoria: enla otra parezca oro. [x^r-x^v]

This discussion belongs within a tradition stretching back to St. Jerome [Russell 1985]. But Guevara goes much further in advocating thought-for-thought ('sentencia de sentencia') translation than earlier writers; and his idea that what is dross in Greek or Latin can become gold in the vernacular is a radical manifestation of the new perception of the relative merits of ancient and modern languages. Guevara's position is the opposite to that adopted by de la Grise. According to Guevara, the translator is free to do whatever he likes to the original work, in order to produce a text which pleases his readers. The distinction between translation, thus conceived, and original composition is indistinct.

In this way de la Grise and Guevara had defined the theoretical positions between which Edward Hellowes and the other English translators had to choose, whether they realized it or not.

Hellowes, like the others except Fenton, chose literal translation, which he practised with more success than the others. But no translation can be literal. In practice, the literal translator is the one who stays as close to the original as circumstances permit. These circumstances include the abilities of the translator, the demands of the publisher and of his readers, and the nature of the languages concerned. On occasions, for instance, Hellowes came across a word or phrase that he did not understand. Faced by this dilemma there are, as examination candidates know, three possible solutions: be brave and make an intelligent guess; be cowardly and omit, in the hope that the omission will not be noticed; be foolhardy and make a wild guess or even a calque.

Hellowes' most intelligent guesses are, of course, unidentifiable. He was not a cowardly translator, and most of the omissions in his work are probably unintentional. And he makes few mistakes, most of them intelligent or at least forgivable, such as the following, from *The Familiar Epistles*:

acordaron todas las mugeres Romanas, de embiar (2ʳ) / all the women of Rome did not forget to sende (1: acordar-acordarse)

paresce mas characteres con que se escriue el musayco, que no carta de cauallero (33ʳ) / it seemeth rather the characters wherwith they write musike, than the letter of a Gentleman (54: musayco-musica).

no es possible menos, sino que se escriuio con caña cortada, o con cañon por cortar (33ʳ) / it is not possible (at the least) but that you did write it with a cane or with a cannon (55: caña grande-arma de fuego).

de tales romerias no podeys sacar sino tales veneras (35^r) / out of such pilgrimage, you can obtaine but like pardons (58: not a bad guess).

Ser vno poderoso de refrenar la yra (68^v) / For a man to be in power and authoritie, and to refraine his anger (118).

ceuase de palabrillas (146^r) / he is blinded with gilefull speeche (240: ceuar-cegar).

el donayre dello (147^r) / the reward of them (241: donaire-don, dello-dellos).

yo os doy mi fe, que mas ayna os acaben los enojos dela amiga, que no los dolores dela gota (147^r) / I assure you of my faith, that sooner you shall be delivered of the displeasures of your Courtizan, than of the paynes of the goute (242: transitive-intransitive).

There are a few unfortunate calques, for example:

la reina germana (12^v) / Queen Germana (20).

un pesce que se llamaba xibia (33^r) / a fishe called Zibia (55).

cardenillo (33^r) / Cardenillio (55).

Al hombre ayrado no le hemos de importunar, que del pie ala mano perdone la injuria (69^r) / With the yrefull we must not be importunate to entreate a pardon, no not from the foote to the hand (119).

Espetable Senor y magnifico caballero (67^r) / Expectable Gentleman and magnificent Knight (115).

The latter calque enjoys the distinction of inclusion in the *Oxford English Dictionary*, even if it is described as 'erron.'.

Hellowes' deliberate departures from what Guevara wrote are also infrequent. Sometimes the English language requires such departures, most notably where Guevara indulges his fondness for puns, alliteration and other plays on words and sounds. No translator could reproduce the intricate wit of:

> no nos han faltado en esta quaresma hartos pescados que comer, y aun hartos pecados que confessar, porque ha venido la cosa a tanta dissolucion y desverguença, que tienen los caualleros por estado y pundonor de honrra, comer carne en quaresma. [51ʳ]

On occasions, however, Hellowes used his ingenuity to try to find, if not an exactly equivalent effect, then a similar enough one. Maybe it was a desire to reproduce the sound-play that led him to translate 'se escriuio con caña cortada, o con cañon por cortar' as he did, but this led him into semantic trouble. The following piece of translation is a much more successful attempt to preserve sound-play:

> Acuerdome que rinendo con un capellan de vuestra muger delante de mi, como el os dixesse, que no le tractassedes mal: pues tenia cargo de animas, & era cura, le respondistes vos: que el no era cura, sino la locura. [145ʳ]

> I remember that chiding with a Chaplayne of youre wiues in my presence, when he said unto you, that it were not conuenient you shuld deale fowly with him, for that he had charge of soules, & was a Curat, you made answer, that he was not a Curat of soules but of fooles. [238]

This is more felicitous than Savage's effort:

> I remember that you quarrelling once with your Wives Chaplain in my presence, and he saying you should not abuse him, for he had the cure of Souls; you answer'd, he was no Priest, but a sot and a Madman. [Boyer 1701: 83]

But most of Guevara's word-plays are, inevitably, lost in translation. An elegant solution to this problem is to create other word-plays, by way of compensation, where there are none in the original text. Hellowes seldom allows himself this luxury, but in this letter he does turn 'amiga' into 'daintie Dame' and then into 'lustie Lasse' [240-241].

This is an example of the other kind of deliberate departure from the original, the one motivated by the translator's own taste rather than forced upon him by the structures of the languages he is dealing with. In the passage just referred to, Guevara creates one of his characteristic rhetorical accumulations, twelve successive questions beginning '¿Para que quereis amiga...?' [146^v-147^r]. All this is too much even for Hellowes, who opts for elegant variation: 'To what ende will you haue a loue...? Wherefore will you haue a daintie Dame...? For what cause wold you haue a loue...? Why will you haue an amorous dame...?' [240-241]. Deliberate changes of this sort are sometimes based on the conviction that the English language will not readily accept the original effect; yet even then they are often misguided changes, because the most exciting and creative part of the translator's enterprise is to stretch and strengthen his language by making it to do things which it does not want to do. More often, however, such changes amount to stylistic correction, something which it is always dangerous and usually impertinent for the translator to indulge in.

To his credit, Hellowes corrects much less than the other English translators of Guevara. Fenton is the great culprit in this respect, excluding passages if they are anecdotal, personal or funny, and inserting in their place cold stern moralistic passages of his own. Such ideological correction is even less defensible than stylistic correction. But this distinction is an artificial one. Guevara's finely-balanced rhetoric is an expression of his vision of the world, an idealized feudal world of God-given symmetries and harmonies, and any disruption of the rhetoric is also a disruption of the vision.

A correction of even the smallest detail can disturb the whole text like a pebble dropped into a pool. At the beginning of a sermon preached to the Queen, Guevara requests:

> pues vuestra alteza es seruida que a esta platica esten presentes las damas que la siruen, y los galanes que las siguen mande les que no se esten cocando, ni señas haziendo: porque han jurado de me turbar o me atajar. [13ʳ]

The patterns of the rhetoric encourage the reader to anticipate 'las damas que la sirven y los caballeros que la atienden'; but Guevara was too witty and intelligent to fall into the rhetorician's trap of writing by numbers. Hellowes, noticing that something strange has happened and wrongly sensing a mistake, writes:

> And since it pleaseth your highnesse, that the Ladies and dames that serue you, and the gallants and Courtiers that attend upon you be present at this communication, that you commaund them that they be not gibing, either making of signes: for they haue sworne to trouble me, or to put me from my matter. [20]

The expansion of 'damas' and 'galanes' is uncharacteristic. Hellowes must have felt that it was unacceptable that a queen, let alone an empress, should be followed by gallants. So he modified 'siguen' and 'galanes' in order to redress the etiquette somewhat, with the minimum disruption of the original text. At least he did not suppress the gallants, as Fenton would have done. So as to keep the rhetorical balance, Hellowes next had to double 'damas'. And the correction, or pseudo-correction, of 'la' for 'las', completes the destruction of the delicious humour of the original, in which Guevara's disturbance of his own rhetorical patterns reflects a disturbance of the social proprieties and harmonies he held so dear: the German Queen is not in charge, or even at the centre, of her Spanish court; the requested command, even if the Queen can issue it, is not going to be obeyed; and the poor plaintive preacher finds himself addressing an uncontrollable gaggle of giggling adolescents. One of the many endearing qualities of Guevara's writing is this willingness of his to direct his humour against himself, a quality lost in this piece of translation because the translator deviated, just a little, from his normal practice of close and faithful rendering. Maybe Hellowes, who was Queen Elizabeth's Groom of the Leash, could not imagine such an unruly royal court, and made his corrections for this reason.

But Edward Hellowes, despite his occasional mistakes and misjudgments, was a thoughtful and intelligent close translator, who knew that his art consisted in an appropriate combination of passivity (allowing himself to be absorbed by the author and his style) and activity (forcing his language to stay as close as possible to what the author wrote). The lack of a bilingual dictionary was the least of his problems, and could even have been an advantage: it made him think about words rather than look them up, and shielded him from the worst dangers of word-for-word translation.

Most contemporary translators, for all our profusion of reference books, make no fewer mistakes than Edward Hellowes, the admirable pioneer of close and faithful translation from Spanish to English.

John Rutherford
The Queen's College, Oxford

REFERENCES

Boyer, A. (ed.), 1701
   Letters of Wit, Politicks and Morality, London
Guevara, A. de, 1534
   Marco Aurelio con el relox de príncipes, Sevilla
————————, 1535
   The Golden Boke of Marcus Aurelius, London
————————, 1540
   Lorloge des Princes, Paris
————————, 1544
   Le Mespris de la court, avec la vie rustique, Paris
————————, 1562
   Epístolas familiares, I, Anvers
————————, 1570
   Le Livre doré de Marc Aurèle, Lyon
————————, 1575
   The Familiar Epistles, London
Martín-Gamero, S., 1961
   La enseñanza del inglés en España, Madrid
Paz y Melia, A., 1890
   Sales españolas, Madrid
Russell, P., 1985
   Traducciones y traductores en la Península Ibérica, Barcelona
Rutherford, J., 1989
   'Teoría y práctica de la traducción literaria: *La Regenta* al inglés', in
   Translation Across Cultures: Actas del XI Congreso de AEDEAN,
   Leon, pp. 159-172
Thomas, H, 1930
   'The English translations of Guevara's works', in *Homenaje a Bonilla
   y San Martin*, II, Madrid, pp. 565-582

La otra voz de la Academia Española: notas sobre el *Diccionario manual*

1 EN EL año 1915, el sosegado transcurrir de la lexicografía académica fue agitado por una pequeña conmoción, producida por el acuerdo de publicar una versión manual e ilustrada del *Diccionario de la lengua castellana*, cuya edición decimocuarta acababa de aparecer en el año anterior. Mas la idea de editar una versión manual del *Diccionario* no era nueva: ya un siglo atrás (1814) se había pensado en su oportunidad, si bien no se llevó adelante [Cotarelo 1928: 30-31]. Y en realidad, el propio *Diccionario* común [DC] nació en parte de presupuestos semejantes a los de un diccionario manual: la necesidad de poner la obra de la Academia—el *Diccionario* por excelencia, es decir, el 'de Autoridades'—al alcance de un público amplio y la conveniencia de hacer más cómodo su manejo, reduciéndola a un volumen. Aparecida en 1780 esa versión *compact*—a la que los académicos se referían como 'el Compendio'—, no tardó en ir borrándose de la memoria colectiva su condición vicaria y abreviadora, hasta el punto de que muy pocos hoy, incluso dentro de la Academia, tienen conciencia de que el actual *Diccionario manual* [DM] no es, en el fondo, sino el compendio de un compendio.

El diccionario manual proyectado en 1915 se proponía llegar a un sector social más amplio que el destinatario tradicional del DC, no solo imprimiendo un determinado giro a su fisonomía interna, sino haciéndolo mucho más económico y físicamente mucho más manejable. Parece razonable no descartar la probabilidad de que como estímulo de la iniciativa académica actuase la aparición reciente [1912] del *Pequeño Larousse ilustrado*, adaptación española, redactada por Miguel de

Toro y Gisbert, del *Petit Larousse* [1906] de Claude Augé. En apoyo de la hipótesis de este influjo están algunas semejanzas visibles entre el nuevo producto académico, tal como se presentó en su primera edición, y el vástago español de la editorial parisiense: la ilustración, el formato idéntico, la información gramatical, la atención especial a los usos hispanoamericanos, y la inclusión de neologismos no presentes en el *Diccionario* académico grande.

2 Publicado por fin en 1927, el *Diccionario manual e ilustrado de la lengua española* se abrió camino con fuerza. Su éxito se debía a que su oferta no solo comprendía la comodidad del manejo, la moderación del precio y las diversas informaciones nuevas que acabo de mencionar, sino, sobre todo, el mantenimiento de la garantía académica, hasta entonces solo ostentada por el DC. El DM reproduce todo el contenido del diccionario mayor, exceptuando las etimologías y todas las voces y acepciones que en este último llevan las marcas de anticuadas o desusadas.

Además de este contenido 'académico', y reemplazando al contingente de las voces y acepciones reputadas fuera de uso, el DM ofrece una información lexicográfica suplementaria nítidamente distinguible para el lector por medio de una señalización que diferencia bien lo 'académico' (es decir, lo que es reproducción del DC) y lo 'no académico' (la aportación propia del DM). Este último sector está constituido por dos subsectores. El primero es el de los 'regionalismos, así de España como de América' y 'muchas otras voces comunes o técnicas que no hay motivo para censurar, pero que la Academia no quiere acoger en su Diccionario general, fundada, las más veces, en que son voces demasiado recientes y no puede presumirse si llegarán a arraigar en el idioma' [DM1: viii].

Un segundo subsector es el de 'los vocablos incorrectos y los extranjerismos que con más frecuencia se usan', con indicación de la 'expresión propiamente española que debe sustituirlos'. Tres ediciones del DM han seguido a la de 1927: 1950, 1983-85 y 1989. Si comparamos estas fechas con las de las ediciones del DC a lo largo de este siglo [1914, 1925, 1939, 1947, 1956, 1970, 1984], lo primero que llama la atención es el contraste entre la relativa regularidad con que se espacian las apariciones del DC y la acusada arritmia del DM. El segundo fenómeno que se observa es que desde el año 1927, en que nace el DM, este no se ha reeditado hasta hoy más que tres veces, mientras que en el mismo período el DC ha salido cinco veces.

La irregularidad en el ritmo de las ediciones del DM se matiza al considerar las circunstancias de la publicación de la tercera y la cuarta. La tercera se presentó en forma de fascículos semanales, de 1983 a 1985. Una vez encuader-nados los 120 fascículos (no 200, como por error dice DM4, [vii]), resultaban seis volúmenes en formato 19,5 x 27 cm, con un total de 2.400 páginas copiosamente ilustradas. Como no era indiscutible que este producto respondiese a su denominación de 'manual', la Academia advertía al frente de él que esta edición presentaba como novedad la 'aparición en fascículos además de la edición normal en tomos' [*sic*]. Pero la publicación de la edición 'normal' se retrasó por razones técnicas. Esta demora forzosa fue aprovechada por el equipo redactor para llevar a cabo una nueva revisión del texto, con lo cual la prevista presentación en un tomo de la tercera edición pasó a ser una cuarta edición. Ahora bien, la hermandad entre una y otra es evidente, hasta el punto de que lo que se ha escrito sobre una de ellas es en líneas generales aplicable a la otra. Tal ocurre, v. gr., con el extenso comentario de Emilio Lorenzo [1984] a la edición tercera y con el artículo de Manuel Casado [1989] a propósito de la cuarta.

La escasez relativa de ediciones del DM frente al DC es otra visible anomalía. El primero nació a la sombra del segundo: 'Este Diccionario Manual—dice la Advertencia de la primera edición—es un resumen y a la vez un suplemento de la décima quinta edición del Diccionario de la lengua española que la Academia acaba de editar' [DM1: vii]. Parecía lógico esperar que las ediciones sucesivas del DC dieran lugar a consiguientes puestas al día de su hermano menor. Salvo la revisión de este en 1950, la Academia solo mostró acordarse de él para reimprimirlo en offset múltiples veces hasta 1983. Afortunadamente, el desinterés de la Academia parece haberse rectificado en los últimos años. Solo es de lamentar, en las ediciones recientes, el olvido de tres características fundamentales de las primeras: el formato reducido, el volumen manejable y el precio económico, que constituían ventajas no desdeñables frente al diccionario grande. El injustificado afán de poner en primer plano lo puramente ornamental es un lastre que pesa perniciosamente sobre aquellas características y, en definitiva, sobre la propia obra. Con este aumento de volumen y de peso contrasta el cuidado que muchos editores, particularmente extranjeros, ponen en que sus diccionarios manuales guarden la línea, a fin de salvar siempre su carácter esencial.

3 Como en el DM las palabras y acepciones no 'oficialmente reconocidas' por la Academia (es decir, las incluidas en él sin que figuren en el DC) se imprimen con signos que las diferencian del resto del vocabulario, no es difícil tomarlas como punto de partida para buscar algunas claves de la actitud oficiosa de la Academia ante los elementos léxicos nuevos o que se le presentan como

nuevos. Con ese propósito he efectuado una exploración de tanteo a lo largo de algunas páginas de la última edición del D M, poniéndolas en contraste, cuando procedía, con las correspondientes de la primera edición. Las entradas estudiadas pertenecen a dos sectores de la letra M, el primero desde *m* hasta *margullo* y el segundo desde *me* hasta *mezquite*.

3.1 En primer lugar, es curioso considerar que el número de entradas del sector acotado, 2.319, no solo supera al de la primera edición, 1.946—lo cual es perfectamente natural—, sino al del último DC, 2.230. Si extrapolamos este dato llegaremos a la paradójica conclusión de que el diccionario pequeño es más extenso que el grande.

3.2 El segundo punto que vale la pena anotar es la actitud ante 'los vocablos incorrectos y los extranjerismos', que llevan un asterisco como indicación de que deben evitarse. La postura censora es bastante acusada en la primera edición. En esta los asteriscos sumaban 49. En cambio, la edición cuarta trae un solo asterisco (*mandolino*, incluido ya en la lista anterior). Algunos de los reprobados en 1927 han sido aprobados con el paso del tiempo y hoy figuran como normales tanto en el DC como en el DM (por ejemplo, *medidor, mensuración, menú, metido*). Otros tampoco son tachados ya de incorrectos, pero, al no haber ingresado en el DC, se registran en el DM con corchete (*mandatario, manito, mansarda, marchantería, mechonear, mediano, medical, melodio, memorista*). Otras voces que llevaban la marca infamante han sido eliminadas; la mayoría eran simples errores fonéticos, generalmente populares y de diversa extensión geográfica, a menudo (no siempre con acierto) localizados por el diccionario en uno o más países de América (*manque, melitar, méndigo, meope*, etc.).

La observación de las variantes en el sector de los
asteriscos nos permite concluir que, en los sesenta y dos
años que separan la primera y la cuarta edición, se ha
producido en la Academia un cambio en su postura de
crítica del lenguaje. En el aspecto metodológico, la
Academia considera ahora inadecuado a un diccionario
general prestar atención a los errores fonéticos de nivel
popular, por lo cual ha optado por prescindir de los que
antaño recogió y no incluir ninguno nuevo. Y en el
aspecto ideológico, el purismo de otro tiempo ha perdido
dureza: parte de las voces antes censuradas están hoy
instaladas en las columnas del DC; otras, aunque no
hayan alcanzado esa dignidad, constan ahora en el DM
simplemente con corchete, como no recogidas en el grande, lo cual en el lenguaje académico no significa condena,
sino abstención provisional.

3.3 La provisionalidad de esa abstención alcanza a veces
una notable estabilidad. Así lo muestra el tercer nivel de
nuestro análisis, que se refiere precisamente a las voces y
acepciones señaladas con corchete. Atendiendo (aunque
no literalmente) a las indicaciones de la microestructura
del propio diccionario, distribuyo esas adiciones en seis
grupos. Los cuatro primeros pertenecen al uso español
general; los dos últimos son de extensión geográfica
limitada.

a Voces y acepciones del nivel culto o medio del
   español general, en número de 239. En realidad, esta
   cantidad hay que rebajarla en una unidad, porque hay
   que dejar a un lado una palabra fantasma: *melga*
   'zahína, planta', que debe su presencia a una errata de
   DM1, donde se imprimió *melga* por *melca* en el lugar
   alfabético de esta última (*melca* en DC de 1925 y
   ediciones posteriores). En las ediciones siguientes del
   DM, en lugar de pensar en un error de imprenta se

pensó en un error de alfabetización; sin embargo, se repuso en su sitio *melca* 'zahína'.

De las 238 voces y acepciones, algunas son viejas inquilinas del idioma y llenan vacíos pendientes desde hace mucho en el DC; por ejemplo, *madrigalesco, magdaleniense, magníficamente, magnificar, maniqueísmo, manivela, manopla, manía de grandezas, hasta mañana, medida, mediocre, mediocridad, melodrama, memez, menchevique.*

Otras pertenecen a un estrato onológico más o menos moderno, y su no inclusión en el DC puede obedecer a la cautela con que este suele tratar las novedades, o bien al recelo académico ante formas que a sus ojos traslucen demasiado su procedencia extranjera; por ejemplo, *macramé, macrobiótico, machismo, magnetofón, manierismo, mansarda, maratón, maratoniano, marchante, marginar* y sus derivados, *mensajero, mentalizar, mesón.*

Algunas voces y acepciones del español general que en este DM figuran con corchete ya se encontraban igualmente en la primera edición: *macfarlán* o *macferlán, magullón* (que en DM1 se calificaba de chilenismo), *magnetizable, mandarinato, mantequería, menear* (que en DM1 era peruanismo), *mesmeriano.* Y ya cité antes los casos de voces que han sido indultadas de su antiguo asterisco y ahora llevan corchete (*mandatario,* etc.).

En DM1, el número de corchetes de español general era mucho más restringido: no pasaba de 20. Figuraban entre ellos palabras hoy tan familiares para nosotros como *malamente, mecanografiar, mefistofélico, memorismo* y *mentalidad.*

b Voces y acepciones con la etiqueta de familiares o vulgares, en número de 68. Tres de ellas ya figuraban en DM1: *malqueda* (que entonces se localizaba en

Álava), *metete* (que se daba como de Chile y Guatemala) y *mezquita* 'taberna'. Otras, aunque no incluidas allí, podían muy bien haberlo sido por su edad, y más de dos de las ahora recogidas ya están marchitas. He aquí algunas muestras de este grupo: *tocar madera, viva la madre que te parió, magín, maldita sea, criar malvas, mamarracho, mamón, a mandar, manduca, mangonear, manos de mantequilla, manojo de nervios, borrar del mapa, menda, mengue, mercachifle, merienda de negros, metedura de pata.* Entre las más decrépitas están *manflotesco, manús* y la citada *mezquita.*

Otro sector, en este grupo, está formado por voces y acepciones cuya vida es más corta y que en algunos casos hemos visto nacer: *macarra, maco, madera* 'la policía', *madero* 'el policía', *de puta madre, magreo, mandanga, manitas, manta, marabunta, marcha, meningítico, meódromo, merluzo, metralla.*

También en DM1 era el grupo de las voces y acepciones familiares, entre las señaladas con corchete, mucho más reducido que en DM4: solo 7 se incluían, entre ellas *mangante, mangoneador, mecachis, melón* 'persona inepta' y *memada.*

c Extranjerismos, solamente 4 marcados como tales: *made in, maillot, maitre* [sic] y *manager.* En DM1 este grupo de palabras se señalaba, no con corchete, sino sistemáticamente con asterisco, según hemos visto en párrafos anteriores.

d Voces y acepciones técnicas y especiales, en número de 113. De las 113, sin embargo, hay que retirar una, *mano-*, elemento compositivo fantasma procedente de DM3 y que es grafía errónea por *nano-* (que por cierto ya está en su sitio). De las 112 que quedan, 4 ya estaban en DM1, pero no han conseguido entrada en el DC: *machihembradora* (que allí era chilenismo), *maimo-na, mamitis, mesenteritis.* Entre los ejemplos nuevos pertenecientes a este sector, tenemos *macromolecular, magnetoscopio, mamografía, mandril* y sus derivados, *mandrinador, mareómetro, mediometraje, menú* (en informática), *mercadotécnico, mesotrofia, metalin-güístico, mezclar* y sus derivados (en cine y televisión). Hay que incluir en este grupo, naturalmente, los términos deportivos y taurinos, como *manoletina, mansurronear, meseta del toril, metisaca, melé, meta.*

En DM1, el número de corchetes dedicados a voces y acepciones técnicas y especiales era solo de 6.

e Voces y acepciones marcadas como regionalismos peninsulares, en un total de 31. De estas, un tercio ya se habían recogido en DM1. De las de DM4, por regiones, 14 corresponden a Andalucía (2 de ellas a Granada), 5 a Salamanca, 4 a Galicia, 3 a Aragón, 2 al País Vasco (una de ellas a Álava), 2 a Santander, 1 a Navarra, 1 a Asturias y 1 a Murcia. (La suma de estas cifras, y la de las que siguen, no corresponden a la global de adiciones, al existir acepciones con más de una localización.)

El número de regionalismos españoles registrados con corchete en DM1 era comparativamente menos breve que otros grupos: 12. Distribuidos por regiones, 6 eran de Salamanca, 2 de Álava, 2 de Murcia, 1 de León, 1 de Santander y 1 de Aragón.

f Voces y acepciones correspondientes al español no europeo, que suman 265. Incluyo aquí no solo las que llevan una marca diatópica ('América', 'Antillas', etc.), sino las que designan realidades—normalmente propias de la botánica o de la zoología—pertenecientes a países determinados. De las 265 voces o acepciones, una sola corresponde a Filipinas. Lo más notable de esta colección, que por el número de sus componentes se coloca a la cabeza de todas, es la elevada proporción de ellos que ya estaban estampados en DM1: 186 del total de 265; a las que aún hay que añadir 15 que datan de DM2. Con lo cual los americanismos con corchete heredados de las dos primeras ediciones ascienden a 201: un 75% de los actualmente presentados. Es decir, solo 64 de las voces y acepciones son de reciente aportación.

En DM1, el grupo de las voces y acepciones del español extrapeninsular introducidas con corchete era, con mucho, el más copioso de aquella edición: 244, frente a las 45 que sumaban todos los demás grupos (general, familiar, técnico y regional de España). De esas 244 adiciones, solo 2 correspondían a Filipinas. La obra nacía, sin duda, con vocación americanista [cf. DM1: vii; Casares 1950: 303]. ¿Por qué en el contingente actual se mantienen 186 de las que ya entraron en 1927, más 15 que entraron en 1950? El proceso normal haría esperar que, si no todos, la mayoría de estos elementos hubiesen acabado instalándose en las columnas del DC. No fue así. La explicación está en la 'liberalidad quizá excesiva' con que se les dio entrada en DM1, la cual produjo 'inclusiones no bien justificadas', a juicio de algunos críticos americanos [DM2: ix; cf. Casares 1950: 303]. La consecuencia de tales censuras ha sido la cuarentena tácita que pesa sobre aquellas propuestas, en virtud de la cual, al cabo de decenas de años, siguen almacenadas con sus corchetes en el DM en una especie de limbo, sin que la Academia termine de decidir si las asimila oficialmente o les retira su interinidad.

En la distribución por áreas y países de los americanismos 'provisionales' del DM siempre se ha traslucido cierta falta de homogeneidad. Las adiciones americanas de DM1 se repartían así: 8 marcadas como americanismos generales, 2 de América del Sur, 3 de América Central, 2 de las Antillas, 75 de Chile, 44 de Cuba, 43 de Méjico, 43 de Honduras, 19 de Argentina, 19 de Colombia, 14 del Perú, 12 del Ecuador, 10 de Bolivia, 7 de Venezuela, 5 de Guatemala y 2 de Costa Rica. (Igual que en las listas anteriores, la suma de estas cifras no corresponde a la global de las adiciones, al existir acepciones con más de una localización.) No hay ninguna adición atribuida a Santo Domingo, Puerto Rico, Nicaragua, el Salvador, Panamá, Uruguay ni Paraguay.

Comparemos la distribución precedente [DM1) con la de los 64 nuevos americanismos con corchete de DM4: 8 se dan como americanismos generales, 2 de América Central, 1 de Antillas, 26 de Méjico, 17 de Argentina, 13 de Puerto Rico, 8 de Cuba, 8 de Venezuela, 7 de Colombia, 6 de Chile, 6 de Bolivia, 5 de Uruguay, 4 del Perú, 2 de Santo Domingo, 1 de Costa Rica, 1 de Guatemala, 1 del Perú y 1 del Salvador. Ninguno del Ecuador, Panamá, Nicaragua y Honduras. Como se ve, ahora está representada la generalidad de los países americanos y, aunque es notorio el predominio de algunos (Méjico sobre todo), el desequilibrio no es tan acusado como el que aparecía en la primera edición.

3.4 En este esbozo de descripción del DM4 nos queda señalar un cuarto aspecto sobre el que nadie, que yo sepa, ha llamado la atención, empezando por la misma Academia.

Una de las características de la obra, como queda dicho, es, en su reproducción del contenido del DC, la exclusión de todas las voces y acepciones que en este llevan la etiqueta de anticuadas o desusadas. Esta norma ha dejado pasar alguna excepción. Ya en DM1 se registraba *man*, ant., 'mano'; y en DM4 se conserva la misma calificación en *melecina*, y la de 'desus.' en *mecánico* 'bajo e indecoroso', *mecánica* 'acción mezquina', *manjorrada* 'cantidad de manjares ordinarios', *mandar* 'ofrecer, prometer'. Otros casos de 'anticuados' del DC han sido objeto de recalificación en el DM: *maldadoso* 'acostumbrado a cometer maldades', ahora 'poco usado' (pero en DM1, como normal en Chile); *malfeita* y *manija* ('manilla de los presos'), así como *manzana* ('pomo de la espada', que para DM1 era de uso normal), ahora los tres 'desusados'; *malsinar* y *mantecón* (que en DM1 se daba como familiar general), ahora 'poco usados'. Por otra parte, algunos 'desusados' del DC han sido ascendidos a 'poco usados' en D M4: *malcaso*, *marea* ('conjunto de inmundicias'), *melampo* ('candelero'); los tres eran para DM1 de uso normal.

Pero lo que quiero señalar aquí es un fenómeno de sentido inverso. La obligación explícita del DM de prescindir de las voces anticuadas y desusadas del DC tiene como reverso la de registrar *todas* las restantes que figuran allí. Por lo que he podido comprobar, este principio se ha cumplido estrictamente. Ahora bien: es sabido que el DC contiene, aparte de las marcadas como tales, multitud de voces y acepciones que son realmente anticuadas y desusadas, aunque nada se indique a este respecto [Seco 1988: 565]. El D M4, sin faltar a la norma de incluirlas todas, ha puesto las etiquetas de 'p. us.' y, con menos frecuencia, 'desus.' en aquellos casos que, a juicio de los redactores, carecen de verdadera vigencia en la lengua actual.

La nota de poco usada se utiliza, dentro de las 2.319 entradas que aquí estudiamos, 180 veces. La de desusada, 43. Hasta en una ocasión se emplea la de anticuada. En total, pues, son 224 las marcas restrictivas de vigencia puestas por el DM4 donde el DC no indica nada. Como ejemplos de las voces que el DM da como poco usadas citaré *madurativo* 'medio que se aplica para inclinar o ablandar al que no quiere hacer lo que se desea'; *malato* 'leproso', con sus derivados *malatía* y *malatería*; *mandoble* 'amonestación'; *manero* 'manejable'; *manfla* 'mujer con quien se tiene trato sexual ilícito'; *manguitería* 'peletería'; *tomar la manta* 'tomar las unciones mercuriales'; *marconigrama* 'radiograma'; *meaja* 'migaja'; *mendoso* 'errado o mentiroso'; *mercadante* 'mercader'; *metamorfosi* 'metamorfosis'; *metedor* 'persona que mete contrabando', con su derivado *meteduría; mezquino* 'desdichado'. Entre las que el DM señala como desusadas están *magancés* 'traidor, avieso', *magdaleón* (en farmacia) 'rollito largo y delgado que se hace de un emplasto', *maguer* y *maguera* 'aunque', *manera* 'abertura en las sayas de las mujeres, para que puedan pasar las manos hasta alcanzar las faltriqueras', *mercantivo* 'mercantil', *muchas mercedes* 'muchas gracias', *metalario* 'artífice que trata y trabaja en metales'. Y la palabra excepcionalmente calificada de anticuada es *máncer* 'hijo de mujer pública'.

Parece que, al menos en las voces y acepciones que acabo de mencionar (y, naturalmente, podría añadir otras) está justificada la advertencia del DM sobre su escasa actualidad.

De este procedimiento oficioso, como antes dije, nada se advierte en ninguna parte. No lo considero criticable, sino digno de elogio, puesto que enmienda discretamente, aunque no sea sino de manera parcial, un defecto evidente del DC. Un pequeño inconveniente es, sin embargo, que las marcas aplicadas por el DM a determinadas voces y acepciones son las mismas que llevan 'de origen' otras voces que con ellas ya estaban en el DC. Entre estas últimas están *machío, maderación, malingrar, marañoso, marchantería* 'comercio de géneros', *manera* 'bragueta', *maniego* 'ambidextro', *medio* 'mellizo', *mediterráneo* 'del interior de un territorio', *meguez* 'caricia', *meritar* 'hacer méritos', *mesto* 'mezclado': todos ellos con la marca 'p. us.'. Añádanse los citados más arriba con la marca 'desus.' (*mecánica, mecánico, mandar, manjorrada*).

4 En los párrafos que anteceden he intentado trazar una somera caracterización del *Diccionario manual e ilustrado de la lengua española*, obra cuya primera edición publicó la Academia Española en 1927 y que hasta el momento ha sido objeto de tres más, la última en 1989. En sus seis decenios largos de vida ha conservado, en general, sus rasgos originales.

Aunque en el aspecto material esa fidelidad es harto discutible [§2], en el contenido se ha mantenido la línea primitiva por la que se daba un sesgo nuevo al corpus léxico del DC. Por una parte, se vuelve la espalda a todo lo que en este se presenta como histórico o antiguo. De ahí la supresión de las etimologías y la exclusión de las voces y acepciones que llevan la etiqueta de anticuadas o desusadas. Por otra parte, se conserva íntegramente todo el material que el DC da como vigente (esto es, sin las marcas de anticuado o desusado). Y por último, a este cuerpo fundamental se añade, con señalización especial, una serie de voces y acepciones que 'todavía' no tienen cabida en el DC. Con ello, abiertamente, el centro de gravedad del DM pasa a ser la lengua viva.

En esa línea de modernidad, no obstante, había en la primera edición un factor conservador: la actitud de censura ante los malos usos, incluyendo los extranjerismos. Tal actitud, manifestada a través del asterisco, ha sufrido un fuerte retroceso a partir de la edición tercera. El DM trasluce así ahora una mirada más objetiva que antes frente a los imprevisibles e incontenibles avances del léxico.

En cuanto a las adiciones propias que, marcadas con corchete, introduce el DM en el corpus que el DC da como vigente, se ha desarrollado notoriamente su proporción en las dos últimas ediciones con respecto a las dos primeras. En DM1, las adiciones eran 289 (un 15%) sobre una muestra de 1.946 entradas; en DM4 son 720 (un 31%) sobre una muestra de 2.319 entradas. Las adiciones que mayor incremento muestran en la última edición respecto a la primera son las de vocabulario general, que pasan de un 7% a un 33%; las de vocabulario técnico, de 2% a 16%, y las de vocabulario familiar, de 2% a 9%. En cambio, el vocabulario del español fuera de España (casi exclusivamente hispanoamericano) baja de un 84% a un 37%. A pesar del fuerte descenso, es aparentemente indiscutible la primacía del factor americano en las adiciones ofrecidas por DM4. Pero la importancia de su proporción se atempera aún más si recordamos que el contingente de este sector es en su mayor parte herencia de DM1 (y algo de DM2); y, en efecto, la aportación nueva se reduce en definitiva a un 9%: porcentaje que sitúa este grupo de adiciones en un nivel igual al del vocabulario familiar.

Para la correcta interpretación de todas las cifras relativas a las adiciones del DM no hay que perder de vista que no reflejan el crecimiento del caudal académico (el del DC), sino que corresponden al plus aportado por esta 'segunda voz' de la Academia. En él podemos ver las direcciones en que se produce un acercamiento más apurado a la realidad actual de la lengua, acercamiento que tal vez sea anticipado espejo de las tendencias del crecimiento futuro del DC.

El dato más destacable de la fisonomía del DM4 (presente ya en DM3) es el reforzamiento de la posición sincrónica señalada como ideal en la edición primera. Tal reforzamiento se realiza no solo ampliando las cuotas del

material léxico complementario, sino también ejecu-
tando una suerte de criba en la masa de usos que el DC da
por sobrentendido que están vigentes. El procedimiento
consiste, en general, en aplicar la etiqueta de 'poco usado'
a aquellas voces y acepciones que, contra lo que supone el
Diccionario grande, no han resistido incólumes el paso
del tiempo.

Son estos movimientos de moderada discrepancia los
que, a mi entender, constituyen el principal interés del
DM y lo hacen acreedor de una atención superior a la que
hasta ahora se le ha concedido por parte de los
estudiosos. Sin olvidar, claro está, su importantísimo y
no siempre bien calibrado papel de divulgación.

Manuel Seco
Real Academia Española

REFERENCIAS

Casado, M., 1989
'La "perestroika" académica', *Nuestro Tiempo* [Pamplona], 425, 34-37.

Casares, J., 1950
Introducción a la lexicografía moderna, Madrid

Cotarelo y Mori, E., 1928
Catálogo de las obras publicadas por la Real Academia Española, Madrid

DC = Real Academia Española, *Diccionario de la lengua española* [=Diccionario común]. (Cito varias ediciones. Cuando no indico fecha, normalmente me refiero a la 20ª, Madrid, 1984.)

DM = Real Academia Española, *Diccionario manual e ilustrado de la lengua española*, [1ª ed.], Madrid, 1927. 2ª ed., Madrid, 1950. 3ª ed. revisada [coordinador, Alonso Zamora Vicente; colaboradores, María Josefa Canellada, Guadalupe Galán, José María Martín], 6 vols., Madrid, 1983-85. 4ª ed. revisada [coordinador, Alonso Zamora Vicente; colaboradoras, María Josefa Canellada, Guadalupe Galán], Madrid, 1989.

DM1 = DM, 1ª ed.

DM2 = DM, 2ª ed.

DM3 = DM, 3ª ed.

DM4 = DM, 4ª ed.

Lorenzo, E., 1988
'Zahorí y notario del lenguaje' en *Homenaje a Alonso Zamora Vicente*, I, Madrid, 425-33.

Seco, M., 1988
'El problema de la diacronía en los diccionarios generales', *Revista de Dialectología y Tradiciones Populares*, 43, 559-67

Changing inflection:
verbs in North West Catalan

AMONG the various linguistic topics I was initiated into under Fred Hodcroft's assured guidance was that of Hispanic dialectology; so I am glad to be able to take up some of its intricacies in my contribution to this volume. Multiple dialect divergence from a common original of linguistic structure presents a challenge to explanatory theories of linguistic change. For Catalan, there is a formidable body of data on verbal inflection collected by Alcover between 1906 and 1928 from 149 localities in the Catalan-speaking domains [Alcover & Moll 1929-1933]. The social and cultural conditions of that time were such that informants were likely to have been relatively little influenced by notions of linguistic prestige or by knowledge of written (standard) forms. In earlier papers I have attempted to come to grips with portions of this data, putting forward a combination of psychological-functional and structuralist concepts to explain the considerable variety of inflectional patterns which had, by the early twentieth century, come to characterize Catalan, in place of the mainly uniform structure which scholars generally attribute to the medieval language [Wheeler 1980, 1985, 1986, and, especially, 1984].

Recent developments in the theory of inflectional morphology now provide, it seems to me, a better known and more highly elaborated framework in which to develop these kinds of account in relation to the data of a dialect area I have not previously dealt with. These approaches attempt to flesh out the notion of *naturalness* in morphology, and are proposed both by those who call themselves natural morphologists [Dressler 1985, 1987; Mayerthaler 1987; Wurzel 1984/1989, 1987; Kilani-Schoch

1988] and by those who do not so label themselves [Mańczak 1980; Andersen 1980; Bybee Hooper 1980, Bybee & Brewer 1980, Bybee 1985; Carstairs 1987]. These approaches also give a prominent role to the traditional concept of the inflectional *paradigm* (in contrast to most Generative and Lexicalist morphology where the paradigm has no theoretical status).

In these theories certain semantico-syntactic concepts are taken to be simpler, or more basic, or less marked, than those they contrast with. Thus, among categories relevant to verbal inflection, singular is unmarked relative to plural, present relative to other tenses, indicative relative to other moods, third person relative to other persons [Mańczak 1980:284-285; Bybee 1985:50-78; Mayerthaler 1987:40-48]. Unmarked categories are revealed in the higher text frequency of the forms which express them, in their earlier acquisition by children, and by their conceptual centrality in the context of communication, among other things. Forms expressing such concepts are likely to have a greater degree of *autonomy* [Bybee & Brewer 1980] and are more likely than marked categories to have zero expression [Bybee 1985:54]. A *natural* morphological system is one in which formal complexity reflects conceptual markedness, that is, which displays the property of diagrammaticity or constructional iconicity [Mayerthaler 1987:48]. Bybee [1985] demonstrates from a representative sample of 50 languages that what is morphologically natural (defined as above) is in fact typologically dominant. Humboldt's Universal—the preference for one form to express one meaning and for one meaning to be expressed by one form—(avoid synonymy, avoid ambiguity; see Wheeler 1980) is likewise a universal natural tendency, referred to by Mayerthaler [1987:49] as the uniformity/transparency principle.

It is clear, however, that not all attested inflectional systems are natural in the sense ('system-independent naturalness') so far discussed. Wurzel [1984/1989, 1987] has introduced the important concept of system-dependent naturalness, the operation of which, alongside the effects of phonological change—itself subject to its own naturalness principles—, can help to account for the survival and expansion of somewhat (system-independent) unnatural morphology in particular languages. The idea is that speakers of a language are sensitive to its predominant structural properties and will tend to behave so as to maintain them or to reinforce them. For example, 'it is evidently more "normal" for N[ew] H[igh] G[erman] that a monosyllabic masculine is inflected according to the *e*-plural class and not the *n*-plural class, and a monosyllabic feminine according to the *n*-plural class and not the *e*-plural class' [Wurzel 1987:62]. This system-dependent naturalness in morphology has two major aspects: system congruity and inflectional class stability. The individual morphological phenomena of a system display system congruity to the extent that they are in accord with the 'system-defining structural properties' (SDSPs) of the inflectional (sub-) system. When an inflectional system is not uniformly structured 'the quantitative relationship of competing structural features is decisive' [Wurzel 1987:64]; that is, the properties of the numerically dominant paradigms or forms are the SDSPs. 'Morphological changes take place in the frame of the respective SDSPs and are induced by them, but there are no morphological changes which cause the change of the SDSPs them-selves. SDSPs are resistant to morphological change' [Wurzel 1987:68]. That is, SDSPs tend to be stable over time; change in them results from extramorphological developments. Non-system-congruous forms and sub-paradigms may survive for centuries, however, if no allomorphs or reanalysable strings are available for new use. Some proposed SDSPs for NW Catalan verb inflection are listed below [page 180].

For Wurzel, inflectional classes are defined by 'implicative paradigm structure conditions', for example, if in Russian a noun ends in /a/, then it has /i/ in the genitive singular, /e/ in the dative singular, etc. 'Stable inflectional classes are classes whose paradigms follow the implicative pattern of a paradigm structure condition which exclusively applies to, or dominates, the words having the respective extramorphological [e.g. syntactic, semantic, phonological—MW] properties' [Wurzel 1987: 80]. Stable inflectional classes are unmarked—they are the ones (provided they are system-congruous) to which neologisms are assigned and to which, over time, words tend to be transferred from unstable complementary classes. Stable inflectional classes tend to become independently motivated, that is, to become based on extramorphological properties, such as the phonological shape of the base, semantic or syntactic properties, etc. The markers found within stable inflectional classes are 'stable markers', but unstable classes may also contain some stable markers: these will be *superstable* markers which are found in stable classes, and elsewhere (for example, /-ém/ and /-éw/ in modern Catalan) [Wurzel 1987:81-2]. Instability may be resolved by remotivation (phonological, semantic) of the inflectional class, or by transfer of lexical items from one class to another, that is, by a process of lexical diffusion which can be very slow. (Some Catalan examples are the replacement of *tòrcer* 'twist' from less stable class II, by *torçar* from stable class I; or the shift of items from IIIa to IIIb, in which Catalan dialects have participated to different extents.) One could suggest also that instability can be lessened by lexical innovation, by which lexical items from unstable classes are particularly subject to obsolescence; examples would be the replacement of *témer* 'fear' by *tenir por*, and of *rompre* 'break' by *trencar*.

Mayerthaler [1987:52] and Wurzel [1987:92] propose that various principles of system-independent and system-dependent morphological naturalness can be hierarchically ordered in terms of their effects, as follows:

I   *The principle of system congruity.* It favours inflectional systems which are structured typologically in a uniform and systematic way with respect to the main parameters of the respective system.

II *The principle of class stability.* It favours inflectional systems whose inflectional classes are independently motivated and whose paradigms follow implication patterns that are as general as possible.

III *The principle of uniformity and transparency.* It favours inflectional systems which are structured according to the formula 'one function–one form'.

IV *The principle of constructional iconicity.* It favours inflectional systems which encode unmarked categories as non-feature-bearing and marked categories as feature-bearing.

Among other things, we shall be looking to see to what extent the facts of Catalan are in conformity with this hierarchy.

Thirty-three of the 149 localities investigated by Alcover [points 63-94] fall within the boundaries of the NW Catalan dialect (as defined by Alcover & Moll and widely accepted; that is, places in Catalonia and Aragon which have IlI in /-o/ and lack vowel reduction of unstressed /o/ to [u]). Not surprisingly, some important structural isoglosses affecting verb morphology diverge from this diagnostic one, and in what follows certain extra localities have been considered, in particular 33, 38, 56, 59, 60 and 95-99, with some attention also to 18, 61 and 100 (see Map, p. 00).[1] The NW area displays an overall consistency which makes the defining of SDSPs a reasonable enterprise. Alcover recorded a significant amount of variation at many localities both among the attested forms for any individual verb, and among verbs of the same inflectional class. (Of class I regular verbs, unfortunately, only *cantar* 'sing' was investigated, though this can be supplemented to a degree by some regular forms of *anar* 'go' and *estar* 'stay, be'.) From other classes we have information on a dozen or so verbs.

Before turning to the paradigms, a reminder of the fundamental sound changes affecting Vulgar Latin unstressed final syllables may be helpful, in order to clarify which inflectional forms are (phonologically) regular, and which due to morphological restructuring.

1 Final -M is lost, as is general in Romance.
2 -O-, -E-, in final syllables are lost. If the subsequent consonant group cannot stand as a syllable rime, a support vowel /e/ appears, preceding any inflectional /-s/ or /-n/.
3 Final -T is lost.

[1] Merger of unstressed /a/ and /e/ as [ə] falls further East than the diagnostic heterogloss, leaving 33, 38, 56, 59 and (variably) 60 to the West. The Valencian points 95-99 have I1I in /-o/, in contrast to the /-e/ of the rest of Valencian. Outside the conventional NW dialect area points 95, 97, 99, 100, and variably 98, display the characteristic NW sound change -AT > /-e/, while within it, points 91, 94, and variably 92 have -AT > /-a/ in common with the rest of Catalan. VL stressed /e/ gives generally /ɛ/ at 87, as in Eastern Catalan. Subjunctives in /-i-/, characteristic of Eastern Catalan, are found at 91, and in competition with alternative formations at 73 and 84-86. The 'infix' of class IIIb is /-éʃ/ at 91, and variably at 66 and 73, as opposed to /-íʃ-/ which is characteristic of NW and Valencian Catalan as a whole.

4 -A- > /e/ before a consonant (i.e. there is merger of /a/ and /e/ in these contexts).[2]

5 In Eastern dialects unstressed /a/ and /e/ are merged as [ɛ].)

In most Catalan dialects changes (3) and (4) operated in the order given, with the result that Latin -AM and -AT fall together, as they do in Spanish. A characteristic, and morphologically highly significant, feature of N W Catalan is that change (4) preceded (3), so that -AT > /-e/, while -AM > /-a/.[3] The consequences of this will be examined below. The dialects of Ribagorça (points 70, 77) resemble Aragonese and Castilian in lacking change (4), a difference which has far-reaching consequences for their inflectional morphology. I shall be concerned in this paper with the inflectional developments of regular verbs (classes I, IIa, III); regular verbs do not have suppletive stems or (except in the case of some IIIa verbs) stem alternation.

[2] The data from persons 4 and 5 of PI, PS, show some interesting divergences from this general statement. Latin -A- (-BAMUS, -BATIS) and -E- (-SSEMUS, -SSETIS) give /-o-/ at 63-69, 71-75 (labialization before /m/, /w/, and neutralization with /o/); they give /a/ [ɛ] at 80, 82, 84-87, 89; the text-book result, namely /e/, is found at 76, 81, 83, 88, 90-99. At 70 and 77, as expected, there is no merger and etymological /a/ and /e/ are retained. At 78 and 79 an unexpected distinction between original -A- and -E- is observed, with the former giving /e/, and the latter /o/ (78) or /a/ [ɛ] (79).

[3] I previously raised [1984:413-414] the possibility of /-e/ in third person forms being analogical. Casanova [1989] takes note of this suggestion, but is inclined, I now think rightly, to reject it. An analogical change affecting, among other forms, the base-form (I3) of the verb paradigm of the stable class I is most unlikely from the point of view of Natural Morphology. I now interpret this characteristic of NW dialects as a matter of distinct historical ordering of sound changes.

The paradigms in Table 1 are the inflectional affixes expected as a result of the regular sound changes (1) to (4) which are typical of NW Catalan generally. They are arranged by T[ense] A[spect] M[ood] and P[erson] N[umber] categories, with subdivision for inflectional classes - technically the allomorphs of each of the TAM and PN combinations. Where stress is not marked it falls on the stem syllable preceding the affix.

table 1: original verb inflections

	1	2	3	4	5	6
I						
I	-	es	e	ám	áw	en
II	-	s	-	ém	éw	en
IIIa	-	s	-	ím	íw	en
IIIb	ísk	íʃes	íʃ	ím	íw	íʃen
S						
I	-	s	-	ém	éw	en
II/IIIa	a	es	e	ám	áw	en
IIIb	íska	ískes	íske	ám	áw	ísken
Im						
I		a		ém	áw	
IIa		-		ám	éw	
IIIa		-		ám	íw	
IIIb		íʃ		ám	íw	
PI						
I	áva	áves	áve	ávem	ávew	áven
II/III	ía	íes	íe	íem	íe w	íen[4]

[4] The forms of PI affixes in the table (which are also those of the standard language) give a misleading picture of the TAM allomorphy

[*table 1, cont.*]

PS

I	ás	áses	ás	ásem	ásew	ásen
I/II	és	éses	és	ésem	ésew	ésen
III	ís	íses	ís	ísem	ísew	ísen

F

I	aré	arás	ará	arém	aréw	arán
II	ré	rás	rá	rém	réw	rán
III	iré	irás	irá	irém	iréw	irán

C

I	aría	aríes	aríe	aríem	aríew	aríen
II	ría	ríes	ríe	ríem	ríew	ríen
III	iría	iríes	iríe	iríem	iríew	iríen

PS'r'

I	ára	áres	áre	árem	árew	áren
II	éra	éres	ére	érem	érew	éren
III	íra	íres	íre	írem	írew	íren

The nature of System-Defining Structural Properties can now be illustrated with the example of the NW Catalan verb system. (The sub-headings are based on those of Wurzel [1987].)

---

current in the NW area. Four sub-dialects can be distinguished: (*a*) the far NW—points 65a, 68-71, 77—with I /-av-/, II /-ev-/, III /-iv-/, as in Gascon and High Aragonese; (*b*) the North East with I /-av-/, II/III /-iv-/—categorical at 63-65, 67, 72, 74-76, 78, and in variation with II/III /-i-/ at 81 (91% /-iv-/), 73 (69% /-iv-/), 80 (56% /-iv-/), 79 (45% /-iv-/) and 82 (33% /-iv-/; (*c*) a central region—79, 80, 82-86, 88-89 —with I /-aj-/, varying with /-av-/ except at 83, II /-ej-/ (86, 89) or /-i-/ and III /-i-/; (*d*) a Southern region—90, 92-93, 95, 97-99—with /v/ → ∅ /___/e/. In *a*, *b*, and *c* we observe a strong tendency to adopt a common -VC- pattern throughout the classes (interpreting /-í-/ as equivalent to /-íj-/).

System Defining Structural Properties of Catalan verbs

a *Categorial systems and categories assigned to them*

Finite:
> *Tense* (T): Present, Future, Past, Conditional
> (*Aspect* (A): Perfective, Imperfective)
>> Perfective, within Past, is expressed by means of a periphrastic 'semi-compound' [DeCesaris 1988].
> *Mood* (M): Indicative, Subjunctive, Imperative
> *Person* (*of Subject*) (P): 1, 2, 3 (Semantic 2 'polite' = Grammatical 3)
> *Number* (*of Subject*) (N): Singular, Plural

Non-finite:
> *Infinitive*
> *Gerund*
> *Participle*: Gender, Number

b *Base-form inflection versus stem-inflection*

Base-inflection (i.e. base = stem) is found in conjugation classes II and IIIa: base = Im2 = I3.
Stem-inflection is found in conjugation classes I (base = stem + V) and IIIb (base = stem + Vsk). Stem-inflection is dominant.

c *Separate versus combined (cumulative/overlapping) symbolization (exponence) of categories*

Tense/Aspect/Mood: cumulative/overlapping
Person/Number: cumulative
> Persons 1,3 are cumulative/overlapping with Tense/Aspect/Mood; Person 2 is cumulative with Imperative Mood. Where PN morphs consist of

-VC, -V- overlaps with TAM. In some verbs in some dialects stem alternation (involving the stem vowel and/or the final consonant) is indexical of PN categories.

Dominant   SDSP: TAM (cumulative/overlapping) distinct from PN.

d *Number and distribution of formal distinctions in the paradigm: presence of syncretism.*

Generally Im45 are identical in form with some other category; traditionally Im4 = S4, Im5 = I5, innovatively Im45 = I45 or S45. There are three patterns of person-syncretism 1 - 3: where -AT > /-a/ we find S1 = 3, Im2 = I3, PI1 = 3, C1 = 3, PS1 = 3; I1 distinct from 3, F1 distinct from 3. This is typical of Eastern Catalan and Valencian; among the points investigated here it is found at 18, 60 (variably), 61, 70, 77, 94 and 96. The typical NW Catalan system (where -AT > /-e/) has 1 distinct from 3 in all TAM categories. It is attested at 33, 38, 63-69, 71-76, 78-90, 92, 93, 95, 97. A mixed system, which is basically the Eastern system, but with Im2I distinct from I3I, is found at 56, 59, 60 (variably), 91 and 98-100. Other syncretisms are not system-congruous: S6 = I6 (archaic system); S23I = I23I (NW primary innovation); S45I/IIa/III = I45 (secondary innovation).

e *Types of markers that occur and their relations to the categorial complexes concerned*

Suffixes (on cumulation/overlapping, see above):
Present: In the traditional system Mood exponence was largely by means of 'relative' markers (Andersen 1980:30; and see below), though /-í-/ was

uniquely indicative. I/Im1236: -ø(C_{PN}), -V(C_{PN}) (V is mid or low) — in IIIa: -ís(k)/íʃ(o), -íʃ ; I/Im45: -VC_{PN}. Subjunctive is marked by -V(C_{PN}) where -V- is distinct from indicative, or by -gV(C_{PN}). In the Present system -VC_{PN} is the dominant marker type; the others are system-incongruous to various degrees.

Future: -(V)rV(C_{PN}); the stressed vowel /é/ or /á/ is an index of PN.

Conditional: -(V)rVV(C_{PN}); the unstressed vowel /e/ or /a/ is an index of PN; or -(V)rVV/C_{PN} for the *cantaria, canataris* type characteristic of the northern part of the NW region—33, 63-67, 69, 72-76, 78.

Otherwise: -V(C)(V(C_{PN})), where the stressed -V- = /á/, /é/ or /í/, the unstressed -V- = /e/ or /a/, an index of PN; PS may have the form -(V)gés(V(C_{PN})

PN 1: -V (or -g, in I1 IIb/IIIb), 2: -(V)s (except Im: -(V)), 3: -(V), 4: -Vm, 5: -Vw, 6: -Vn.

f *Presence versus absence of inflectional classes: if present, paradigm-structure conditions [Wurzel 1984/89: 119] which define the inflectional classes*

For regular verbs I3 /-e/ → I, I3 /-iʃ/ → IIIb; I3 /-Ø/ & I4 /-ém/ → II; I3 /-Ø/ & S4 /-gém/ → IIb; I3 /-Ø/ & I4 /-ím/ → IIIa, where I, II, etc. stand for sets of further implicational relations. Though I3 probably does serve as the base form, the other cues are not exclusive; infinitives, gerunds could also be used.

Class I is the dominant stable class: it acquires neologisms and its forms spread to other classes. Within class III, IIIb is stable relative to IIIa. For many Western dialects IIb is stable relative to IIa, probably because its subjunctive is more unique/

transparent and its verbs are among those of highest frequency.

With respect to these sub-types *a–f* of system-defining structural properties, I should like to suggest that issues relating purely to formal structure, such as *b*, or *e* in part, or purely to semantic organization *a* are secondary, that is, less important in conditioning morphological change than issues relating to exponence—the relation of meaning and form—, namely *c* and especially *d* (+ *e* in part, possibly), which are primary. Types *a-e* relate to system congruity, type *f* to inflectional class stability. From the point of view of *b*, stem-inflection is dominant, that is, an SDSP of Catalan. However, there is no tendency to replace base-inflection (I2II/IIIa /-s/, I3/Im2II/IIIa /-ø/) provided the primary SDSPs of *d* are maintained.

On the whole, the system in Table 1 displays a fairly high degree of morphological naturalness. Most category combinations are adequately distinguished and the differences in marker types (in syllable structure, stress pattern, etc.) correlate with extramorphological (morpho-syntactic) categories. There are certain elements in this inflectional system which are not system-congruous; aspects *d* and *e* of SDSPs are particularly involved.

The syncretisms I1II/IIIa = I3II/IIIa (-ø), S1I = S3I (-ø), and PS1 = PS3 (-ás/és/ís) are not congruous with the SDSP of NW Catalan that 1 is distinct from 3. It is with this in mind that it becomes easy to account for the adoption of, e.g., /-o/ in I1II,IIIa—on the origin of this element see, most recently, Casanova [1989]; it is to be expected that S1I should also acquire some vocalic ending, such as /-e/ where the model is verbs in -CC stems such as *llaure* 'I plough' or /-a/ from S1II/IIIa. The reasons for the choice between these are explained below where the solution is related to other changes in the Present system. An addition to person 1 forms is the minimum change which would restore system congruity; retaining zero in 3 as opposed to 1 is in accord with the constructional iconicity aspect of system-independent naturalness. Likewise, the adoption in PS1 of an ending /-a/, available in S1II/III or in 1 of Past paradigms generally, was a straightforward solution to the system incongruity of the inherited forms. So we arrive at these widespread modifications of Table 1 paradigms, with the innovations italicized:

		1
I	I	-
	II/IIIa	*o*
S	I	*a* (or *e*)
PS		V*sa*

The syncretisms S1I = I1I (-ø) and S6I/II/IIIa = I6I/II/IIIa (-en) are not congruous with the SDSP that subjunctive is distinct from indicative. The first of these would have been immediately cured by the resolution of S1 = S3 syncretism previously mentioned; i.e. S1I /-a/ versus I1I /-ø/. S6 = I6 was not so easily dealt with, in the absence of plausible alternative allomorphs in either function; the extension of stable subclass IIIb at the expense of IIIa was the one possible development which could overcome this incongruity. (The absence of available morphological material doubtless helps to explain why syncretism of Im45 with some other category has been retained almost universally; with noteworthy exceptions at 92 (II /-ám/, SI /-ásem/, ImI /-ém/) and 93 with similar options but II variably /-ém/.)

Within the Present system the category of Mood was originally expressed by means of relative markers

[Andersen 1980:30]: in the pairs of affixes 2 <-es, -∅s>, 3 <-e, -∅>, 4 <-ám, -ém>, 5 <-áw, -éw> each marker is ambiguous. For example /-es/ denotes indicative only by contrast with /-∅s/ attached to the same lexeme (e.g. *cantar*); attached to, e.g., *batre* 'strike' the same markers have the opposite meaning. Though the relative marker type was not dominant within the verb paradigm as a whole, it could be argued that it was dominant in the less marked, Present, system, and hence system congruous and stable, as of course the corresponding markers are in Spanish. However, it was already the case that the elements which comprised the relative Mood marker system displayed a notable lack of transparency: the set <∅, ∅, é, e> (I1, 2-3, 4-5, 6 in II; S1, 2-3, 4-5, 6 in I) contrasts with the sets <a, e, á, e> (SII) and <∅, e, á, e> (II)— defective uniqueness too in the ambiguity of the last element (-e-) in 6, as mentioned above, and of the first element (-∅-) in class I. This marker system is surely particularly confusing for a learner, and even if not sufficiently unnatural in itself to trigger reform, was ripe for replacement as soon as it came to be undermined even further by changes to class I, shortly to be mentioned.

Other original forms of class I do not appear to violate any SDSP, e.g. I1 *cant* 'sing' is distinct from I3 *cante* 'he/she sings', S2 *cants* is distinct from I2 *cantes*; S3 *cant* is distinct from I3 *cante* (and distinct from S1 *canta* or *cante* after the reform mentioned above). As system-congruous forms they should, according to Wurzel's theory, be resistant to change (or, if the only system-incongruity was the use of non-syllabic markers, then this should be equally resolved in SI and III/IIIa). In fact these forms are all obsolete (as are the parallel forms in all continental dialects—the zero subjunctives survived on the islands until Alcover's investigation, by which time they were obsolescent there too). However, these forms are notably unnatural in the system-independent sense, since they are in conflict with constructional iconicity. The forms are not just *non*-iconic (as is the case, for example, with 1 /-a/ versus 3 /-e/ where the greater markedness of 1 as compared with 3 is not symbolized). These forms are *counter*-iconic. The marked categories (1, S) are expressed by zero, in contrast to the unmarked categories (3, I) which are expressed by /-V/. In fact these counter-iconic forms of I1I and S123I were among the earliest to have been replaced in mainland dialects, probably by the sixteenth century [Casanova 1989]. When I1I is replaced by /-o/, then /-∅/ in S1I (if surviving) would itself have become counter-iconic. The resulting forms are (again with innovations italicized) as follows:

		1	2	3
I	I	*o*	es	e
I	II/IIIa	o	s	-
S	I/II/IIIa	a	*es*	*e*

The counter-iconic zeros in S23I seem originally to have been replaced universally in NW Catalan with /-es/, /-e/, as mentioned above; the source of these forms is equally S23II/IIIa and those -CC verbs of class I like *llaures*, *llaure* 'plough'. In the light of the general viewpoint of Natural Morphology these changes do not look odd or unexpected. What is at fault is Wurzel's hierarchy which incorporates constructional iconicity only at one point—it is illustrated with the example of OHG plural formation in monosyllabic stems, where zero plural marking was extended even though non-iconic. But *counter*-iconicity is intuitively much more unnatural than just non-iconicity. The Catalan example suggests that counter-iconicity should go to the top of the strength hierarchy. (The much longer survival of counter-iconic present subjunctive and first-person present indicative formation in Balearic remains a problem, of course.)

We can now attempt to account for the replacement of /-∅/ in S1I, previously mentioned, in the following way: two forms were potentially available: /-a/ (from S1II/III), or /-e/ from S1I in -CC stems. Both these innovations are attested. Where the sound change -AT > /-a/ operated, the SDSP 1 = 3 becomes dominant (Eastern/ Valencian syncretism system), and /-e/ would be favoured in S1I. This would be expected at 70, 77, 94, 96 and is indeed found there; at 91 the typical Eastern subjunctive system in /-i-/ obtains (in which also S1 = S3). Where the sound change -AT > /-e/ operated, the SDSP '1 distinct from 3' was strongly dominant (general NW system), so S1I /-e/ (= S3I), even if favoured at one stage, would be less acceptable after the adoption of /-es/, /-e/, in S23I, and the choice would come down to /-a/. This is generally what is found. At 98, 99, 100, despite apparent -AT > /-e/, the principle 1 = 3 has evidently become dominant (perhaps borrowed from general Valencian) and S1I is in /-e/ (99, 100). Localities 33, 38, share the SDSP '1 distinct from 3' with most of NW Catalan, but have adopted the prestigious /-i-/ subjunctive from the East, though there are remnants of S1 /-a/ (distinct from S3) at 38, as indeed there are also at 84, 85 where subjunctive /-i-/ is also used. That is, the combination of the SDSP '1 distinct from 3' with the prestige pressure towards /-i-/ subjunctive results in a mixed paradigm. A third innovation is also found where S = I is acceptable: /-o/ (98: S1 = I1 = S3I). The form /-o/ is also found at 95, 97 (S1 = I1 distinct from S3I).

It is likely that the morphological resolution of the major system-independent unnaturalness and system incongruity of S123I was achieved many centuries ago in NW Catalan by the universal adoption of the forms of S123II/IIIa. However, the negative consequences of this change were themselves not by any means wholly resolved by the early decades of this century—nor indeed have they been today. The first consequence seems to have been that the change to S123I fatally undermined the already precarious system of relative markers for Mood in the Present of classes I, II and IIIa. The pattern now looked like this:

```
                1    2    3    4    5    6
   I   I            es   e    ám   áw
       II    } o { }s    -  { ém   éw }
       III   )   ( )        { ím   íw  }
                                        } en
   S   I            {      ém   éw  }
       II/III } a   es   e { ám   áw  /

   Im  I              a         ém   áw
       II       } -         ám { éw
       III      )             { íw
```

Leaving aside the cross-person syncretisms (S1 = Im2I, I3 = Im2II/III) which are unlikely to have been problematic, we note that /-s/, /-∅/, are now unambiguous indices of indicative (and have tended to survive though they are not dominant and are incongruous with the SDSP *b* of stem-inflection or the SDSP *e* of syllabic marker types); /-o-/ is unambiguous, acceptable by the SDSP *e* of marker type but less so by reason of cumulation of TAM with PN *c*; the affix /-en/ is ambiguous but not relative; all the markers /-es/, /-e/, /-ám/, /-ém/, /-áw/, /-éw/ are ambiguous and relative only in a very complex way; (/-ím/

alone is unambiguous and entirely system-congruous). The selection of /-á-/ or /-é-/ in persons 4 and 5 of the three mood categories is particularly opaque. It is reasonable to propose that, as a result of the change to S123I previously discussed, the relative marker type ceased to be inducible from the data and evidently ceased to be system-congruous. Subsequent changes have sought to replace the anomalous forms, even though this itself has continued to produce further system-disorienting consequences. It seems that at an early stage /-ám/ and /-áw/ were eliminated from forms of classes II and III, where the vowel /á/ was itself anomalous, in favour of the corresponding indicative forms: /-ém/, /-éw/ in II, /-ím/, /-íw/ in III; (though see below on /-(i)gém/, /-(i)géw/). (Where the relative marker type is better preserved, as at points 70 and 77 which lack the sound change -A- > /e/, /-ám/ and /-áw/ survive in II and III.) The preexisting syncretisms between Im and S (4) and between Im and I (5) form the Trojan horse (for further details see Wheeler 1984, 1985; remember also that negative Imperative = Subjunctive). For /-ám/, /-áw/, in the subjunctive of class II there was also the pressure of the now established subjunctive paradigm of the dominant class I which was already identical to that of II in four persons out of six (*-a, -es, -e, -ém, -éw, -en*) and displayed a coherent use of the vowel /e/.

The gradual replacement of the forms /-ám/, /-áw/, in I451 is attested by variation at individual localities and differences in geographical distribution in Alcover's data. Information collected subsequently confirms that /-ém/, /-éw/, have become categorical in nearly all of the area [Gimeno Betí 1986; Martí 1970; Coromines 1936/1976; DeCesaris 1988]. The attested geographical distribution and presence of variations can at this point be suggestive of the historical process by which one morphological pattern comes to be replaced by another; that is, we can use socio-geographical variation as an indicator of morphological change in progress, in a sub-Labovian way, though we lack information on the social status of the users of the variants, or of social attitudes towards the variants. The original functional distribution, as in Table 1, of the forms /-ám/, /-ém/, /-áw/, /-éw/ in *cantar* was attested by Alcover at 68 and 70—the latter, of course, outside the area of merger of /a/ and /e/. On the principle that the Imperative is the weak point at which /-é-/ may attack, the next logical stage is variation /-áw/ ~ /-éw/ in Im5I. This variation alone is not attested, but the nearest thing to it is at 90, with /-ám/ ~ /-ém/ in Im4I as well as /-áw/ ~ /-éw/ in Im5I. After that we could expect two possible developments: *a* categorical /-éw/ in Im5I alone, or *b* variation /-áw/ ~ /-éw/ in Im5I plus variation /-ám/ ~ /-ém/, /-áw/ ~ /-éw/ in I45I. (Categorical Im4 /-ám/, Im5 /-áw/, at 63-64 is against the general NW trend.) Pattern *a* was attested at 65, 73, 80, 89 and 92; pat-tern *b* at 69, 71, 74, 77 (where despite lack of /a/ - /e/ merger, the subjunctive in /e/ has made considerable headway in class II), 83, 94 (which also has variation /-ám/ ~ /-ém/ in Im4I) and 75 which has variation /-ám/ ~ /-ém/, /-áw/ ~ /-éw/ in class I for all three Mood categories. A subsequent stage: categorical /-éw/ in Im5I with variation /-ám/ ~ /-ém/, /-áw/ ~ /-éw/ in I4,5I was attested at 67, 72, 76, 82, 86 and 93. The last stage: categorical use of 4 /-ém/, 5 /-éw/, in all three categories in class I was attested at the E Catalan points, at the Valencian points (95-100) and at 78, 81, 85, 88, 91. As a result of the progressive substitution of relative markers of Mood in the Present system (replacement of /-ø-/ by /-e-/ in the subjunctive and of /-á-/ by /-é-/ wherever it occurred) by stable or superstable markers, the Present systems of classes I and

IIa come to differ only in the forms of I23, where class I has /-es/, /-e/, and IIa has /-s/, /-∅/. Likewise, within these two inflectional classes, except in person 1, it is only in 23II that subjunctive is distinct from indicative. In such a system, syncretism S = I in the Present and syllabic inflectional endings are properties which have become system-congruous through numerical dominance. Pressure to replace /-s/, /-∅/, in I23II/IIIa can be expected. The form /-es/ in I2 is an especially stable marker since it is already found not only in class I but already (morphophonologically justified) in classes II and III after stems ending in sibilants, e.g. II *coneixes* 'you know', *vences* 'you defeat', IIIa *cuses* 'you sew', IIIb *partixes* 'you divide'. Cases of 2II /-es/ were attested at 33, 63, 64, 66, 67, 69, 74, 85, 91, 94, and cases of both 2II /-es/ and 3II /-e/ at 65a, 68, 71, 83, 86 and 87, being particularly numerous at 65a and 68. There is no particularly strong correlation with the presence of /-ém/, /-éw/ in class I.

The second negative consequence of the early spread of /-a/, /-es/, /-e/, as subjunctive inflections in the singular of class I is the extension of syncretism S = I (now in 236I). Though S = I syncretism was already present in person 6, it was not system congruous; subjunctive was distinct from indicative in the Present of other inflectional classes, and throughout the Past system, where subjunctive had a consistent marker /-s-/. (When /-á-/ was replaced by /-é-/ (II) or /-í-/ (III) the syncretism S = I spread to persons 45 (IIa, III). Where /-á-/ was replaced by /-é-/ in class I we have S45 = I45 in class I also.) The syncretism pattern S236I = I236I is attested at 63-69, 71-74, 76, 78, 81, 86, 88-90, 94-97, 99-100, there being variation with some innovative form at 66, 71, 73, 86, 89 and 95. It seems to be possible for speakers to perceive S=I236 as a congruent structural property. Thus they may extend the pattern to persons 2 and 6 at least in the next most stable inflectional class after I, namely IIIb, by levelling the /ʃ/ ~ /sk/ alternation characteristic of that class so as to give /-íʃes/ S = I2 IIIb, /-íʃen/ S = I6 IIIb. This pattern is found at 66, 73, 78, 85, 86, 89, 90, though it is only at 90 that the pattern is categorical for both inflectional classes.

There have been significant moves, however, to try to restore the congruous 'S distinct from I', by means of the /-o-/ subjunctive which is a speciality of NW Catalan (S2 /-os/, S3 /-o/, S6 /-on/) or the /-i-/ subjunctive (S13 /-i/, S2 /-is/, S3 /-in/) which is characteristic of E Catalan and Balearic, and of the standard language. Gulsoy [1976] gives the most plausible account of the etymology of the /-o-/ (and the /-i-/) subjunctives. Unstressed final-syllable /-o-/ would originally have been a phono-logically conditioned variant of /-e-/ after stems with rounded vowels, that is, it would have been due to vowel harmony, a phenomenon which is only sporadically attested in contemporary Catalan. In verbs, however, this /-o-/ element has been thoroughly morphologized. (It is word-final /a/ which is more likely to become [o] phonetically nowadays: in our area, at 69, 74 and 81, resulting in syncretism S = I in 1I/IIa/IIIa; these localities do not use the /-o-/ subjunctive, which would result for them in non-congruent 1 = 3.) There is an interesting issue concerning the geographical distribution within NW Catalan of the /-o-/ subjunctive, to which is related its distribution within the inflectional classes. Allières [1970] pointed out a geographical correlation between the presence of /-o-/ subjunctives and the front articulation of word-final /a/ as [ɛ] or sometimes [e]. This correlation is not quite as strong as Allières implies, and his explanation of why it should exist can be improved on. Table 2 sets out the association and includes information on places where either of the two phenomena is variable.

table 2

Localities where the fronting of /-a/ or subjunctive in /-o-/ is attested

	/-a#/ not [ε] ~ [e]	/-a#/ variably [ε] ~ [e]	/-a#/ categorically [ε] ~ [e]
no /-o-/ *subj*	33, 38, 56, 59, 60, 63-65a, 67-72, 74, 77, 81, 90, 94, 97	76, 78, 88, 91, 96, ?99, 100	
variable /-o-/ *subj*	66, 73, 95 (I only)		85, 86, 89, 92
categorical /-o-/ *subj*	87, 93 (I only) 98 (I only)	75, 80	79, 82, 83

The data in Table 2 suggest some connection of the kind Allières mentions, particularly if we exclude from consideration those points (93, 95, 98) where the /-o-/ subjunctive is attested in class I only. Here the /-o-/ subjunctive can be seen exclusively as a solution to the problem of S = I syncretism in I. Where /-a/ → [ε] the distinction between /a/ [ε] and /e/ [e] is not great; in fact at 82 word final /a/ and /e/ have indeed merged completely as /e/ and at various other points [e] is occasionally transcribed by Alcover where [ε] ← /a/ might be expected. The danger is that the SDSP '1 distinct from 3', maintained by 1 /-a/ versus 3 /-e/ might be obliterated. The adoption of /-o-/ forms avoids this in the Present subjunctive at least; it also resolves the system-incongruity of S6 = I6. This would account for the general use of /-o-/ subjunctives across the three inflectional classes, as opposed to its use (original?) only in I where it contrasts S236 with I236. The attestations at 66, 73, would reflect geo-lectal spread from 75 (Organyà) up the valley of the Segre and Valira rivers to Andorra, and that at 87 from nearby 85 and Les Borges Blanques [Arqués i Arrufat 1910/1983]. Of the places where /-o-/ might be expected but is not found, 91 has (along with other Eastern features) the subjunctive in /-i-/; 96, 99 and 100 are within the Valencian area, where 1 = 3 is the norm outside the Present indicative and where 1 /-e/, 2 /-es/, 3 /-e/, 6 /-en/, is the pattern for subjunctives in classes I, IIa, and III. Points 76, 78 and 88 are at the NW (conservative) edge of the area affected by /-a#/ → [ε].

Where /-á-/ has been replaced, by /-é-/ in class II, by /-í-/ in class III, in persons 4 and 5 of the Present subjunctive, S45 = I45 syncretism results. This is indeed a persistent structural property of the regular verbs in E Catalan (and of the standard language). In the NW area it is categorically found at 84, 85, 87 and 91, that is, at localities which share other phonological and morphological isoglosses with E Catalan. Elsewhere, there are two devices which are exploited to reestablish contrast 'S distinct from I' in persons 4 and 5.

The first involves taking over into the Present system forms of the Past subjunctive /-ásem/, /-ésem/, /-ísem/, /-ásew/, /-ésew/, /-ísew/, or, with /-g-/ in addition, /-(i)gésem/, /-(i)gésew/. This phenomenon, attested here at 90, 92-94, 98, is an idiosyncratic feature of the area of South Catalonia and North Valencia. It results, of course, in tense syncretism (PS = S), except at 93 where the -r-type of Past subjunctive typical of Valencian is now used. (At 98 the -r- type appears alongside the -s- type.) These dialects, then, when faced with a choice between Mood syncretism and Tense syncretism have opted for the latter, although it is not system-congruous; in general, Present, Past and Future are kept rigidly apart. The innovation does have the virtue of being as well applicable to class I as it is to the other classes. However it remains rather surprising and is in need of further investigation.

The second device available for re-establishing contrast between subjunctive and indicative does have the defect of not being readily available for—of having no model in—class I. It consists of the element containing a velar obstruent, which is normally found in Catalan in class IIb (I1, S1-6, PS1-6, and regular Participle). It appears variously as /-eg-/, /-ig-/, /-g-/ and /-k-/, the conditions for each being partly phonological, partly lexical, and partly dialectal. I shall not consider further here the conditions for the variants, nor the issue of their source [see Wheeler 1984:414-416], but will refer generally to the velar extensions as /-g-/. In analyses within the tradition of generative grammar [most recently DeCesaris 1988] this element has been treated as an 'empty morph'. This viewpoint, however, makes it hard to explain why such an element should spread in morphological change, as it has to a considerable degree in all Catalan dialects. It now seems to me that an analysis which involves 'empty morphs' is not psychologically plausible, and the school of Natural Morphology seems, implicitly, to forbid such a segmentation. The /-g-/ in question occurs between stems and suffixes. One question, therefore, is: does it belong with the former or the latter? Are we dealing with stem allomorphy or suffix allomorphy? The Catalan evidence strongly suggests the latter. If /-g-/ were psychologically part of the stem, in e.g. /dig-/ ~ /diw-/ ~ /di-/ 'say', as the etymology suggests, then we might expect to see levelling through the verb on the basis of this stem /dig-/ (which corresponds to the canonical CVC pattern for verb stems) without particular regard to the form or content of the following suffix, for example, into I2 /*digs/, PI /*digia/, Inf /*digre/, F /*digré/, etc.

We should not expect /-g-/ to remain strongly associated with particular inflectional categories, nor could we account for the spread of stem-alternation, such as /di-/ ~ /dig-/ to other verbs. The all-but-unique case of the spread of /-g-/ to the PI of *córrer* 'run' giving *corregueva*, etc., as a variant of *correva*, at 68, confirms the point. Rather, /-g-/ in Catalan is associated with, or is an index of, specific morpho-syntactic categories or category bundles: I1, S, PS, Past Perfective (synthetic), Participle, and non-standard Gerund. It is also strongly associated with a particular inflectional vowel /-é-/, such that /-g-/ can ride on the back of /-é-/; that is, /-gé-/ and /-é-/ are seen as valid alternatives. This association may partly explain too the extension of /-g-/ to the Gerund of II to give /-gént/, and the rather rare cases of /-gém/, /-géw/, as 45 Indicative forms. I suggest that /-g-/ in Catalan has come within verbs to be an index, indeed, a superstable marker within classes II and III, of *derived* (non-basic, secondary) categories, such as 1 versus 3, S versus I, PS versus PI, Past Perfective versus PI (if Imperfective is less marked in Catalan), and Participle and Gerund versus Infinitive within the non-finite categories.

If the Catalan development is at all typical of morpho-logical change, we might propose as a general principle of system-independent morphological naturalness the 'Empty Morph Attachment Principle' (EMAP):

EMAP: Where $X_{Stem} + Y + Z_{Affix}$ alternates with $X_{Stem} + Z_{Affix}$, Y is much more likely to be taken to be an index of Z than of X, that is, YZ will be developed, if at all, as an allomorph of Z, rather than XY as an allomorph of X.

This principle is reflected in the well-known cases of reanalysis of Maori passives or French adjectival gender, and corresponds to the general unnaturalness of subtractive processes. I suggest that it is the principle which often gives rise to the presence of inflectional classes within a language (and which indirectly may explain Carstairs' [1987] Paradigm Economy Principle). Verb conjugation classes would have come to exist in (proto-) Latin when Xa:, Ye:, Zi: ceased to be invariant throughout verb paradigms, as a result of phonological changes which, among other effects, conflated long vowels with following affixes.

The source for the spread of /-g-/ as mentioned above is most obviously class IIb, where it is generally found in S and PS (and I1 and Participle); /-g-/ had already spread very commonly to the S of *saber* 'know', *cabre* 'fit', and *córrer* 'run'. One might have expected spread, if attested, to be even across the S and PS categories and to be more firmly established in IIa, the closest associate of IIb, than in IIIa (or those forms of IIIb where the -SK- element is absent). The data from Alcover [1929-1933] show that this is not always so, and that further explanation is required. We may first distinguish six contexts in the finite paradigms in which /-g-/ may be found to different degrees:

A: S1236II
B: S45II
C: S1236III
D: S45III
E: PSII
F: PSIII

Alcover's data provide no evidence for differences *within* each of these six groups (except for lexical conditioning, that is). Why should S1236 and S45 be treated separately? The reason is partly phonological: /-g-/ precedes stress in 45, and follows it in 1236 in the Present

system, while from the morphological point of view S = I
(= Im) syncretisms in 45 tend to be of a different kind
from those in 1236, where unstressed vowel variation
can be exploited. In 45 /-g-/ is the only device available
(after the banishment of /-á-/) to mark subjunctive. We
can pool the attested variation and lexical differences
within each of the six sets to give a percentage of /-g-/
usage, and then group the percentages on a scale from 0
to 4 points to make comparison easier (and to emphasize
categorical presence: 4, or absence: 0): 0 = 0%, 1 = 1-33%, 2
= 34-66%, 3 = 67-99%, 4 = 100%. On this basis most localities have either the same score for A and B, and the same
scores for C and D, or a difference of at least 1 point in
favour of B and D (the S45 sets) as at 18, 33, 59, 61, 65a, 66,
71-73, 75, 78-83, 89, 90 (two or more points difference at D
versus B 78-80, 82-83). The mean scores are: A 1.85, B 1.72,
C 1.98, D 2.33. Some occasional differences of no more
than one point in the other direction are probably not
significant (64, 65, 67, 74, 88, 95). But at 93, 94, 96, 97 and 99
there is a difference of at least two points in one or both
classes in favour of S1236; that is, there is a dialect
tendency, not very far advanced, to associate /-g-/ with S
only in 236 and to allow S = I syncretism in 45. The /-g-/
element is somewhat more widespread in class III (mean
score C + D + F: 2.28) than in class II (mean score A + B +
E: 1.75), with two or more points difference at 65a-67, 69,
73, 75, 78-83, 94, though again in the southernmost
region (92, 93, 95, 97-99) there is a slight tendency in the
opposite direction, favouring class II.

　　Perhaps the predominant favouring of /-g-/ in S45III
goes back to the period when /-ám/, /-áw/, were being
replaced. Whereas the primary replacements used in II
(/-ém/, /-éw/) were already subjunctive markers (in class
I), that is, were allomorphs (stable markers) extending
their lexical range from the stable class I, the class III

form /-ím/ was originally exclusively and unambiguously indicative, and /-íw/ only indicative and imperative. The alternative /-gém/, /-géw/, being already subjunctive forms, could have been preferred. The even stronger predominance of /-g-/ in PSIII (mean score for F: 2.52) as opposed to PSII (mean score for E: 1.67) is even harder to account for, since /-ís-/ would appear coherent and well-integrated. I suspect that in fact the alternative between /-í-/ and /-igé-/ in class III dates back into the mists of time when 'strong' preterits in /-g-/ were being replaced by 'weak preterits' in /-gé-/ so that when Pret3 *volc* 'wanted' was replaced by *volgué*, a form like Pret3 *partic* 'divided' became *partigué*. This form subsequently provided a base for PS *partigués*, PS'r' *partiguera*, and in due course S4 *partiguem* etc. Here as elsewhere historical grammars of Catalan have concentrated on the standard language and give little help in the history of non-standard usage.

Conclusions

1 Principles of Natural Morphology are helpful in the explanation of morphological change. Morphological change in NW Catalan can be seen to result from pressures to restore system congruity, inflectional class stability, and system-independent naturalness.

2 Flagrant violations of system-independent naturalness, in particular counter-iconicity, may provoke morphological change even in sub-systems which are system-congruous.

3 The Empty Morph Attachment Principle is a candidate for incorporation within system-independent naturalness.

4 There should probably be a strength hierarchy within the SDSPs defining system congruity, distinguishing primary SDSPs which are concerned with exponence from secondary SDSPs which are concerned with content or form separately.

5 The pattern of synchronic variation and geographical distribution can assist in the recovery of sequence within historical change.

6 In NW Catalan /-g-/ is becoming a stable marker (within 'non-stable' classes II and III) of derived categories.

Max Wheeler
University of Sussex

ABBREVIATIONS

I	Present Indicative
S	Present Subjunctive
Im	Imperative
F	Future
C	Conditional
PI	Past Imperfective Indicative
PS	Past Subjunctive
1-6	1st, 2nd, 3rd person singular, 1st, 2nd, 3rd person plural respectively
I	Conjugation class I [*-ar*]
IIa	Conjugation class II—regular verbs, with I1 in /-o/, e.g. *batre* 'strike', *córrer* 'run', *rompre* 'break'
IIb	Conjugation class II—irregular verbs with I1 in /-g/, e.g. *prendre* 'take', *creure* 'believe', *dir* 'say'
IIIa	Conjugation class III without -SK- element, e.g. *sentir* 'hear'
IIIb	Conjugation class III with -SK- element, e.g. *partir* 'divide'. The lexical membership of classes IIIa and IIIb varies considerably in NW dialects: for verbs other than *partir* 77 scores 0% for IIIb; at nearby 81 the only class IIIa verb is *eixir* 'go out'.

LIST OF LOCALITIES

18	Martinet (Baixa Cerdanya)
33	St Llorenç de Morunys (Solsonès)
38	Solsona (Solsonès)
56	Sta Coloma de Queralt (Conca de Barberà)
59	Valls (Alt Camp)
60	Reus (Baix Camp)
61	Vilanova d'Escornalbou (Baix Camp)
63	Alòs de Gil (Pallars Sobirà)
64	Isavarre (Pallars Sobirà)
65	Esterri d'Àneu (Pallars Sobirà)
65a	Caldes de Boí (Pallars Jussà)
66	Andorra la Vella (Andorra)
67	Llavorsí (Pallars Sobirà)
68	Vilaller (Pallars Jussà)
69	La Torre de Cabdella (Pallars Jussà)
70	Bonansa (Alta Ribagorça, Aragon)
71	El Pont de Suert (Pallars Jussà)
72	Sort (Pallars Sobirà)
73	La Seu d'Urgell (Alt Urgell)
74	La Pobla de Segur (Pallars Jussà)
75	Organyà (Alt Urgell)
76	Tremp (Pallars Jussà)
77	Benavarri (Baixa Ribagorça, Aragon)
78	St Salvador de Toló (Pallars Jussà)
79	Ponts (La Noguera)
80	Artesa de Segre (La Noguera)
81	Tamarit de Llitera (Llitera, Aragon)
82	Balaguer (La Noguera)
83	Pradell de Sió (La Noguera)
84	Cervera (Segarra)
85	Bellpuig d'Urgell (Urgell)
86	Lleida (Segrià)
87	St Martí de Maldà (Urgell)
88	Fraga (Baix Cinca, Aragon)

89   La Granadella (Les Garrigues)
90   Riba-roja d'Ebre (Ribera d'Ebre)
91   Falset (Priorat)
92   Gandesa (Terra Alta)
93   Calaceit (Matarranya, Aragon)
94   Tortosa (Baix Ebre)
95   Morella (Els Ports, País Valencià)
96   Vinaròs (Baix Maestrat, País Valencià)
97   Benassal (Alt Maestrat, País Valencià)
98   Alcalà de Xivert (Baix Maestrat, País Valencià)
99   Llucena (L'Alcalatén, País Valencià)
100   Castelló de la Plana (La Plana Alta, País Valencià)

NW Catalan and adjacent points considered in this paper.
Dotted line marks language frontier.
(From Alcover & Moll, 1929-33)

REFERENCES

Alcover, A. M., & F. de B. Moll, 1929-33
'La flexió verbal en els dialectes catalans', *Anuari de l'Oficina Romànica de Lingüística i Literatura*, 2, 1929:73-184; 3, 1930:73-168; 4, 1931:9-104; 5, 1932:9-72.

Allières, J., 1970
'Le subjonctif en -*o*- du catalan occidental', *Estudis Romànics*, 12. 1963-68:255-65.

Andersen, H., 1980
'Morphological change: towards a typology', *in* Fisiak [1980:1-50].

Arqués i Arrufat, R., 1910/1983
'Variants de la llengua catalana parlada a les Borges d'Urgell y pobles veins de la Plana', *Bolletí del Diccionari de la Llengua Catalana*, 6, 1910 [reprinted in *Butlletí de Dialectologia Nord-Occidental*, 1, 1983:39-72].

Bybee Hooper, J., 1980
'Child morphology and morphophonemic change', *in* Fisiak [1980:157-88].

Bybee, J. L., 1985
Morphology. A Study of the Relation between Meaning and Form., Amsterdam/Philadelphia.

————., & M. A. Brewer, 1980
'Explanation in morphophonemics: changes in Provençal and Spanish preterite forms', *Lingua* 52:201-42.

Carstairs, A., 1987
Allomorphy in Inflexion, London.

Casanova, E., 1989
'Gramàtica històrica i història de la llengua. A propòsit de l'evolució de la desinència de la 1a persona del present d'indicatiu', *in Segon Congrés Internacional de la Llengua Catalana*. Vol. 8. València, 343-57.

Coromines, J., 1936/1976
'El parlar de Cardós i Vall Ferrera', *Butlletí de Dialectologia Catalana* 23, 1936:241-331 [reprinted in J. Coromines, *Entre dos llenguatges*. Vol. 2. Barcelona, 1976:29-67].

DeCesaris, J. A., 1988
Regular Verb Inflection in Catalan. Doctoral dissertation, Indiana University.

Dressler, W. U., 1985
'On the predictiveness of natural morphology', *Journal of Linguistics*, 21:321-37.

————., (ed.) 1987
Leitmotifs in Natural Morphology, Amsterdam/Philadephia

————., 1987a
'Introduction', *in* Dressler [1987:3-22].

Fisiak, J. (ed.), 1980
Historical Morphology, The Hague

Gimeno Betí, L., 1986
'El tortosí septentrional', *in* J. Veny, & J. M. Pujals, (eds), *Actes del Setè Col·loqui Internacional de Llengua i Literatura Catalanes. Tarragona-Salou, 1-5 octubre 1985*. Montserrat, 619-32.

Gulsoy, J., 1976
'El desenvolupament de les formes del subjuntiu present en català', *in* R. B. Tate & A. Yates (eds), *Actes del Tercer Col·loqui Internacional de Llengua i Literatura Catalanes*, Oxford, 27-59.

Kilani-Schoch, M., 1988
Introduction à la morphologie naturelle, Berne.

Mańczak, W., 1980
'Laws of analogy', *in* Fisiak [1980:283-288].

Martí i Castell, J., 1970
Contribució a l'Estudi del Dialecte Occidental, Tarragona.

Mayerthaler, W., 1987
'System-independent morphological naturalness', *in* Dressler [1987: 25-58].

Wheeler, M. W., 1980
'Analogy and inflectional affix replacement.', *in* E. C. Traugott *et al*. (eds), *Papers from the Fourth International Conference on Historical Linguistics*. Amsterdam, 273-83.

————, 1985
'Sincretismo entre categorias modales y cambio desinencial en el verbo románico', *in Linguistique Comparée et Typologie des Langues Romanes. Actes du XVIIème Congrès International de*

Linguistique et Philologie Romanes (Aix-en-Provence, 19 août - 3 septembre, 1983), Vol 2, Aix, 449-60.

————, 1986

'Analogy and psychology: morphological change in Balearic Catalan', *Sheffield Working Papers in Language and Linguistics*, 3, 1-16.

Wurzel, W. U., 1984/1989

Flexionsmorphologie und Natürlichkeit. Ein Beitrag zur morphologischen Theoriebildung, Berlin, 1984., English translation: *Inflectional Morphology and Naturalness*, Dordrecht, 1989. Page references are to the English edition.

————, 1987

'System-dependent morphological naturalness in inflection', *in* Dressler [1987:59-96].

Versatility and vagueness in early Medieval Spain

IT used to be taken for granted that the development of the Romance languages out of spoken Latin, and their divergence from each other, was caused, or at least precipitated, by the break-up of the political empire. This idea is no longer taken seriously, for it is generally agreed that many 'Romance' phenomena appeared much earlier than the end of the empire, whereas for all practical purposes the linguistic divergence of different geographical areas happened much later than the end of the empire. Vàrvaro [e.g. 1991] has contributed most to the solution of this problem, in essence through the application of common sense and the sociolinguistic experience of widely-spread modern speech communities. All such speech communities have wide variation–geographical, sociolinguistic and stylistic–and when new linguistic developments arise (as they do all the time) they fit into the existing complex mosaic. Non-Classical developments could begin before the end of the Western Empire without the older forms of similar function necessarily dying out of normal usage for several centuries (Menéndez Pidal's *estado latente*). Thus there continues to be one Western Romance speech-community until the late eighth century or so, of increasing complexity but without any explicitly-expressed idea arising that geographical or stylistic differences are such as to impede the normal communications possible in any complex but monolingual area [cf. Van Uytfanghe 1989, Wright 1991]. Banniard [1989] makes the point from the viewpoint of a cultural historian; the inhabitants of Romania (before 800) belonged to one 'ensemble linguistique' [187], with 'une symbiose suffisante entre la forme écrite et la forme parlée du latin' [197], in which—for example—the illiterate had sufficient passive expertise to follow sermons as they were read aloud by a kind of 'connivence entre les producteurs de la communication et ses consommateurs' [204]. We can call this perspective 'complex monolingualism'.

It has also often been implied that the early medieval Romance languages were of a lesser linguistic quality than Imperial Latin had been. Salvador has recently summed up this view with stunning baldness [1988: 645]:

> ...esta devastación...es fenómeno bien conocido y explicado. La desaparición de las declinaciones, la reducción del sistema verbal, el naufragio de las estructuras sintácticas, con la necesidad de reinventar luego, como quien dice, todos los elementos de la relación, no son más que la otra cara...de la descomposición sufrida por la lengua latina al desintegrarse. Si la gramática originaria ofrece...el desolado panorama que todos conocemos...

As Banniard points out, the societies of the fifth to the eighth centuries were ones in which writing tended still to be done on wax tablets and papyri, which are biodegradable and have left no trace. The number of surviving pieces of (non-degradable) slate [recently studied by Díaz y Díaz 1986 and Isabel Velázquez: see Fontán and Moure 1987: 135-38] also suggests that writing was commoner then than we tend to think. Even so, it is still reasonable to conclude that they were less literate societies than those that preceded and followed. This is not in itself necessarily a bad thing. Oral styles in any society have flexibilities and nuances of intonation, word order, topicalization, deictics, discourse pragmatics, style, register, effects based on the interplay of old and new information, dyadic interaction with audiences, etc., of a complexity and exuberance rarely achieved in writing, even in the work of the most gifted dramatists. It is not difficult to believe in the existence of early medieval Spanish oral literature, however unattested it may seem [Wright 1986, 1990b]. The earliest written 'Romance' texts were usually specifically designed for oral reproduction of some kind. Standardization, however, of necessity involving the reform of the language of written texts, usually takes the form of a limitation on permissible options, with the consequence that many of the features of oral language which seem ill-disciplined to the grammarians, who perceive a moral order in such details, tend to disappear from texts but survive in real life. This was the main effect of Aelius Donatus's fourth-century *Ars Minor*: to banish from written respectability, for centuries afterwards, all sorts of ordinary spoken usages. And even if they appeared, copyists such as those instructed by Cassiodorus were trained to 'emend' them later.

It would be unfair to regard the spoken usage of early medieval Romance areas in any general sense as 'worse' than spoken Imperial Latin. Indeed, the observable features of early Romance morphology and syntax often seem to have had the effect of making speech more complex, versatile and sophisticated than it had been before; Romance uses of *se* with a passive function, which arose long before the synthetic passives disappeared, or multiple auxiliaries such as in Castilian *habrían sido hechas*, made the language semantically more flexible and richer in nuance than before [Green 1982, 1991]. The analysis of the compound perfect form (HABEO FACTUM > *he hecho*) as a regular paradigm available for any lexical verb did not lead to the loss of the synthetic forms (FECI > *hice*) previously used to express the same meaning (except over a millenium later in France); the continuing coexistence of old and new led in this case, as in others, to a greater flexibility and subtlety in the resources of spoken Early Romance than had existed in earlier spoken Latin.

Thus the new is not necessarily inferior. Even within the temporal limits of the Empire, non-canonical written features can speak to modern investigators who have a sympathetic eye. Herman, of course, is the prime master in seeing the rationale behind non-Classical usages which the school of Donatus and B. H. Kennedy [1930] prefer to dismiss as mere barbarism and symptoms of a lack of culture; in a recent study, for example, Herman [1989] explains that those 'Late' writers who use *quod* or *quia* clauses, rather than the accusative and infinitive clauses that would appeal more to nineteenth-century schoolmasters, were in fact using a language of greater subtlety and pragmatic versatility than previously available (in that the *qu-* alternative can be exploited only when the agent of the subordinate clause is not the pragmatic topic). The advent of the new had added to the resources of the language by providing useful material for a contrast with the still-existing previous alternative. If we can consider the data from perspectives that Donatus and Kennedy knew nothing about (such as functional grammar and pragmatics), and accept that supposedly 'non-Classical' usages found in early manuscripts genuinely had a function and deserve not to be 'emended' out of existence (as they often are in editions prepared by historians rather than linguists), many of the features which are traditionally thought of as unacceptably 'Romance' (or 'Vulgar') can be seen to have had a role even in the speech of the Empire.

The most inappropriate word in Salvador's comment quoted above is *luego*: he assumed that Latin grammar 'collapsed' [*al desintegrarse*] and Spanish grammar then needed to be rebuilt laboriously on the ruins, whereas it often seems reasonable to postulate that the new turned up long before the death of the old which it seems in retrospect to have neatly replaced. And insofar as we can conclude anything from the evidence, it seems reasonable to claim that Imperial Latin, post-Imperial Early Romance (Late Latin), Old Castilian speech-communities and others contained variation of a normal type that was in no sense dysfunctional. This claim will here be examined for the three main areas of language; phonetics and syntax briefly, semantics at greater length.

As far as phonetics is concerned, there is no reason to suppose that variability in any medieval speech community was so great as to cause a practical problem. This contention is slightly circular, in that the speech communities after the ninth century are usually defined as being smaller in geographical terms than the whole of Romania, on the grounds of diminished mutual intelligibility; but given this restriction, there is no sense in concluding that Romance in Romania as a whole, and early medieval Ibero-Romance phonology in the Peninsula, were in any meaningful sense 'inferior' to that of Imperial Latin. But in Castilian-speaking areas, the period of wide variety and versatility did not continue untrammelled beyond the late thirteenth century. Politics had an effect here. Politicians cannot directly guide speech, but they can affect writing, which is an artificial accomplishment, taught and learnt in controllable circumstances. Alfonso *el Sabio* and his scholars eventually felt, for practical reasons, that they had to do to some extent what Donatus had done before, and what 'reformers' usually aim to do [Marcos 1979]; that is, to impose artificial limitations in writing on the options available in the spoken diversity, thereby regarding some features of speech as inadmissible in writing. In this way they hoped to achieve some kind of standardization of the written form (*derecho*, of which the famous *drecho* is probably only a misprint; see the enlightening study by Cano Aguilar, 1985). Henceforth written norms would once again disguise the versatility of speech.

There can be little objection in general to standard-ization of spelling, even when it obscures phonetic variations. All orthographies in practice crassly under-represent nuances of intonation, length, stress, etc., and even the most ostensibly 'phonetic' orthography tends to be anisomorphic with actual phonetics and even with phonology. One example of these restrictions has been well studied; pre-Alfonsine Spanish texts and the early Alfonsine works up to Chapter 116 of the *General estoria* [Echenique 1979, Lapesa 1982] vary between writing -*e* and *Ø* after final clusters (*adelante* ~ *adelant*, etc.). At that point they felt they ought to decide whether or not to write a final -*e* corresponding to a sound that was some-times apocopated in speech, and which even if it existed in the lexical entry always underwent synalepha where applicable then as now, and (possibly even at the King's own initiative) they chose to include the letter regularly. This variation must have corresponded to variation in speech (between [-*e*], *Ø*, and perhaps also [ə] [as suggested by Allen 1976]). The variation in speech can in no circumstances have been awkward, and would have given rise to all sorts of flexibility and nuance for soci-olinguistic and pragmastylistic effects. Here too the new form had arisen before the disappearance of the old, and the coexistence of both, though partly hidden eventually by the standardizations of grammarians, led to the spoken language being (as usual) more versatile than the written.

As regards syntax, variation between old and new in early medieval Spain is no more dysfunctional than it had been a thousand years before or than it was in contemporary phonetics. The fact that, for example, perfect auxiliaries could either follow or precede their participle (in the years before the reanalysis as a compound tense-form led to the actualization of a fixed order) almost certainly led to possibilities that could be exploited in oral discourse, for pragmastylistic purposes rather than being a reflection of contemporary grammatical 'barbarism' and indiscipline. For example, the fact that there were two pluperfects (*fiziera, avia fecho*) might seem at first sight to be a symptom of unnecessary confusion; but Lunn and Cravens [1991] have recently distinguished their pragmatic functions in the *Poema de Mio Cid* (essentially, *avia fecho* for new information and *fiziera* for old), demonstrating the existence of a sub-conscious sophistication at the time higher than that operated hitherto by modern analysts, and essentially based on the presence of an audience (pre-Alfonsine Castilian literature being an orally-delivered genre, however composed).

Semantics might seem to be a special case. If there is indeed some kind of relative practical insufficiency in the speech used between the end of the Roman Empire and the twelfth-century Renaissance, it could perhaps be in the greater vagueness of a number of words. Vagueness in itself is not a bad thing. Every vocabulary structure needs generic words at the top of its hyponymic scales, and there are many circumstances in which choosing the vaguer word 'animal' is preferable to choosing the more precise word 'cat' [*pace* Aitchison 1987: ch. 7]. In tenth-century Spain everyone who could write, and the greater number who could read, met old-fashioned lexical usages which were not totally outside their passive experience despite being absent from their active everyday colloquial usage, and of whose original precise meaning they could not have always felt entirely sure, despite grasping the main gist (including synthetic morphology: e.g. in the passive, which—as both Stengaard [1991: 5.2.1] and Green [1991] show—must have been largely intelligible). This happens to most people in Modern Britain who inadvertently chance upon an eighteenth-century text (or a Daily Telegraph leader). Such words could thus, for many people, have a vaguer potential reference than might have been the case when they were in many people's active vocabulary centuries before. Writers were aware of this problem. The Great Scholars of the age often felt that their most pressing task was to explain semantic distinctions that contemporary usage was becoming unaware of; this tradition is represented by Isidore of Seville's *Differentiae* and Bede's mis-named *De Orthographia* [see Wright 1989: 132-33, 158-61]. The famous Visigothic delight in piling up synonyms is partly based on the hope that one of them at least might be intelligible. Writers were often inspired to solve this problem by imitating works of an earlier time. As modern scholars investigate the 'literary' texts of the age, they usually unearth such models even for the most apparently insignificant phraseology. For example, the famous hymn to St James *O Dei verbum, patris ore proditum* [c. 784] has been shown by Díaz y Díaz to have borrowed much of its wording from hymns composed considerably earlier [1976: 237-72]. This procedure was safer from the point of view of achieving 'correctness', but had the inevitable effect of making the precise details of the real-world referent less clear. This technique was equally applicable to prose: in the ninth chapter of the *Chronicle of Alfonso III*, for example, Pelayo at Covadonga is described in terms taken from martyrs' *Passiones* [Gil *et al.*, 1985: 124-27]. In the tenth century, Vigila, abbot of Albelda, described his predecessor Salvo in terms taken almost directly from the *De Viris Illustribus* tradition of Saints Isidore and Ildefonsus. Vigila had the admirable aim of emphasizing the continuity of tradition between the great men concerned, but from a semantic point of view this technique necessarily led to vagueness in words that might seem to be precise. If almost any abbot can be described as 'lingua nitidus et scientia eruditus...cuius oratio...plurimam cordis compunctionem et magnam suaviloquentiam legen-tibus audientibusque tribuet' [*sic*], the result is infuriatingly lacking in individuality [Díaz y Díaz 1979: 282; Wright 1989: 286-87].

In its natural state, linguistic semantics is usually imprecise. Rothwell pointed out [1962: 30], with reference to Medieval France, that 'in a language untrammelled by grammarians and academies the development of the vocabulary can often be quite undisciplined'. I quoted this comment of Rothwell's in my own study of semantic change in Spanish words for parts of the face, and began the conclusion there as follows: 'it is worth considering whether semantic fixity is more rigid at some times than others. Times of comparatively wide education and high literacy...may encourage professionals to impose clearer distinctions than naturally exist otherwise' [Wright 1985: 287-88]. The point is that, without the encouragement of teachers, lawyers, grammarians, lexicographers and allied pedants, firstly, different items can slide around from one part of our semantic structure to another, and secondly, the manner in which we superimpose that structure on the outside world can be inconsistent. The semantic history of *boca* (< BUCCA, 'cheek'), *mejilla* (< MAXILLA, 'jaw'), etc., shows that on the whole the modern vocabulary structure embodies the same distinctions as were made two thousand years ago, but that several forms have moved from one part to another of the framework which the semantic structure hopes to impose on the flux of perceived reality.

A later study looked at the Romance words for 'cut' [Wright 1990a], a part of the vocabulary which is structured on hyponymic scales rather than simply on an attempt to divide a continuum of reality into individuated areas of reference. The data led to a general conclusion that here in semantics, as in phonetics and syntax, time brought versatility rather than disintegration. There seems to have survived through the ages, in all areas studied, a more or less consistent structure intended to contain a word meaning 'strike', superordinate to several subordinate co-hyponyms including a word meaning 'strike [with the specific criterion of] successfully with a sharp edge'; this latter word is in turn superordinate to an unspecified and extensible number of hyponyms of its own. The structure itself is roughly constant over time (as the 'face' one seems to have been), although the words filling the slots have often moved, usually via generalization (moving up to the less precise levels of the hyponymic scale), or specialization (moving down). The structures of Latin, French, Italian, Old Spanish and Modern Spanish were discussed in detail in that study, and are merely summarized here. The Latin superordinate term CAEDERE 'strike' disappeared eventually from active usage. Its usual original hyponym for 'cut' was SECARE, which in turn had hyponyms of its own, such as METERE, 'cut corn'. Old Spanish had a superordinate *golp[e]ar* 'strike' (originally formed off *golpe* < COLAPHUS, 'blow'), and a hyponym *tajar* meaning 'cut' (originally formed off TALEA, 'plant cutting'), with hyponyms of its own including *cortar*, 'shorten by cutting' < CURTARE, *segar* < SECARE, 'cut corn', and *(a)serrar*, 'cut with a saw' (originally formed off SERRA). Italian emerges with *colpire*, *tagliare* and *segare* in the same structural position as their Spanish cognates, although in Italy *segare* specialized to mean 'cut with a saw' (originally), for *mietere*, 'cut corn' (< METERE) survived. In French *couper*, however, unlike its Spanish and Italian cognates (*golp[e]ar* and *colpire*), specialized as 'cut' (that is, no longer usable for blows that did not involve a sharp edge) and a new superordinate *frapper* came to be preferred. *Couper* 'cut' now has its own hyponyms in the ordinary way, such as *moissonner*, 'cut corn', *scier* (< SECARE), 'saw', and *tailler*, more specialized than its Italian and Old Spanish cognates (*tagliare, tajar*), 'cut carefully'. Modern Spanish has since moved *cortar* (< CURTARE 'shorten') to the intermediate superordinate slot, 'cut', and specialized *tajar* as 'chop' (in Spain). Other words have turned up on the more precise level also, such as *talar* from Germanic, . *amputar* from Early Renaissance Latin, *tallar* from Renaissance Italian; but the essential structure seems to have remained intact throughout the ages [cf. also the superb discussion in Stengaard 1991 on STARE, *estar* and *estar de pie*].

Salvador discussed cases where the structure has indeed changed in part over the last 2000 years, in words for 'kiss', 'wall', 'height' and 'hair', and as a consequence takes the same line on semantics as on morphosyntax: 'la historia semántica del léxico español es la historia de la lenta reedificación de una nueva lengua sobre los restos des-moronados de los campos semánticos latinos' [1988: 644]. The postulation of a semantic vacuum after this hypothesized collapse and before the supposed rebuilding is patronizing and needlessly ungenerous. The suggestion that features of early medieval linguistic practice can legitimately be explained with the assumption that everyone between AD 400 and 1200 in Spain must have been as thick as two short planks is not one which appeals to any serious historian of the age, continually aware of an enormous number of serious and intelligent individuals of many types struggling hard to operate effectively in a world full of obstacles. Instead we can envisage that in semantics, as in phonetics and syntax, as elsewhere in Early Romance, and as envisaged by Banniard for the culture of the age in general, old and new coexisted for a long while; not only is there not a Salvadorean gap of many hundreds of years in which people were hardly able to talk effectively at all, and even the most 'patrimonial' words had no meaning, but the linguistic communities of the time had remarkable vitality and versatility, combining the old—surviving longer, at least in a passive mode, than Salvador implies—with the new, beginning earlier than the age of definitive Romance languages.

In every semantic change (not only in Early Romance) there is a period where the word has potentially both the older and the newer use. For example, SECARE (> *segar*) in Spain for a long time was probably used mostly in reaping contexts, but was still perfectly intelligible if found in a written text with its older unspecialized use, e.g. referring to 'cutting hair'. Such uses seemed gradually more metaphorical, no doubt ('harvesting hair'), but still comprehensible. In addition, new words were coined and borrowed all the time, increasing versatility and 'ruining' (*desmoronar*) nothing at all; even in this small field, *talar* ('cut down trees') was originally Germanic; *aserrar* and *acortar*, 'shorten' (coined to replace CURTARE (> *cortar*) when the latter specialized to mean specifically 'shorten with a knife'), are merely two examples among thousands of the convincingly reconstructable exuberance of derivational morphology in Early Medieval Spain. These new words coexisted with the old, jostling over the frameworks provided by existing structures, each contributing another stone to the complex monolingual mosaic and further possibilities for sophistication and versatility in speech. Such semantic indeterminacy as there was resulted from an *embarras de richesses*.

Some semantic imprecision is normal anyway, and certainly not confined to the years between AD 500 and 1200. For example, the standard areas of vocabulary structure whose hyponymic organization is thought by modern analysts to be clearer than most concerns the natural world; birds, fish, etc. Yet Whinnom [1966] shows an astounding variety in the way different people apply the same Spanish words to different actual birds. Similarly, experts on fish regularly complain about the Academy Dictionary's lack of ichthyonymic expertise, pointing out that the same word can be used in practice to refer to . different fish in different ports, as well as different words being used to refer to the same fish [Mondéjar 1982, 1989; Barriuso Fernández 1981: Ríos Panisse 1977/83; Martínez González 1977; Alvar 1985; for Catalonia, Veny 1980]. What we have here is a lack of standardized fit between the hyponymic criteria and the world (reference), but the structure itself (sense) stays the same; for the words concerned remain hyponyms of *pez*. Similarly, García Mouton [1987] found people who use *ardilla* (supposedly 'squirrel') to refer to weasels. The referential vagueness over the names of creatures may well be worse now than it was in the tenth century. There is in practice little certain way of knowing whether the Roman Empire had greater internal consistency in orthonymic and ichthyonymic usage, but it probably did, if only because the language once belonged to a much smaller geographical area. It could thus have been the case that in natural history terms it was the Empire itself that led to vagueness, rather than its dissolution. Further diversification and confusion is inevitably reported from Latin America [e.g. Ronchi March 1980]. Even if the early Middle Ages saw wide imprecision in such areas, it is probably no less culpable in this regard than Modern Spain.

Early Medieval Christian Spain was not merely a time of intellectual barbarism, decadence and stupidity. It was a time of complex monolingualism, a mosaic of old and new linguistic usages, with an essentially oral culture abetted by a widening anisomorphic gap between speech and writing, and between active and passive skills, but individuals were in general not obviously less intelligent then than they are now; and even if modern scholars might feel justified in their common patronizing attitude towards the speakers of Early Medieval Spanish, the features referred to are not in themselves particularly medieval. As Klein [1989] and others have observed, modern Spanish speech and writing are also very different from each other; and yet most Spaniards can understand the written form of their own language when read aloud in 1990, as, I suggest, they also could in 990. It is time for us to be far more generous, and admit that the communities of those centuries were linguistically fully viable, and included what Spaniards now call *protagonismo*; let us restore to the millions of Early Medieval Spaniards their self-respect, their intelligence, their linguistic versatility, their voice, their ears, their very participation in society itself. Let us, in short, accept the perspective of Alarcos Llorach [1982: 15, 42]:

> Nuestros viejos antecesores se entendían entre sí tan bien (o tan mal, según se mire) como nos entendemos nosotros...esos hablantes se expresaban y se entendían entre ellos tan bien como nosotros.

Roger Wright
Liverpool

REFERENCES

Aitchison J., 1987
  Words in the Mind, Oxford
Alarcos Llorach E., 1982
  El español, lengua milenaria, Valladolid
Allen J. H. D., Jr., 1976
  'Apocope in Old Spanish', *Estudios ofrecidos a Emilio Alarcos Llorach*, vol.I, Oviedo, 15-30.
Banniard M., 1989
  Genèse culturelle de l'Europe: Ve-VIIIe siècle, Paris,
Barriuso Fernández E., 1981
  'Ictionimia y diccionario académico: pargo, pagel y rubiel', *BRAE*, 61: 141-54.
Cano Aguilar R., 1985
  'Castellano ¿drecho?', *Verba*, 12: 287-306.
Díaz y Díaz M. C., 1976
  De Isidoro al Siglo XI, Barcelona
Díaz y Díaz M. C., 1979
  Libros y librerías de la Rioja altomedieval, Logroño
  ———————., 1986
  'Algunos aspectos lingüísticos y culturales de las pizarras visigóticas', *Myrtia*, 1: 13-25.
Echenique Elizondo M. T., 1979
  'Apócope y leísmo en la *Primera crónica general*. Notas para una cronología , *Studi Ispanici*, I, 43-58.
Fontán A. and Moure Casas A., 1987
  Antología del latín medieval, Madrid
García Mouton P., 1987
  'Motivación en nombres de animales', *Lingüística Española Actual*, 9: 189-97.
Gil Fernández J., Moralejo J. L., and J. I. Ruiz de la Peña, 1985
  Crónicas Asturianas, Oviedo
Green J. N., 1982
  'Vers une théorie du renouvellement morphologique. Nouvelles perspectives sur la *voix impersonelle*', XVI Congrès Internacional de Lingüística i Filologia Romàniques: *Actes*, vol. 2, Palma de Mallorca 85-93.

Green J. N., 1991
    'The collapse and replacement of verbal inflection in Late Latin/Early Romance: how would one know?', in Wright (ed.) 83-99.
Henman J., 1989
    '*Accusativus cum infinitivo* et subordonnée a *quod, quia* en latin tardif—nouvelles remarques sur un vieux problème', in G. Calboli (ed.), *Subordination and other topics in Latin*, Amsterdam, Benjamins: 133-52.
Kennedy B. H., 1930
    The Revised Latin Primer, London
Klein Andreu F., 1989
    'Speech priorities', in L. Hickey (ed.), *The Pragmatics of Style*, London, 73-86.
Lapesa R., 1982
    'Contienda de normas lingüísticas en el castellano alfonsí', in W. Hempel y D. Briesemeister (eds), *Actas del coloquio hispano-alemán Ramón Menéndez Pidal*, Tübingen, 172-90.
Lunn P. V. and T. D. Cravens, 1991
    'A contextual reconsideration of the Spanish -*ra* "indicative"', in S. Fleischman and L. R. Waugh (eds), *Categories of the Verb in Romance: Discourse Pragmatic Approaches*, London
Marcos Marín F., 1979
    Reforma y modernización del español, Madrid
Martínez González A., 1977
    'Notas de ictionimia andaluza', *RDTP*, 33: 165-243.
Mondejar J., 1982
    'Congrio y zafio: un capitulo de ictionimia mediterranea y atlantica, *Vox Romanica*, 41: 206-19.
Mondéjar J., 1989
    'Robalo y lubina [*Morone labrax* L.]: otro capítulo de ictionimia mediterránea y atlántica (ALEA 1109; ALEICan 465; ALM 541W)', *RFE*, 69: 61-95.
Ríos Panisse M. C., 1977, 1983
    Nomenclatura de la flora y fauna marítimas de Galicia, 2 vols, Santiago de Ccmpostela
Ronchi March C. A., 1980
    'Sobre la incorporación de los nombres científicos de plantas y animales en el Diccionario de la Real Academia Española', *VIII Congreso de Academias de la Lengua Española*, Lima: 437-40.
Rothwell W., 1962
    'Medieval French and modern semantics', *MLR*, 57: 25-30.

Salvador G., 1988
'Lexemática histórica', *Actas del I Congreso Internacional de Historia de la Lengua Española*, Madrid: 635-46.

Stengaard B., 1991
Vida y muerte de un campo semántico: un estudio de la evolución semántica de los verbos latinos STARE, SEDERE y IACERE del latín al romance del siglo XIII, Tübingen

Van Uytfanghe M., 1989
'Les expressions du type quod vulgo vocat dans des textes latines anterieurs au Concile de Tours et aux Serments de Strasbourg', *ZRP*, 105: 28-48.

Varvaro A., 1991
'Latin and Romance: fragmentation or restructuring?', in Wright (ed.), 44-51.

Veny J., 1980
Transfusió i adaptació d'ictionims en el *Dictionarium* de Pere Torra (segle XVII)', in *Homenatge a Josep M. Casacuberta*, vol. I, Badalona, Montserrat:69-102.

Whinnom K., 1966
A Glossary of Spanish Bird Names, London

Wright R., 1985
'Indistinctive features (facial and semantic)', *RPh*, 38: 275-92.

————., 1986
'How Old is the Ballad Genre?', *La Corónica*, 14: 251-57.

————., 1989
Latín tardío y romance temprano, Madrid

————., 1990a
'Semantic change in Romance words for "cut"', *Papers from the 8th International Conference on Historical Linguistics*, Amsterdam, 553-61.

————., 1990b
'Several ballads, one epic and two chronicles (1100-1250)', *La Corónica*, 18, 21-37.

————., 1991
'The conceptual distinction between Latin and Romance: invention or evolution?', in Wright (ed.), 103-13.

————., (ed.) 1991
Latin and the Romance languages in the Early Middle Ages, London

TABULA GRATULATORIA

David Bernal Rodríguez
Biblioteca de la Real Academia
  Española
Leslie Brooks
Xosé Ma. Castro Erroteta
Agustín Coletes Blanco
Silvia Coll-Vinent
Lia N.R. Correia Raitt
Alan Deyermond
Steven N. Dworkin
Paloma García-Bellido García
  de Diego
Regina af Geijerstam
Peter Glare
John N. Green
Ray Harris-Northall
Thomas R. Hart
Pat Harvey
Leo Hickey
J.R.L. Highfield
Richard Hitchcock
Lynn Ingamells
Mrs. Cyril Jones
Ron Keightley
Elspeth Kennedy
King's College, London
Jeremy Lawrance
Pippa Mayfield
Brian Mott
Taylor Institution, Oxford
Exeter College, Oxford

New College, Oxford
St. Anne's College, Oxford
The Master and Fellows of
  Saint Cross College, Oxford
St. Edmund Hall, Oxford
Lady Margaret Hall, Oxford
St. Hugh's College, Oxford
St. Peter's College, Oxford
Queen's College, Oxford
Worcester College, Oxford
Frank Pierce
Robert Pring-Mill
Mrs. Joyce Reid
Xon de Ros
Nicholas G. Round
Peter Russell
Miss E. M. Rutson
Rodney Sampson
Dorothy S. Severin
Harvey L. Sharrer
E.A. Southworth
Colin Thompson
Ronald Truman
John & Laura Wainwright
Geoffrey J. Walker
C.J. Wells
Clive Willis
Margaret Wilson
John & Gaynor Woodhouse
Alonso Zamora Vicente, Madrid,
  Real Academia Española